THE SHAPESHIFTING CROWN

The Crown stands at the heart of the New Zealand, British, Australian and Canadian constitutions as the ultimate source of legal authority and embodiment of state power. A familiar icon of the Westminster model of government, it is also an enigma. Even constitutional experts struggle to define its attributes and boundaries: who or what is the Crown and how is it embodied? Is it the Queen, the state, the government, a corporation sole or aggregate, a relic of feudal England, a metaphor or a mask for the operation of executive power? How are its powers exercised? How have the Crowns of different Commonwealth countries developed? *The Shapeshifting Crown* combines legal and anthropological perspectives to provide novel insights into the Crown's changing nature and its multiple, ambiguous and contradictory meanings. It sheds new light onto the development of the state in postcolonial societies and constitutional monarchy as a cultural system.

CRIS SHORE is Professor of Anthropology at Auckland University and Guest Professor of Public Management at Stockholm University's Centre for Organisational Research (2018–19). He has taught at Perugia University (1986), Oxford Brookes University (1987–90), Goldsmiths College (1990–2003) and Auckland University where he was also Head of Department and founding Director of the Europe Institute. His research specialisms include political anthropology, organisations, higher education, the anthropology of policy, corruption and Europe. He is author/co-editor of 140 articles and 14 books, including *Building Europe: The Cultural Politics of European Integration* (2000); *Corruption: Anthropological Perspectives* (2005); *Policy Worlds: Anthropology and the Analysis of Contemporary Power* (2011); *Up Close and Personal: Peripheral Perspectives and the Production of Anthropological Knowledge* (2013) and *Death of the Public University? Uncertain Futures for Higher Education in the Knowledge Economy* (2017). He has held visiting appointments at the universities of Harvard, Bristol, Aarhus, Sussex, University College London, Malta and the European University Institute in Florence. In 2017 he was awarded the Royal Society of New Zealand's Mason Durie medal for contributions to the social sciences.

DAVID V. WILLIAMS is Professor of Law at the University of Auckland. He has taught and researched at the University of Dar es Salaam

(Tanzania) and then the University of Auckland since 1972. He has been an independent researcher and barrister specialising in research relevant to Treaty of Waitangi claims by indigenous Maori concerning historic acts or omissions of the Crown. He has authored five books, including *Te Kooti tango whenua: The Native Land Court 1864–1909* (1999) and *A Simple Nullity? The* Wi Parata *Case in New Zealand Law and History* (2011). Additional publications include 18 book chapters, 37 refereed journal articles and 10 major technical reports submitted to the Waitangi Tribunal. He has held visiting appointments at Exeter College, St John's College and Corpus Christi College in the University of Oxford, and at the University of Dar es Salaam, Tanzania. He was elected an honorary fellow of the American Society for Legal History in 2017 and a Fellow of the Royal Society of New Zealand in 2018.

THE SHAPESHIFTING CROWN

Locating the State in Postcolonial New Zealand, Australia, Canada and the UK

Edited by

CRIS SHORE

University of Auckland

DAVID V. WILLIAMS

University of Auckland

CAMBRIDGE
UNIVERSITY PRESS

Cambridge
UNIVERSITY PRESS

University Printing House, Cambridge CB2 8BS, United Kingdom

One Liberty Plaza, 20th Floor, New York, NY 10006, USA

477 Williamstown Road, Port Melbourne, VIC 3207, Australia

314–321, 3rd Floor, Plot 3, Splendor Forum, Jasola District Centre, New Delhi – 110025, India

79 Anson Road, #06–04/06, Singapore 079906

Cambridge University Press is part of the University of Cambridge.

It furthers the University's mission by disseminating knowledge in the pursuit of education, learning, and research at the highest international levels of excellence.

www.cambridge.org
Information on this title: www.cambridge.org/9781108496469
DOI: 10.1017/9781108677738

First published 2019

Printed in the United Kingdom by TJ International Ltd, Padstow, Cornwall

A catalogue record for this publication is available from the British Library.

ISBN 978-1-108-49646-9 Hardback

CONTENTS

FIGURES

Cover Image 'Heritage' by Barry Ross Smith, 2008. The image depicts Queen Elizabeth with imagined moko. The roman numerals identify the date [6 February 1840] when the Treaty of Waitangi between Queen Victoria and Maori was first signed [Moko is a permanent facial marking for Maori women of high status. This one is similar in style to those done according to traditional Maori protocols].

ACKNOWLEDGEMENTS

Books always owe a debt of gratitude to people far beyond those whose names appear in the table of contents. This book began its journey in 2012 with a pilot study that set out to map the Crown's multiple meanings in New Zealand and analyse the different ways in which that term is understood and used by political elites and state actors today. What we learned from that first foray into the world of constitutional monarchy was just how fluid, ambiguous, contested and yet symbolically potent the concept of the Crown can be. This led us to probe further into the nature of the Crown, the different space that it occupies in the constitutional orders of other postcolonial societies, and the legal, political and cultural ramifications of its ambiguity and shapeshifting character. The result was an anthropological study spanning four years (2013–17) and involving over 220 in-depth and face-to-face interviews with civil servants, politicians, government ministers, legal experts, academics, indigenous rights activists and Crown officials across four countries.

We would like to thank the Royal Society of New Zealand (RSNZ) Marsden Fund without whose generous financial support and encouragement our study would not have been possible. We also wish to acknowledge the University of Auckland's *Te Wharekura* research initiative, which funded the pilot study, 'The Crown in New Zealand: Legal, symbolic and demotic perspectives on an essentially contested concept'. This was a good example of how seed funding for cross-disciplinary research, in this case anthropology and law, can produce innovative partnerships that push disciplinary research and conceptual boundaries in interesting new directions.

We want to express our gratitude to Margaret Kawharu, Corinna Howland, Sam Taylor-Alexander, Courtney Addison, Marama Muru-Lanning and Matthew Davie who provided research assistance for different parts of the project and shared in the interviewing and wider conversations, and to Nat Daddy and Claire Black for their tireless and indispensible work transcribing the interviews. Warm thanks are also owed to Mona-Lynn Courteau whose forensic attention to detail and copy-editing skills helped to iron out any glitches and inconsistencies in the manuscript and ensure scrupulous academic rigour.

One of our biggest debts of gratitude is to the many interviewees in Australia, Canada, New Zealand and the United Kingdom who so generously contributed their time and thoughts and responded with patience and enthusiasm to our sometimes naïve questions. Meeting face-to-face, collecting stories and engaging in sometimes highly personal conversations with this diverse collection of actors provided key insights as well as valuable moments for reflection and analysis: it was also one of the most enjoyable aspects of the project that has laid the ground for what we hope will be a conversation that will continue into the future.

Some of the ideas in this book were road tested at workshops and conferences, including a two-day symposium held at the University of Auckland in November 2017. We would especially like to thank for their valuable and generous feedback the discussants and participants at that event: Anne Twomey, Phillipe Lagassé, Sebastian Payne, Janet McLean, Richard Hill, Fiona McCormack, Sean Brennan, Mike Dreaver, Margaret Kawharu, Noel Cox, Steven Winter, Morgan Godfery, Keith Locke, Matthew Hooton and Sir Anand Satyanand.

It has been a pleasure to work with the editors at Cambridge University Press, particularly Marianne Nield and Finola O'Sullivan, and we are grateful for the comments provided by the two anonymous reviewers of our proposal. Above all, we wish to express our thanks to Sally Raudon and Jai Patel. They started out in 2015–16 as MA students studying the role of the Crown in Australia and New Zealand, respectively, but continued to work on the project as team members and active participants at all stages of the research. This was a uniquely collaborative initiative and members of the team contributed to developing the ideas of the book and framing the arguments. Every Thursday, over a period of many months and aided by coffee and pastries, we would meet in the Anthropology Meeting Room to thrash out the arguments and workshop the individual chapters. This made the writing process much more interactive, dialogic and reflexive – terms often associated with postmodernism, yet this is by no means a work of postmodernist writing. Our book is therefore unlike most edited collections. It can either be read as a series of individual chapters each of which examines a particular theme or issues relating to country-specific dimensions of the Crown, or it can be read from beginning to end as an integrated and holistic study of the

Crown as an anthropological concept as well as an historical and contemporary set of institutions and practices and the way these developed in each of the four realms covered in our story.

Finally, we should also acknowledge a debt of gratitude to the Crown itself: that mysterious, arcane, multifaceted, shapeshifting and yet curiously contemporary entity which has provided us with such a rich and interesting object of study. As Carol Duffy wrote in her poem to mark the 60th anniversary of the Queen's coronation, 'Time-gifted, the crown is old light, journeying from skulls of kings to living Queen . . . Not lightly worn'.

TABLE OF STATUTES AND CASES

Statutes

Cases

1

Introduction

A Shapeshifting Enigma: The Crown in Australia, Canada, New Zealand and the United Kingdom

CRIS SHORE

From Colonial Aggressor to Postcolonial Apologist: The Many Faces of the Crown

On a cold afternoon on 22 August 2014 an event of major historic significance in relations between the New Zealand government and its indigenous people took place in the small town of Taneatua in the North Island Bay of Plenty region. Chris Finlayson, New Zealand's attorney-general and minister for Treaty of Waitangi negotiations, stood before a crowd of over three thousand people, mainly members of the Tūhoe *iwi* (tribe), but also including former prime minister Jim Bolger, Police Commissioner Mike Bush, members of Parliament from across the spectrum and descendants of Premier Richard Seddon to deliver a long-awaited apology on behalf of the government for historical grievances of the Māori people, reflecting what are often considered the most deplorable episodes in New Zealand's colonial history. This official apology followed a Treaty of Waitangi settlement between the *iwi* and the government agreed a month earlier which included a financial and commercial redress package totalling NZ$170 million and formal acknowledgement of the mistreatment of Tūhoe carried out by successive New Zealand governments over 140 years. Speaking with calculated solemnity and humility from the rostrum under a large marquee, Mr Finlayson (2014) declared:

> The Crown unreservedly apologises for not having honoured its obligations to Tūhoe under te Tiriti o Waitangi (the Treaty of Waitangi) and profoundly regrets its failure to appropriately acknowledge and respect *te mana motuhake o Tūhoe* [Tūhoe autonomy] for many generations.
>
> The relationship between Tūhoe and the Crown, which should have been defined by honour and respect, was instead disgraced by many

> injustices, including indiscriminate *raupatu* [confiscation], wrongful killings, and years of scorched earth warfare. The Crown apologises for its unjust and excessive behaviour and the burden carried by generations of Tūhoe who suffer greatly and carry the pain of their ancestors.

Tūhoe's leaders had, in Finlayson's words, acted 'honourably', whereas the Crown had 'subverted' the Urewera District Native Reserve Act of 1896 to purchase much of Te Urewera illegally and later excluded Tūhoe from the establishment of Te Urewera National Park. The Crown, he continued, was 'remorseful for the suffering it has caused' and 'deeply sorry' for its failure to make amends. It would never forget its unwarranted and gratuitous behaviour and now wished to compensate for its sins. The Crown would 'work hard to regain the trust of Tūhoe' and 'build afresh its relationship' with the *iwi*. Mr Finlayson then thanked Tūhoe for providing the Crown with this opportunity to do this, adding, 'We take responsibility for that suffering. Today, I seek your forgiveness. And I reiterate the Crown's commitment to your settlement' (Figure 1.1).

Figure 1.1 The Honourable Christopher Finlayson delivers the Crown's formal apology to Tūhoe for breaches of the Treaty of Waitangi as the Maungapōhatu flag is unfurled; 23 August 2014
(© Auckland War Memorial Museum – Tāmaki Paenga Hira)

As he finished speaking, with head bowed, the assembled delegation on the stage stood up and gathered around Finlayson to sing a mournful *waiata* (song), thus bringing this official part of the ceremony to a close.

What is striking about Finlayson's speech was not its candour in acknowledging the full extent of wrongs perpetrated against generations of Tūhoe by successive New Zealand governments but its personification of the body responsible for those violations. Nowhere in the attorney-general's 3,300-word apology did he use the term the 'state'; nor was there any mention of 'government' (except for two references to Tūhoe 'self-government'); nor was the apology given on behalf of the people of New Zealand. By contrast, 'the Crown' was named no less than 64 times as the guilty party. Equally striking is the extraordinary range of different emotions and dispositions attributed to the Crown. It is, by turn, 'disgraced', 'dishonoured' and 'deeply sorrowful' for its behaviour; it confesses to having acted illegally and immorally, yet is eager to 'atone' for its duplicity; it 'regrets' its failures; it is 'humbled' and profoundly 'remorseful' yet 'grateful' for this opportunity to make amends; above all, it 'hopes' to build afresh its relationship with the Tūhoe people, a relationship that will endure for future generations. The narrative was reminiscent of a court trial in which a lawyer, speaking on behalf of the offending party, expresses the client's contrition and desire for forgiveness.

Events of this kind have become regular features of the postcolonial political landscape and settlement process in New Zealand and highlight important issues about the process of historical reconciliation and the recognition of indigenous rights. But they also raise some fundamental philosophical, legal and anthropological questions about governance, the state and the nature of sovereignty in those countries whose political systems are based on the Westminster model of constitutional monarchy. In these highly ritualised deeds-of-settlement ceremonies, past wrongdoings are acknowledged and forgiveness sought for the suffering these have caused, but the wrongdoing is always attributed to the Crown, never to the government or its officials or to any named individuals. The incantation accompanying each public deed-of-settlement agreement generally follows a prescribed format that must be read aloud without deviating from the script. Notwithstanding the choreographed manner of their delivery, these apologies are deeply felt and highly significant, often evoking raw emotions among those present.[1] Some participants say the apology is of equal if not greater significance than the financial compensation. In these orations, the Crown 'unreservedly' apologises to members of the *iwi* and their ancestors for the many failures to 'honour its obligations' and proclaims its desire to restore its 'reputation' and 'honour'.[2] 'Honour' in this context is very different from the more diffuse cultural concept of honour that featured so prominently in early anthropological studies of peasant societies and the Mediterranean (Schneider 1971; Davis 1977). The complex meanings of the term 'honour of the Crown', and the problems associated with that category, are addressed later in this book. But as these and other public events show, the Crown often occupies a central place in the national imaginary of postcolonial settler societies. Like Thomas Hobbes's Leviathan, it is often understood as a reified, distant, powerful and overarching sovereign that straddles the whole of government and operates at a level of reality above, and separate from, everyday life. The nature of these realities and the work that the idea of the Crown performs in New Zealand and other Commonwealth countries is the subject of this book.

While New Zealand represents perhaps an extreme case of reification, the concept of the Crown plays no less an important role in the constitutional orders of Australia, Canada and the United Kingdom (UK). However, there are often wide discrepancies between constitutional orders and how everyday political life is understood and enacted. One of the most important findings of our study, in fact, was just how differently the Crown features in the national imaginaries, cultural understandings and contemporary usages of these four countries. For example, in Australia the Crown was absent from the political discourses and imaginaries of most Australians. Anne Twomey (2006) has shown how central the Crown remains as a legal entity in Australia and how it continues to discreetly underpin Australia's state institutions. Yet almost all of our Australian interviewees did not see, did not understand or did not want to be reminded of that fact because the Crown is seen as a

[1] A good example of this was the recent Crown apology and reconciliation package offered to the people of Parihaka, a Taranaki-region settlement which, in the late 1800s, became a focus of non-violent Māori resistance to settler land confiscations and was brutally sacked by government troops while its leaders were imprisoned and deported to the South Island. As one Radio New Zealand journalist observed, 'people openly wept as the apology was read out by Treaty Negotiations Minister Chris Finlayson' (Haunui-Thompson 2017).

[2] See Hickey 2012. The attorney-general used almost exactly the same formula of words in an earlier oral apology given to Ngai Tāmanuhiri (McLean 2015: 193).

colonial relic that has limited legitimacy in Australia. Even some Australian monarchists prefer 'Crown Republic' to 'the Crown'. In Canada, we found that the Crown appears to play almost no role at all in the political imaginary of the state. The metonym for the federal state is 'Ottawa'; for Ontario it is 'Queen's Park', which is the location in Toronto of the executive and legislative branches of the provincial government; and so forth for each province. The Crown in Canada is a concept largely linked to the entrenched position of the monarchy in the patriated Constitution Act, 1982. Canadian monarchists have made huge efforts to imagine a Canadianised sovereign, the 'Maple Crown' (MacLeod 2008; Lagassé 2014). And in Canada too the judiciary has in recent years coined 'the honour of the Crown' as crucial to relationships between governments and the various aboriginal peoples (First Nations, Métis and Inuit). As in New Zealand – but not Australia – the indigenous peoples of Canada have put the Crown at the forefront of many issues. But there is nothing in Canada that compares with the usage of the Crown in New Zealand, or the complex set of relationships and responsibilities that Chris Finlayson's speech invokes. The UK is different again, although the non-federal Westminster constitutional order is very similar to that of New Zealand. The actual person of the reigning monarch is much more important than the constitutional framework within which the Crown sits for almost everyone we spoke to there.

It is not so much the constitutional similarities of the Crown as the differences in the Crown's meanings and manifestations in each of these four countries that interest us and which constitute the problem we seek to address. As we will illustrate in subsequent chapters, the historical, genealogical and cultural character of the Crown and its unstable and competing meanings are issues rich in anthropological, legal and political importance.

Legal Fiction or Social Fact: The Crown as Metonym for the State

Since 1840 the Crown has stood at the heart of New Zealand's constitutional order as the embodiment of state authority and power and key signatory to the Treaty of Waitangi. That treaty, agreed to in 1840 between a British consul and some 540 leaders of indigenous Māori tribes, has come to be the basis of bicultural public policy objectives, and it is often considered to be practically, if not legally, the country's founding document. Yet, as former New Zealand attorney-general

Margaret Wilson (2011: 1) notes, the Crown is also 'a useful fiction that enables government to distance themselves from direct responsibility for obligations under the Treaty'. The implications of this contradiction are profound and yet have rarely been explored. How can the Crown, as the constitutional heart of the political system, be a 'useful fiction' and enable governments to distance themselves from their legal obligations? Perhaps before trying to analyse the Crown's contribution to the art of government and the machinery of state power, we must first pose the question, what exactly *is* the Crown, as an imagined entity and as a subject for political and anthropological study? If it is a 'legal fiction', how is that fiction made real and how is it put to use, by whom and in whose interests? These questions are relevant to all those countries that share the system of constitutional monarchy and Her Majesty Queen Elizabeth as their head of state,[3] but nowhere more so than in the UK and three of its former dominions, Australia, Canada and New Zealand.

Legal theorising on the nature of the Crown generally sees it as a metonym for government and the state. According to Stephen Sedley (2011: 270), '[t]he Crown, for good historical reasons, is simply the visible icon which stands for that intangible but very real entity, the State'. However, the individual who wears the crown 'is a separate person, recognised by law, who is divorced . . . from all but the formalities of state power' (270). While this idea of the separation of the 'King's two bodies' has become deeply institutionalised and axiomatic in British legal thought, Sedley suggests that lawyers find the Crown 'a source of continuing and unnecessary puzzlement' (270). For Janet McLean (2012: 2), writing on the state in British legal thought, the Crown is 'common law's closest approximation to the state'. This suggests that the concept of the Crown is the nearest equivalent to the State in public law, but just how overlapping and interchangeable are these concepts? As we show in Chapter 3, this question has important practical as well as theoretical implications for understanding postcolonial states, the construction of political authority and the challenges for constitutional reform in Westminster-style political systems. Martin Loughlin (1999: 33), another leading constitutional historian, argues that 'the Crown has, in practice, provided a poor substitute for the idea of the State'. Both he and Sedley

[3] These are, in alphabetical order Antigua and Barbuda, Australia, Barbados, Belize, Canada, Grenada, Jamaica, New Zealand, Papua New Guinea, Saint Kitts, Saint Lucia, Saint Vincent and the Grenadines, Solomon Islands, The Bahamas, Tuvalu and the United Kingdom.

note that 'English law does not recognise a concept of the State' (Sedley 2015: 210). While this is not entirely accurate,[4] it nonetheless highlights the conceptual and legal complexities – and obscurity – of constitutional monarchy. In the chapters that follow, we examine these assumptions by questioning not only the extent to which Crown and State are equivalent, but also what the 'realities' of the Crown entail from an ethnographic as well as an analytical perspective. Indeed, the concept of the State is just as ambiguous and problematic as that of the Crown. As the legal historian F. W. Maitland wrote over a century ago, 'the Crown is a convenient cover for ignorance: it saves us from asking difficult questions, questions which can only be answered by study of the statute book' (Maitland [1908] 1965: 418). Maitland was wrong in proposing that the statute book provided answers to the mystery and meaning of the Crown. He was also wrong about the Crown being simply a cover for ignorance. As Philippe Lagassé (2014: 271) remarks, what the Crown covers is not 'ignorance' so much as 'complexity', as it is inherently obscure and multifaceted. Yet Maitland's observations about the powers of the Crown, the uncertainties surrounding the uses of the royal prerogative and the need for scepticism towards things claimed in the *name* of the Crown are as relevant today as they were in 1908. One of those particularly 'difficult questions' concerns the meaning and ontology of the Crown itself and what that concept makes possible in the spheres of politics and law. That is, the Crown not only opens up novel ways of conceptualising authority and power and endowing personhood on the institutions of governance but it also forecloses other ways of knowing the state. As academic and prominent Māori leader Sir Tipene O'Regan described, the Crown is 'the decent face of Leviathan' (Patel 2016: 168).

Maitland's observation was made in a time when there was but a single Crown, the British Crown, which encompassed the dominions of empire. His bemusement may have increased by the invention of the Crown's divisibility after various British dominions adopted the Statute of Westminster 1931 during the 1930s and 1940s. This statute codified the divisibility of the Crown, for previously semi-independent states known as dominions to become independent nation-states with their own Crowns. The Queen is now the head of state of 16 realms, each with its own Crown. However, some realms have even divided their own

[4] As Anthony Bradley noted (Interviews, 2016), there are a few instances in English public law where the State is referred to, such as State secrets and the pensions of civil servants of the State (see Bradley, Ewing and Knight 2015).

Crowns. For instance, as we discovered in the course of our investigations, the number of Crowns in Australia is still a matter of some dispute. Each state has its own Crown, and state governors are appointed by the Queen on the advice of individual state premiers (Stokes 1998; Twomey 2008). The Northern Territory and Australian Capital Territory (ACT) are not states but have their own separate body politics, and Norfolk Island has its own executive, so Australia arguably has at least nine Crowns including its federal one (Twomey 2008: 7). In Canada's federal arrangements, by way of contrast, there are separate Crowns for each province, but it is only the governor-general who is appointed by the Queen on the advice of the federal prime minister. Lieutenant governors of each province are viceregal representatives appointed by the governor-general on the advice of the prime minister without the involvement of the Queen. The commissioners of Canada's three territories represent the federal government, not the sovereign.

In New Zealand, as in other former British colonies, the Crown appears as an abstract, polysemous entity which, like the state, is positioned both 'above' society yet within it. Like other 'key symbols' (Ortner 1973) it has a spectrum of meanings that are fluid, condensed, polyvalent and ambiguous. Historically, the Crown embodied the British Empire; today it serves more as a compendious cloak for aligning contemporary governmental authority with the trappings of archaic ceremonies, rules and meanings (Boyce 2008; McLean 2008). Cox (2008a) calls it the 'conceptual placeholder' or proxy for the state and highlights its shifting connotations. But if the Crown is a proxy for state authority with fluid and shifting meanings, what is the nature of that authority? How and when do those meanings shift? Who 'speaks' for the Crown, and where does it begin and end? For example, does it refer to the executive branch of government, or does it include the courts, Parliament, local government, provinces and states? How does this ambiguity affect those who have to deal with the Crown in its different guises? And what remains of the doctrine of the 'indivisibility' of the Crown, or the idea of 'Crown immunity', the historic doctrine that the 'Crown can do no wrong'?

Hidden in Plain Sight

Despite major interest in the history of the Crown and its legal status (Sunkin and Payne 1999; Twomey 2006; Boyce 2008; Cox 2008b; McLean 2012), there have been few comprehensive accounts of the Crown as a socio-political institution and cultural entity. This is an important omission, for while the Crown is a familiar icon and commonly used idiom in many Commonwealth countries, particularly New Zealand, Australia, Canada and the UK, it is also a constitutional enigma with confusing and often contradictory meanings. In New Zealand, for example, most people assume that they know what the Crown is and therefore seldom bother to think about it. It is treated as a given: it is the ultimate source of legal authority; it is the head of state; it is an institution with a history that connects the country all the way back to the Westminster model of government, to British colonialism, to Queen Victoria and the British Empire, and ultimately back to the divinely anointed kings of medieval England. It is a fundamental organising principle of New Zealand society (and Canadian, Australian and British society for that matter), and a major actor in the nation's political life. In New Zealand, the media refer to the Crown almost daily. It is mentioned in the context of the courts and criminal prosecutions, state finances, trade deals, land and resource use, oceans, rivers, lakes and seabed, as well as relations with indigenous peoples. In each of these instances, the Crown acts, negotiates, thinks, agrees, arbitrates, argues and articulates particular dispositions. In short, it is an actor as well as an *actant* in the actor-network theory sense of that term, i.e., an object in a network which, although 'silent and invisible', nevertheless 'acts or shifts actions' and performs tasks (Callon 2002: 63).

Yet the Crown is also inherently ambiguous and chameleon-like (Twomey 2006). Despite its high public visibility and its seeming omnipresence, it typically passes unnoticed or misrecognised. As we found repeatedly in the course of our fieldwork[5] in New Zealand, Australia, Canada and the UK, most people when asked struggled to define the institutions of the Crown beyond simple associations with Queen Elizabeth and the monarchy. Those that did tended to regard the Crown as obsolete, residual and largely irrelevant to contemporary life. At the same time, the symbols of the Crown are everywhere present (see Figures 1.2–1.6). It is the first thing a visitor sees when arriving at the airport in these four countries: it is there on the uniforms of border security officials and customs control officers; on the gateways through which returning citizens or visitors enter the country; on the face of coins and on banknotes in their wallets. The Crown features on the coat of arms; it is on the logos and lapels of the country's police, armed forces and courts.

[5] Details of our methodology and research methods for this study are outlined later in this chapter.

Figure 1.2 Crown on the badge of Australian police uniform, Sydney, Anzac Day, 25 April 2015
(Sally Raudon)

Figure 1.3 Symbols of nationhood on the New Zealand Dollar: a kiwi and Elizabeth II (Rusm/Getty Images)

It may even be there on the front cover of one's passport. Like a chameleon, it blends into its background and becomes invisible to the undiscerning eye.

Given its diffuse and extensive presence, how can we define the Crown or explain its key qualities? Is it Queen Elizabeth II, the governors-general and viceregal representatives, the government of the day, the State, a 'corporation sole' or a 'corporation aggregate', a residual term from medieval England, a metaphor or simply a mask for the use of executive power? If the public struggles to define it, so too do legal experts. For example, in the UK Stephen Sedley in his book *Ashes and Sparks* observes that '[t]he United Kingdom may be a constitutional monarchy, but an uninstructed observer today might well find difficulty in discerning either the constitution or – except in its ceremonial form – the monarchy' (Sedley 2011: 269). As Colin Turpin (2000: 203) puts it, the Crown is 'an ancient, enduring, omnipresent "something" at the centre of our constitution', but the nature of that 'something' remains elusive.

Apparitions and Shifting Forms: The Multiple Personalities of the Crown

Rather than seeking a precise or final definition of the Crown it is perhaps more analytically productive to accept that the Crown is

Figure 1.4 Canadian coat of arms, a protected symbol
(Reproduced with the permission of the Government of Canada)

not one thing but several. As Chief Justice Elias of the Supreme Court of New Zealand summed it up, the Crown 'has different meanings according to context' (*Attorney-General* v. *Chapman*

Figure 1.5 Commonwealth Australian coat of arms
(Reproduced with the permission of the Department of the Prime Minister and Cabinet)

[2011]: 78).[6] For example, as our opening vignette showed, the Crown in New Zealand is often embodied in the figure of a chastened minister delivering the Crown's public apology to Māori. One of the paradoxes of reconciliation with indigenous peoples is that the Crown appears simultaneously in multiple guises and, in the case of Waitangu tribunal hearings, in the same room (see Figure 1.7). Not only is it the 'defendant' or 'accused' (the 'thief in the room', responsible for stealing land), it is also a source of expert witnesses, the authority that appoints the presiding judge, the owner of the asset under claim, and the entity that made possible the creation of the redress in the first place. In this respect, the Crown provides a convenient mechanism for the state to

[6] Chief Justice Elias's argument appears to be based partly on the work of Janet McLean who observes that '[t]he common law itself contains distinct and competing versions of the Crown' (McLean 2008: 58).

Figure 1.6 New Zealand coat of arms
(New Zealand Ministry for Culture and Heritage) (ullstein bild / Contributor / Getty Images)

enter into conversation with itself in order for the government of the day to find a face-saving way to resolve historical grievances and tensions.

Elsewhere, the Crown appears as the nation's bookkeeper and insurer of last resort; the metonymic holder of the Treasury's finances (typically referred to as 'Crown accounts'). It is the ultimate holder of all lands – including the 'radical title' of all freehold and leasehold lands – and of precious resources that lie beneath them ('Crown minerals'). Even in respect of moveable property, under common law that applies in many Commonwealth jurisdictions the property of those who die with no will or family passes to the Crown as *bona vacantia*. The Crown also owns outright vast tracts of land ('Crown Lands'), but also can manage particular parts of the country (such as the Crown Red Zone properties in

Figure 1.7 A Waitangi Tribunal hearing at the meeting house at Ōrākei marae, Auckland, in 2007 for the Wai 262 claim into Māori rights to traditional fauna and flora, and intellectual property. As with most other tribunal hearings, tribunal members are seated at rear centre, with representatives of the Crown on one side and claimants on the other
(Courtesy of New Zealand Herald/newspix.co.nz)

the earthquake-struck parts of Christchurch, New Zealand[7]). In Australia, current laws grant the Crown, not Aboriginal people, the right to decide what happens to Aboriginal culture and heritage. In New South Wales (NSW), for example, the National Parks and Wildlife Act (1975) stipulates that Aboriginal objects are considered to be 'property of the Crown'. According to indigenous activists and reformers, this gives the NSW Office of Environment and Heritage 'the power to authorise the damage or destruction of Aboriginal objects and places, through the issuing of consents' (Thorpe 2017). Elsewhere the Crown is a prosecutor and privileged legal adviser ('the Crown Law Office')[8] whose actions are

[7] The Central City Red Zone in Christchurch, New Zealand's second largest city, was an area of land and buildings so badly damaged by the February 2011 earthquake that it was deemed unsafe and designated a public exclusion zone.

[8] In Australia, these lawyers are often referred to as 'Crownies'.

sometimes described as 'dishonest' and 'vindictive' (Kidd 2016). It upholds the rule of law and settles disputes; bestows honours on some citizens and incarcerates others; demands oaths of allegiance from its judges, ministers and civil servants; and makes deals with international trade organisations and private companies and investors. Indebted students in New Zealand might be surprised to find that their loans are owed to the Crown. Finally, the Crown also represents sovereignty and the sovereign herself: Her Majesty the Queen in Right of New Zealand, Canada, the United Kingdom or Australia (or her representatives, the governors-general and viceroys).

Even in statutes passed by what is sometimes known as 'the Crown in Parliament', what constitutes the Crown is often far from clear. According to the Copyright Act 1994 (NZ), the Crown 'means Her Majesty the Queen in right of New Zealand' including Ministers of the Crown, government departments and the Offices of Parliament. The Public Finance Act 1989 (NZ) defines the Crown as the 'Sovereign in right of New Zealand' including ministers, but *excludes* offices of Parliament. The Constitution Act 1986 (NZ) mentions the Crown only in regard to 'Ministers of the Crown'. And the Crown Entities Act 2004 (NZ) draws a distinction between the Crown, Parliament and 'Crown entities'; for example, the Productivity Commission and Air New Zealand are bodies owned by the Crown ('Crown entities'), but they are not considered part of the Crown itself.

Arguably the most expansive definition of the Crown is provided by New Zealand's Office of Treaty Settlements (OTS)[9]:

> While 'the Crown' is a convenient way of referring to one party involved in settlement negotiations, it can seem to be something rather abstract or impersonal. Because of our democratic system it can also be said that ultimate authority or sovereignty in fact rests with voters. In this sense *the Crown also symbolises the people of New Zealand.*
>
> (OTS 2015: 17, my emphasis)

The paradox of this statement is neatly captured by Janet McLean, who concludes that the Crown 'can sometimes be imagined as a concept that embraces "the people" and acts according to their collective will . . . and sometimes as a concept that stands apart from the people and appears to

[9] The main role of the Office of Treaty Settlements is to negotiate Treaty of Waitangi settlements. It also advises and requires claimant groups to obtain negotiation mandates so that they are ready to enter negotiations.

exercise a "will of its own". In other words, it can enjoy pre-democratic and post-democratic meanings – sometimes both at the same time' (McLean 2008: 36–37). This is an intriguing proposition which, if taken literally, challenges the idea of the Crown as a separate entity (and moral person) positioned above society and the government of the day. The logic here is that the democratic system renders all subjects of the Crown as *part of the Crown*. This notion not only has curiously metaphysical underpinnings but it also recalls the seventeenth-century conservative philosopher Thomas Hobbes and his image of the modern state as a giant crowned sovereign who looms over the land and its people (as we illustrate in Chapter 3). All this serves to highlight yet again the shape-shifting, ephemeral and ambiguous qualities of the Crown as an entity that is simultaneously singular yet multiple, concrete yet abstract, part of everyday society yet set apart from society, and historically continuous yet temporally bounded.

These apparent contradictions and definitional imprecisions pose substantial difficulties and challenges for lawmakers, politicians and policy professionals. Indeed, in its response to a recent Law Commission report proposing a new Crown Civil Proceedings Act for New Zealand (Law Commission 2014), the New Zealand Law Society (2014) highlighted a series of problems with current definitions of the Crown. It declares that 'continued use of an outdated and amorphous expression such as "the Crown" will not assist the Commission's purpose of modernising the law'. Despite these warnings, it nonetheless concludes that the terminology and concept of the Crown is 'time-honoured and should continue – rather than moving to the use of more modern expressions such as "the Government" or "the State"' (New Zealand Law Society 2014). Part of their argument (or perhaps a reply to an Interpretation Act discussion paper from the Parliamentary Counsel Office [PCO]) was that it is the ambiguity of the Crown that makes it legally potent. Switching to another term, or formulating a single definition of the Crown, would ultimately make the term unworkable.

This brings us back to the question of what the Crown makes possible. Some political and constitutional theorists argue that such countries as Australia, New Zealand and Canada should abolish the Crown to clarify and demystify their political systems in order to bring them into the twenty-first century. However, this may come at a cost. The Crown can lend an aura of dignity and authority to the grubby workings of politics, as constitutional theorists have long observed (Bagehot [1867] 2001). Part of that aura arises from the idea of tradition, which, as Hobsbawm and Ranger (1983) noted long ago, is often essential for institutions seeking legitimacy and authority. The idea of a sovereign located above the arena of mundane politics, providing a sense of historical continuity (unlike governments, which come and go), can be reassuring and politically useful for the settlement of historical grievances with indigenous peoples.

As we argue in this book, the concept of the Crown in New Zealand – as in Canada, Australia and the UK – performs a number of important political, legal and symbolic functions that go beyond the creation of a sense of unity or nationhood. It gives the government of the day a great deal of latitude for manoeuvre. It bestows a sense of history, legitimacy and continuity on the institutions of the postcolonial settler state. In many respects, the Crown is the functional equivalent of what social scientists call the 'state idea' and 'state effect' (Abrams 1988; Mitchell 2006): it lends stability, authority and the illusion of concreteness to the often amorphous workings of government. It also provides a useful vehicle for the reconciliation of historical grievances and enables the appearance of a more just relationship between indigenous peoples and the settler state. At the same time, the Crown provides the moral basis for a discourse about the State's fiduciary relationship and obligations to indigenous peoples. In New Zealand and Canada (but not in Australia) the 'Honour of the Crown' is now a key principle of common law. It is often invoked by indigenous claimants to pursue rights and justice in respect of historic treaty agreements, and also as political leverage to require governments to consult and accommodate indigenous interests when making decisions in relation to contemporary resource management issues.

The Crown idea helps to cloak institutions (and those who speak for them) with an aura of authority and mystique. As Peter Boyce (2008: 5) observes of both Canada and New Zealand, 'the enshrining of state authority in "the Crown" has provided an effective mask for the steady expansion of power within the political executives'. Bagehot ([1867] 2001: 70) illustrated this over a century ago when he described how the 'dignified' elements of the English constitution (i.e., those old and venerable parts like the Queen and House of Lords) served to 'excite and preserve the reverence of the population' and thereby deflect attention from the 'efficient' parts (i.e., Parliament and government), which for him were the real locus of power and decision-making. The use of the 'royal prerogative' is perhaps the best contemporary example of how the Crown still provides cover for certain key decisions, such as the government's pronouncement that Britain would join the US-led invasion of Iraq, or the triggering of Article 50 of the Treaty of Lisbon initiating Britain's withdrawal from the European Union. In both these cases the UK government sought to implement its decisions using the powers of the royal prerogative, though in the second instance the Supreme Court ruled that the royal prerogative alone did not suffice and Parliament had to enact legislation (see Chapter 10 and the discussion of the *Miller* case).

Finally, constitutional reformers sometimes argue that the idea of the Crown is too complex and archaic and needs to be simplified: 'Realism requires that we remove the mystery and the confusion', as former New Zealand prime minister Geoffrey Palmer explained to me (Interviews, 2016). But would substituting the term 'Crown' for 'state' be any less complex, archaic or mysterious? In fact, many of the experts that we interviewed in the course of our research expressed the view that political constitutions generally need an element of majesty, mystery and ambiguity to operate effectively.

Viewing constitutional monarchy from a comparative, historical and anthropological perspective helps remind us that the Crown, like the modern state, is a social and symbolic construct, an unfinished project or work in progress that is constantly being reinvented. It also highlights the point that symbols do not passively reflect or represent political reality: they actively constitute our political worlds and make possible all sorts of political programmes and practices.

Problematising the Crown: Methodology and Approach of This Study

Our study begins from the observation that the Crown, as a legal entity and socio-political category, is typically treated as an unexamined given. This book sets out to deconstruct that category by examining the different forms that the Crown takes and the work that it performs in shaping and legitimising the constitutional order and political decision-making. A secondary aim, more theoretical and comparative in scope, is to use ethnographic insights drawn from our fieldwork as a lens for exploring wider questions concerning democracy, constitutionalism and the transformation of the modern state, particularly in those societies whose political systems are based on the Westminster model of constitutional monarchy.

Our book brings together anthropological, legal and political perspectives to explore the Crown, as a social institution, political idea, legal construct and set of cultural practices, and how it has developed historically in the realms of New Zealand, Canada, Australia and the United Kingdom. Through these combined perspectives we examine the Crown's multiple meanings, the social and political relations that it creates and the legal and political 'grey zones' that it conceals: those 'states of exception' that allow sovereign power to transcend the rule of law in the name of the public good (Schmitt 1985; Agamben 2005).

Our findings draw on theoretical and ethnographic work carried out over four years (2013–17) as part of a Royal Society of New Zealand Marsden Fund project on the contested nature of the Crown and its constitutional and cultural significance. That study included extensive fieldwork and over 220 face-to-face interviews with senior government officials, serving and former ministers, judges, legal experts, journalists and writers, political reform activists, historians, indigenous leaders and constitutional scholars from across New Zealand, Canada, Australia and the United Kingdom.[10] We also carried out numerous interviews with key individuals who represent, embody or personify the Crown: government ministers, senior judges, current and former governors-general, state governors (Australia), lieutenant governors and their official secretaries, and senior representatives of the monarchy. For each of these countries we carried out rigorous analyses of the documents, discourses and debates around the Crown, drawn from sources ranging from government archives, legislative statutes and policy texts to newspaper articles, radio reports and media interviews – in short, we adopted a 'follow that' (Marcus 1995) and 'studying through' (Wright and Reinhold 2011) approach, tracking the discourse of the Crown in its various manifestations and back and forth across different sites.

This comparative, multi-sited and ethnographically informed approach provides the basis for deeper reflection on the nature of constitutional monarchy as a system of government and its past, present and future. In each of these countries, albeit for different reasons, pressure for constitutional reform is growing, yet the reforms themselves are deeply problematic as the constitution is often poorly understood. In addressing these issues we ask, to what extent is the Crown an obstacle to constitutional reform, and what are the implications for understandings of the state if a constitutional monarchy introduces republican reforms? While we acknowledge that the powers of the Crown – in black-letter law – are

[10] Unless otherwise stated, the unreferenced quotes cited in this book are drawn from our fieldwork interviews. A small number of our interviewees asked to remain anonymous.

real and substantial, we are particularly interested in the symbolic power and the conceptual work that the idea of the Crown performs, that is, in what we term the 'Crown effect' (see Chapter 3). In the chapters that follow, we set out the political issues and conceptual problems raised by the study of the Crown and outline our approach to tackling these questions.

Aims and Scope of This Volume

The book is set out in three sections. The first examines the nature and development of the Crown from historical, legal, political and anthropological perspectives. Chapter 2 ('Genealogies of the Modern Crown: From St Edward to Queen Elizabeth II') begins by tracing the genealogy of the modern Crown in English legal and political thought. Starting with the actual crown – now a closely guarded tourist attraction in the Tower of London – we trace its development as a political symbol of constitutional monarchy and its statues within the Westminster model of parliamentary democracy. We track the Crown's key transformations from an absolute monarch who embodies sovereignty to the idea of the 'King's two bodies' in which the institution of the Crown is separated from the person of the monarch. As a singular 'corporation aggregate' presiding over its territory, we trace the Crown's geographical dispersal through colonialism. If the Crown once symbolised the cohesion and unity of Empire, today it is the sovereign head of state in sixteen independent countries. This narrative of an indivisible Crown evolving into multiple, divisible entities explains how postcolonial governments have successfully harnessed the Crown's symbolic potency to legitimise their power and authority.

Chapter 3 ('The Crown as Metonym for the State?') uses theories of the modern state (Abrams 1988; Nagengast 1994; Steinmetz 1999; Mitchell 2006) to interrogate the 'reality' of the Crown. Like the state, the Crown is an 'ideological artefact attributing unity, morality and independence to the disunited, amoral and dependent workings of the practice of government' (Abrams 1988: 81). According to leading constitutional reformers, including former New Zealand prime minister Geoffrey Palmer, the term state can readily substitute for Crown and in a way that would strip away the mysticism surrounding the constitution, providing much-needed clarity and transparency (Palmer and Butler 2016). However, we challenge the claim that the Crown is simply a proxy for the state, arguing that these terms are not coterminous as they entail different semantic fields and often perform different kinds of political work. For example, for indigenous peoples in particular, the Crown has major significance for mediating relationships with governments and states.

This theme is developed in Chapter 4 ('Indigenous Peoples and the Crown: The Sacred Duty'). One of the major paradoxes here is that, while the Crown was responsible for the alienation and dispossession of indigenous people's lands, livelihoods and autonomy, it is nonetheless the vehicle for remedying these historical wrongs. We argue that the Crown's functional ambiguity allows it to perform a plethora of moral and relational obligations that are often seen as exceeding legal provisions, such as notions of honour, trust and sacred duties. In this sense, much of the Crown's relevance is that it can be held responsible for the past. The Crown's importance to indigenous peoples is a key factor in elevating its role in settler societies.

The second part of the book examines how the Crown is embodied, symbolised and performed in each of our sites. Chapter 5 ('The Rituals of Crown and State in New Zealand') analyses the personification of the Crown, particularly in those rituals that serve to buttress state authority. Here the Crown takes on meanings that are particularly associated with the person of the monarch, in this case embodied by the governor-general. These rituals are also invented traditions that combine the pageantry of parliamentary tradition with the protocols of *tikanga Māori*. However, they are also designed to evoke the ideology of a bicultural nation unified under the Crown. Chapter 6 ('Locating the Crown in Australia: The Swag of Camp Gallipoli') turns to the Commonwealth of Australia, where despite this ubiquity in everyday life, the Crown is often regarded as a relic of little importance. In a country where constitutional reform is vigorously debated, we examine the often banal ways that this taken-for-granted symbol has shaped nationalism. For example, the Crown provides a visual anchor for national commemorations. We explore how the Crown sits ambivalently in Anzac Day, a ritualised performance of a purportedly unified Australian identity. Using examples of Camp Gallipoli (a privately operated Anzac event) and ceremonies at Canberra's Australian War Memorial, we show how the Crown is continually reinvented in different contexts. Finally, Chapter 7 ('Localising the Crown: Royals and (Re)Patriation') examines efforts by governments, monarchists and others to 'patriate' their Crowns and endow them with an explicitly national character. While some of these nationalistic projects succeed, such as the Canadian revivals of heraldry and First Nations' efforts to popularise the institution, others have proved less successful, including the Australian knighthood of Prince Phillip on Australia Day 2015. As we illustrate, for monarchists the challenge is to present the monarch – who technically is not a citizen of any country – as a cherished member of the national family.

Part III explores the Crown's role and influence in questions of constitutional reform. Chapter 8 ('The Republican Move: Cutting Colonial Ties') looks at republican initiatives to replace constitutional monarchy. Many see the Crown as an outdated, anachronistic legacy of the colonial era and view republicanism as inevitable. We consider the practical constitutional limits to reform, including demonstrations from recent history. Examples include successes such as Canadian Patriation (1982), and failures including the Australian constitutional referendum (1999) and the New Zealand Head of State Referenda Bill (2010). Chapter 9 ('Constitutional Reform and the Politics of Public Engagement') explores the conditions that promote or inhibit meaningful constitutional deliberation. Taking up theoretical debates over deliberative democracy, and in the context of growing scepticism about democratic institutions, we propose a concept of 'performative constitutionalism' as an alternative framework for evaluating how reform initiatives are carried out in practice. Using examples from New Zealand's 'constitutional conversation' (2013–14) and referendum on a proposed flag change (2016), we illustrate how these initiatives actually foreclosed meaningful deliberation on issues of constitutional importance.

Chapter 10 ('Crown Prerogative: Reining in the Powers') focuses on Britain and the Crown's prerogative powers. What these residual powers are, and when they can be appropriately used, are vigorously debated and yet remain ambiguous. Is the Crown's chief merit its ability to act as a check on the executive, or it simply the mask used to legitimate and hide the controversial use of executive power – such as the decision to go to war or ratify an international treaty? The British exit from the European Union (Brexit) and the question of who had authority to invoke Article 50 of the Lisbon Treaty, thereby triggering Brexit, illustrated these tensions between political and legal constitutionalism. Taking this analysis further, we explore the Crown's controversial role in Britain's overseas dependencies such as the Chagos Islands in the Indian Ocean. We ask: What is the responsibility of the Crown towards the people of these small island domains? What significance can be drawn from the fact that some 85 per cent of the tax havens mentioned in the Panama Papers are British Overseas Territories?

As the longest reigning monarch in history, Queen Elizabeth II's popularity as a sovereign has been shored up by her longevity. Chapter 11 ('The Queen Is Dead, Long Live the King?') considers how the death of the Queen may precipitate initiatives for new constitutional arrangements across the Commonwealth. We ask, why is it taboo to canvas constitutional reform while Queen Elizabeth lives? What are the temporal implications of the sovereign's death and succession? Both monarchists and republicans recognise the death of the sovereign as a time of risk to the constitutional order. From lobbyists advocating a change to public servants charged with ensuring a smooth transition, we examine the potential issues of Prince Charles' succession, and efforts to smooth or disrupt his accession to the throne.

The concluding chapter (Chapter 12: 'The Future of the Crown in an Age of Uncertainty: Sempiternal or Crumbling Foundation?') returns to the paradoxes that lie at the heart of the system of constitutional monarchy and asks, 'What is the future of the Crown?' Constitutional monarchy is often described by its supporters as 'the best of all systems of government', and yet it also generates opacity, confusion and contradiction. To what extent is the Crown a unifying force and indelible part of national identity in those countries where the Queen is head of state? Drawing together the findings of our study, we show how the Crown makes possible certain relationships and political arrangements and why many regard it as irreplaceable. Eradicating the ambiguity and mystique of the Crown, as constitutional reformers insist, may come at a considerable political cost. Against a background of constant laments regarding the 'need to educate the public' about their constitution, we ask whether constitutional reform would make the political system any more rational or legible.

References

Abrams, Philip. 1988. 'Notes on the Difficulty of Studying the State (1977).' *Journal of Historical Sociology* 1(1): 58–89.

Agamben, Giorgio. 2005. *State of Exception*. Translated by Kevin Attell. Chicago: Chicago University Press.

Attorney-General v. *Chapman* [2011] *NZSC 110* (Supreme Court, New Zealand).

Bagehot, Walter. [1867] 2001. *The English Constitution*, edited by Paul Smith. Cambridge: Cambridge University Press.

Boyce, Peter J. 2008. *The Queen's Other Realms: The Crown and Its Legacy in Australia, Canada and New Zealand*. Annandale, NSW: The Federation Press.

Bradley, Anthony Wilfred, Keith D. Ewing and C. J. S. Knight. 2015. *Constitutional and Administrative Law*. 16th edition. Harlow: Pearson Education.

Callister, Paul. 2011. 'Attitudes towards Biculturalism in New Zealand: Asking the Wrong Questions, Getting the Wrong Answers?' Working Paper, August 2011. Wellington: Callister & Associates.

Callon, Michel. 2002. 'Actor-Network Theory.' In *International Encyclopedia of the Social & Behavioral Sciences*, 62–66. Elsevier/ScienceDirect.

Cox, Noel. 2008a. 'The Legitimacy of Government and the Normative Influence of the Crown on a Political Construct.' Paper presented at the 43rd Association of Law Teachers Conference, March 2008, St. Anne's College, University of Oxford.

2008b. *A Constitutional History of the New Zealand Monarchy*. Saarbrücken, Germany: VDM Verlag.

Davis, John. 1977. *People of the Mediterranean: An Essay in Comparative and Social Anthropology*. London: Routledge and Kegan Paul.

Finlayson, Christopher. 2014. 'Address to Tuhoe-Crown Settlement Day in Taneatua.' 22 August. Accessed 18 May 2018 at www.beehive.govt.nz/speech/address-tuhoe-crown-settlement-day-taneatua.

Haunui-Thompson, Shannon. 2017. 'Tears as Crown Apologises for Parihaka Atrocities.' *Radio New Zealand*, 9 June. Accessed 10 June 2017 at www.radionz.co.nz/news/te-manu-korihi/332613/tears-as-crown-apologises-for-parihaka-atrocities.

Hickey, Maureen. 2012. 'Apologies in Settlements.' In Treaty of Waitangi Settlements, edited by Janine Hayward and Nicola R. Wheen, 62–74. Wellington: Bridget Williams Books.

Hobsbawm, Eric and Terence Ranger (eds.). 1983. *The Invention of Tradition*. Cambridge: Cambridge University Press.

Jackson, D. Michael and Philippe Lagassé (eds.). 2014. *Canada and the Crown: Essays on Constitutional Monarchy*. Montreal: McGill-Queen's University Press (MQUP).

Kidd, Robb. 2016. 'John Banks Fails to Recoup Court Costs.' *New Zealand Herald*, 14 July. Accessed 26 May 2017 at www.nzherald.co.nz/nz/news/article.cfm?c_id=1&objectid=11674655.

Lagassé, Philippe. 2014. 'Conclusion: The Contentious Canadian Crown.' In *Canada and the Crown: Essays on Constitutional Monarchy*, edited by D. Michael Jackson and Philippe Lagassé, 271–87. Montreal: McGill-Queen's University Press (MQUP).

Law Commission – Te Aka Matua o te Ture. 2014. 'A New Crown Civil Proceedings Act for New Zealand.' *Issues Paper 35*. Wellington.

Loughlin, Martin. 1999. 'The State, the Crown and the Law.' In *The Nature of the Crown: A Legal and Political Analysis*, edited by Maurice Sunkin and Sebastian Payne, 33–76. Oxford: Clarendon Press.

MacLeod, Kevin. 2008. *A Crown of Maples: Constitutional Monarchy in Canada*. Gatineau, QC: Department of Canadian Heritage.

Maitland, Frederic W. [1908] 1965. *The Constitutional History of England: A Course of Lectures Delivered*. Cambridge: Cambridge University Press.

Marcus, George. 1995. 'Ethnography in/of the World System: The Emergence of Multi-Sited Ethnography.' *Annual Review of Anthropology* 24: 95–117.

McLean, Janet. 2008. '"Crown Him with Many Crowns": The Crown and the Treaty of Waitangi.' *New Zealand Journal of Public and International Law* 6(1): 35–58.

2012. *Searching for the State in British Legal Thought: Competing Conceptions of the Public Sphere*. Cambridge: Cambridge University Press.

2015. 'Crown, Empire and Redressing the Historical Wrongs of Colonisation in New Zealand.' *New Zealand Law Review* 2015(2): 187–212.

Mitchell, Timothy. 2006. 'Society, Economy and the State Effect.' In *The Anthropology of the State: A Reader*, edited by Aradhana Sharma and Anil Gupta, 169–86. Oxford: Blackwell.

Nagengast, Carole. 1994. 'Violence, Terror and the Crisis of the State.' *Annual Review of Anthropology* 23: 109–36.

New Zealand Law Society. 2014. 'Problems if "the Crown" Is Defined.' *Law Talk no. 850*, 12 September. Accessed 18 May 2018 at www.lawsociety.org.nz/lawtalk/lawtalk-archives/issue-850/problems-if-the-crown-is-defined.

Office of Treaty Settlements (OTS). 2015. *Healing the Past, Building a Future: A Guide to Treaty of Waitangi Claims and Negotiations with the Crown*. Wellington: Office of Treaty Settlements

Ortner, Sherry. 1973. 'On Key Symbols.' *American Anthropologist* 75(5): 1338–46.

Palmer, Geoffrey and Andrew Butler. 2016. *A Constitution for Aotearoa New Zealand*. Wellington: Victoria University Press.

Patel, Aaron Jai. 2016. 'Imagining the Right to Rule: The Crown as a Political Symbol in New Zealand.' MA thesis. University of Auckland.

Schmitt, Carl. 1985. *Political Theology: Four Chapters on the Concept of Sovereignty*. Chicago: University of Chicago Press.

Schneider, Jane. 1971. 'Of Vigilance and Virgins: Honor, Shame and Access to Resources in Mediterranean Societies.' *Ethnology* 10(1): 1–24.

Sedley, Stephen. 2011. *Ashes and Sparks: Essays on Law and Justice*. Cambridge: Cambridge University Press.

2015. *Lions under the Throne: Essays on the History of English Public Law*. Cambridge: Cambridge University Press.

Steinmetz, George (ed.). 1999. *State/Culture: State-Formation after the Cultural Turn*. Ithaca, NY, and London: Cornell University Press.

Stokes, Michael. 1998. 'Are There Separate State Crowns?' *Sydney Law Review* 20(1): 127–43.

Sunkin, Maurice and Sebastian Payne (eds.). 1999. *The Nature of the Crown: A Legal and Political Analysis*. Oxford: Clarendon Press.

Thorpe, Robbie. 2017. 'NSW: The "Crown" Owns Aboriginal Culture and Heritage.' *Treaty Republic*. Website. Accessed 25 May 2017 at treatyrepublic.net/node/988.

Turpin, Colin. 2000. 'Review of Sunkin and Payne's *The Nature of the Crown*.' *Cambridge Law Journal* 59(1): 203–5.

Twomey, Anne. 2006. *The Chameleon Crown: The Queen and Her Australian Governors*. Sydney: Federation Press.

2008. 'Responsible Government and the Divisibility of the Crown.' *Public Law*, 742–67. Sydney Law School Research Paper No. 08/137.

Wilson, Margaret. 2011. 'Treaty Settlement Process for Historical Grievances Relating to Land 1999–2005: A Crown Perspective from a Former Minister.' Unpublished conference paper. Between Indigenous and Settler Governance conference, 18–20 August, University of Western Sydney, Sydney.

Wright, Susan and Sue Reinhold. 2011. '"Studying Through": A Strategy for Studying Political Transformation. Or Sex, Lies and British Politics.' In *Policy Worlds: Anthropology and the Analysis of Contemporary Power*, edited by Cris Shore, Susan Wright and Davide Però, 86–104. New York: Berghahn.

PART I

The Nature and Development of the Crown

2

Genealogies of the Modern Crown

From St Edward to Queen Elizabeth II

DAVID V. WILLIAMS

Introduction

This chapter analyses some key moments in the transition from feudalist royal autocracy to constitutional monarchy in English legal history. It is important because there remain to this day, in all four realms we have studied, significant (though often ill-defined) Crown prerogative and reserve powers. Once the personal powers of a feudal king, they remain in the hands of the sovereign, or vice-regal representatives of the Crown, who are required, by written constitution or convention, to act on the advice of ministers of the Crown. It is often suggested that those who run the executive branch of government are keen to preserve and enhance its powers whilst at the same time avoiding accountability either to parliaments or to the courts. Geoffrey Palmer's career-long efforts to move New Zealand from 'unbridled power' (Palmer 1979) to 'bridled power' (Palmer and Palmer 2004) have focussed on such issues, culminating in his advocacy for a republican written constitution in his most recent books (Palmer and Butler 2016, 2018).

The oftentimes controversial reliance on Crown or royal prerogative powers by those acting in the monarch's service in the executive branch of government is discussed in Chapter 10. Examples include such disparate matters as the dismissal of Gough Whitlam as Prime Minister of Australia by Governor-General John Kerr (1975); the expulsion of Chagos Islanders from Diego Garcia in the Indian Ocean by an Order in Council to make way for a United States war facility (1968–73); the decision of the British Government to authorise the invasion of Iraq prior to support from a House of Commons vote (that was explicitly stated to be purely symbolic and not binding on the government) and without the necessary United Nations Security Council authorisation (2003); the response of the Governor-General of Canada to the request of the Prime

Minister, Stephen Harper, to prorogue Parliament when a vote of no confidence seemed imminent (2008); the light shone by the Panama Papers on international tax evasion and offshore banking operations in tiny British Crown colonies lacking any forms of democratic accountability (2016); and the attempt by the British Prime Minister, Theresa May, to invoke article 50 of the Treaty of Lisbon, thus enabling the United Kingdom to begin exiting from the European Union without the need for parliamentary scrutiny of the Government's decision (2017).

What these diverse examples have in common is a contemporary reliance on Crown prerogative powers that are remnants of absolute powers once vested in divinely ordained medieval English monarchs, which have since developed into a form of government termed 'constitutional monarchy'. An important reason to focus on these residual prerogative powers is that the lack of effective constraints on executive government powers remains a major issue in many liberal democracies. Indeed, Campbell Sharman (1994) has argued that the focus of Australian debates on whether or how to move to a republican constitution entirely misses 'that part of our constitutional structure most in need of change: the limited role of representative institutions in checking the exercise of executive power' (113).

Crowns

Some of those we interviewed responded initially by identifying the Crown with the material objects on display in the Tower of London. The display there – protected by high-level security – is not 'the' Crown but nine crowns on display in the Jewel House. First and foremost is the St Edward's Crown, crafted in 1661 by Sir Robert Vyner, with later alterations and additions (Keay 2002) (Figure 2.1).

The original St Edward's Crown, a medieval relic reportedly dating back to Edward the Confessor, had been melted down on Cromwell's orders along with other regalia in an effort to eradicate symbols of monarchy and replenish the war-depleted coffers of the Commonwealth. When Charles II was restored to the throne, his coronation committee revived the rituals with as much majesty as possible. Chief of these tasks was to 'direct ye remaking such Royall Ornaments and Regalia' to recreate, in the same 'fashion', what had been lost and to 'retain the same names' (Keay 2002: 35). Those who knew better encouraged the pleasing, but unprovable, myth that the St Edward's Crown of 1661 included materials recycled from the original St Edward's Crown – a link in a

Figure 2.1 St Edward's Crown, used to coronate the monarch (GraphicaArtis/Getty Images)

perpetual chain of sovereignty anchored by a medieval saint (Barclay 2008). Though not invariably used in coronations since then, this was the crown used at the moment of coronation in 1953. It is depicted on the New Zealand Coat of Arms to symbolise Her Majesty as Queen of New Zealand under the Royal Titles Act 1953. Though this crown was recycled from the metals and stones of previous models, the physicality of a crown has endured for centuries of English history. Ornately fashioned by artifice, it is an enabling ritual object in state ceremonies. For our purposes, however, it is not the qualities of crowns as material objects but the Crown as a metaphor for monarchy itself, and a metonym for the entire constitutional order in Commonwealth realms. The Crown has evolved into a political symbol of secular constitutional monarchy, combining the distinctive features of the Westminster model of parliamentary governance and representative democracy with the separation of executive, legislative and judicial branches of government.

A Journey of Fits and Starts

The journey towards the modern divisible Crown in Commonwealth nations was not the result of a smooth evolutionary development over the centuries. It is a common conceit that the British constitution can be distinguished from other modern constitutions because it has not been birthed in revolutionary turmoil. Thus a British journalist in 2008 asked, 'Why don't we have a written constitution?' and provided this answer:

> Essentially because the country has been too stable for too long. The governing elites of many European nations, such as France and Germany, have been forced to draw up constitutions in response to popular revolt or war.
>
> Great Britain, by contrast, remained free of the revolutionary fervour that swept much of the Continent in the 19th century. As a result, this country's democracy has been reformed incrementally over centuries rather than in one big bang. For younger countries, including the United States and Australia, codification of their citizens' rights and political systems was an essential step towards independence. Ironically, several based their written constitutions on Britain's unwritten version.
>
> (Morris 2008)

'Because of the relative absence of discontinuity here', as British constitutional expert Robert Morris reflected, 'we have kept the apparatus of feudal government' (Morris, Interviews, 2016).

The evolution of English conceptions of the Crown was punctuated by periods of considerable instability, fractious interruptions and significant loss of life in civil wars and revolutions. It is just that these violent events occurred well prior to the modern era. The rules of royal succession were by no means clear, and warfare often settled the issue. The contest in 1066 to succeed the saintly, childless Anglo-Saxon king Edward the

Confessor, whose name continues to hold a place of primacy in royal regalia, was settled in favour of one of the two military forces that invaded England that year. It was the Duke of Normandy, William the Conqueror, who seized power and was crowned with St Edward's crown. He introduced a feudal order with Crown ownership of the radical title to all the land of the kingdom. Crown radical title continues as the basis of real property law in common law jurisdictions to this day. The death of William I's son Henry I in 1135 led to a succession struggle between his daughter Matilda and his nephew Stephen. This was initially settled by an invasion and coup d'état in Stephen's favour, but a civil war – sometimes known as 'the Anarchy' – ensued for most of two decades until the Treaty of Wallingford 1153 left Stephen as king, but with Matilda's son as his designated heir. Half a century later John's reign as king was interrupted by civil wars that Magna Carta failed to quell and a period (1216–17) when Louis of France was proclaimed as king in St Paul's cathedral and controlled much of England. The fifteenth century saw utter instability as the kingship alternated from one contender to another in spasms of extreme violence between Yorkist and Lancastrian lineages in conflicts known as the War of the Roses – though its impact in terms of death and destruction was more severe in some regions than others. However insecure the incumbent monarch may have been during many of those conflict-filled decades in the centuries after 1066, the king's legal powers over his barons, bishops, burgesses and subjects were subject to few constraints. Royal absolutism was firmly entrenched with the feudalist form of governance. The king ruled with virtually unbridled power in his own hands.

The Tudor Constitution

The victory of Henry Tudor at Bosworth Field in 1485 ended the War of Roses. Henry VII and the Tudor monarchs who followed him brought peace to the country and bolstered the powers of the state. Yet political and economic earthquakes in the Tudor era led to transformations in how the powers of the Crown came to be exercised and implemented. Henry VIII had been granted the title Fidei Defensor [Defender of the Faith] by Pope Leo X in 1521 as a reward for defending the supremacy of the papacy in matters of faith and Catholic doctrines on sacraments, including marriage. Circumstances changed in the 1530s when the king sought to repudiate both his own marriage and the pope's authority in England. He defied the papacy, declared himself Supreme Head of the

Church of England, ordered the dissolution of most monasteries and confiscated their assets, resulting in an economic reordering and political transformation of massive proportions. This break from centuries of fidelity to the most sacred institutions of Christendom in western Europe were for reasons quite different from the religious inspirations of Protestant reformers in other parts of Europe. He needed lawful mechanisms of awe and majesty to legitimate his continuing authority. He found it in the English Parliament.

Parliament was an institution that had played a not overly important role in the constitutional arrangements of the state and occasional law-making from the middle of the thirteenth century. This changed dramatically in the 1530s when Henry VIII turned to Parliament to provide an autochthonous source of legitimation for his repudiation of papal authority, to render lawful his divorce from Queen Catherine and to proclaim himself Head of the Church of England. This was accomplished through the Act of Supremacy 1534. Subsequently, Parliament complied with the king's requests – called Bills of Attainder – to condemn to death without trial many of those with whom Henry fell out, including his consort Catherine Howard and his chief minister Thomas Cromwell. Parliament passed acts to alter the rules of royal succession to suit the king's ever-changing circumstances and desires in Acts of Succession 1533, 1536 and 1544. In the preamble to the 1544 Act, Parliament also reinstated 'Defender of the Faith' as one of Henry's titles – in explicit defiance of Pope Paul III's excommunication of the monarch. Oddly, this title remains a royal title to this day – not just for the United Kingdom but also in several Commonwealth realms that have never had an established church. In Canada, for example, the Royal Style and Titles Act 1985 provides that the Queen of Canada is 'Elizabeth the Second, by the Grace of God of the United Kingdom, Canada and Her other Realms and Territories Queen, Head of the Commonwealth, Defender of the Faith.'

Decisive Inventions in the Seventeenth Century

The increased role for Parliament in the Tudor constitution was the precursor to even more dramatic constitutional changes in the seventeenth-century Stuart era. By the end of that century royal absolutism had been curtailed and replaced by the emergence of a constitutional order within which parliamentary supremacy became the cornerstone. There was a high degree of 'revolutionary fervour' at the time, but those who promoted, argued about and fought for those dramatic changes were inspired by an imagined medieval past rather than a vision of a modern future. An anthropological axiom is that all peoples and communities – and now nations – have myths about their origins and what binds them together (Malinowski 1926, 1944). Some constitutional lawyers too acknowledge the key role that myth and legal fictions play in girding constitutional orders. As barrister and public law specialist Richard Gordon put it, the sovereignty of Parliament, the rule of law and the American Constitution all embrace mythic notions that have become sacrosanct and treated as a 'separate force in society' (Gordon, Interviews, 2016). Origin myths may arise from a slow process of sedimentation, but often they are created consciously as part of a political project to invent traditions (Hobsbawm and Ranger 1983). Political myths, French philosopher Georges Sorel wrote, 'are not descriptions of things, but expressions of a determination to act . . . A myth cannot be refuted since it is, at bottom, identical with the convictions of a group, being the expression of these convictions in the language of movement' (Sorel 1908 [1999]: 28–29). Myths, particularly political myths, provide charters for action and narratives that legitimise power. They also offer a deep structure that reconciles the eternal problem of ceding authority to a sovereign in order to legitimate organised social control.

Those who write about nations and national identity, therefore, invent and mould stories from the past to explain and justify the present. Aspects of those stories may purport to have their source in historical events – or at least in a latterly revised version of the significance of those events. The myths that will be articulated most persuasively are likely to suit those who are now the governing elite. At various times the myths may be recontested and reframed by wars, usurpations, marriages of royal convenience or inconvenience, witch hunts, pogroms, persecutions, invasions, conquests and such like. Historians, lawyers, politicians and activists remould and recontest myths to suit contemporary conditions and resolve contemporary problems.

In seventeenth-century England, political actors contested the powers of the Stuart kings and the extent of Crown prerogatives. In the Ship Money Case (*R* v. *Hampden* 1637) the Court of Exchequer Chamber decided (by a narrow majority) that the King's government did have power to impose financial levies on subjects without obtaining parliamentary approval (Keir 1936). As Stephen Sedley (2017), a retired appellate judge, put it: 'It took the rest of the 17th century – a civil war, the king's execution, the implosion of the republic, the restoration of the monarchy and the coup d'état we know as the Glorious Revolution – to establish that government enjoyed no such extra-legal power' (26). Debates raged, petitions were enacted and members of the House of Commons were imprisoned for indefinite terms by the Court of Star Chamber under prerogative powers exercised by the King's Privy Council. Civil war broke out twice, causing severe devastation in many counties. Though Charles I won the battle in the Ship Money Case, he lost the war that followed. After a trial by the rump of parliamentarians remaining in Westminster – whose authority to sit in judgment on their king he denied – he was executed in 1649 for being a 'tyrant, traitor, murderer and public enemy to the good people of this nation' (Robertson 2010: 186–87).

One of Charles I's sons was restored to the throne (Charles II), but another (James II) lost it in 1688. At that point the Tories – those who had supported the Stuart kings – lost political power to the Whig gentry. Whig parliamentarians invited a large Dutch force to invade England. Following James II's abdication, the leader of the invasion force – Prince William of Orange, son of Charles I's daughter Mary – became king (reigning alongside his wife, Mary II, a daughter of James II). For the Whigs, though, William III's distinctive merit was not his Stuart connections but that he was a Protestant. In the nature of myth-making, this foreign invasion and unlawful revolutionary seizure of power was transformed in the history books to become the 'Glorious Revolution' and the origin of Westminster constitutional monarchy whereby government is in the name of the king but the executive branch of government is accountable to those elected to parliament. Parliamentary sovereignty had displaced royal absolutism.

Constitutional conventions have enabled incremental evolution in Westminster parliamentary democracies since the seventeenth century. Yet from time to time those in power need reminding about the foundational principles of constitutional monarchy. Thus, in New Zealand in 1975 Robert Muldoon had just led the National Party to a landslide victory in a general election and become prime minister. Immediately after being sworn in, he purported to suspend an Act of Parliament by issuing a press statement promising retrospective legislation to undo the law of a previous government that his party had vowed to overturn. In private litigation before the courts the Chief Justice declared Muldoon's actions to be unlawful. The judge cited just one law to support his decision – the Bill of Rights 1688 – and declared:

> It is a graphic illustration of the depth of our legal heritage and the strength of our constitutional law that a statute passed by the English Parliament nearly three centuries ago to extirpate the abuses of the Stuart Kings should be available on the other side of the earth to a citizen of this country which was then virtually unknown in Europe and on which no Englishman was to set foot for almost another hundred years.
>
> (Chief Justice Wild cited in Kós, 2014: 243)

The 'Ancient Constitution' of St Edward

Odd though it may seem, much of the seventeenth-century debate about extirpating the abuses of the Stuart kings focussed not on taxes imposed at the time, nor on religion as such, but on an event that took place about six centuries earlier. The year 1066 is a significant date in English history, but was it the date of a *conquest*? It transpired that this question was much more than a matter of mere abstract theory. In the midst of war, rebellion and regicide, enormous efforts in speech-making, litigation and pamphlet writing were devoted to the question of whether the common law could rely upon pre-Norman norms to restrain the prerogative powers of Stuart kings. All agreed that kings were anointed by God to rule. Yet supporters of parliamentary rights and liberties – and, more especially, the members of the House of Commons – who perused the historical record convinced themselves that the notion of a clean constitutional break in 1066 could not be sustained. Many protagonists in the debates were lawyers. A particularly influential advocate of parliamentary rights against the prerogative powers claimed by Charles I was Sir Edward Coke, a former Lord Chief Justice who had been peremptorily dismissed by James I for failing to uphold the King's view of his royal prerogative powers. Judicial tenure at that time was purely at His Majesty's pleasure, and numerous judges were dismissed for failing to support the king. In a previous century Coke might have been executed for treason, but as it was he lived to play a major role in challenging royal autocracy.

The myths surrounding 1066 start from the undoubted historical fact that William, Duke of Normandy, entered England with an invasion force to vindicate his claim to the English throne. His common name – William the Conqueror – assumes that this invasion was a clean break from the law and government of the Anglo-Saxon and Danish kingdoms that he and his barons displaced. The French-speaking Anglo-Norman elite created a feudal system. Royal courts developed and judges applied a system of rules that we now refer to as the English common law. This common law – the law common to the entire realm of England – eventually displaced local customs and baronial jurisdictions but not until well after 1066. Yet it was generally taken for granted by its practitioners that the common law had been established from time immemorial. John Baker (2002) quotes the words of an English serjeant-at-law in 1470 who maintained that 'the common law had been in existence since the creation of the world'. As Baker observes 'it is not improbable that he believed it literally' (1). Again, when considering Coke's writings, J. G. A. Pocock noted:

> The English supposed that the common law was the only law their land had ever known, and this by itself encouraged them to interpret the past as if it had been governed by the law of their own day; but in addition the fact that the common law was a customary law, and that lawyers defined custom in a way which heavily emphasized its immemorial character, made even more radical the English tendency to read existing law into the remote past.
>
> (1987: 30–31)

In their bitter contest with Charles I, Coke and his colleagues were most determined to undermine royal prerogative powers – such as the alleged rights of the king to prorogue or dissolve parliament at will and to raise revenues without parliamentary assent. If William I once had absolute power over the realm of England by dint of conquest, then all his successors might legitimately claim absolute power as God's anointed, ordained to rule as they thought prudent and just. If, however, kings of England since time immemorial were required to legislate with the houses of Parliament as three coordinate estates in the government of the kingdom – King, Lords and Commons – then matters were rather different. Bracton could be, and was, cited for his views on the bridles on a king's powers:

> For he is called *rex* not from reigning but from ruling well, since he is a king as long as he rules well but a tyrant when he oppresses by violent domination the people entrusted to his care. Let him, therefore, temper his power by law, which is the bridle of power, that he may live according to the laws, for the law of mankind has decreed that his own laws bind the lawgiver.
>
> (Thorne 1968: 305)

Presumably, Geoffrey and Matthew Palmer had Bracton's metaphor in mind when entitling their books cited earlier on unbridled and bridled power in New Zealand.

But Bracton was a thirteenth-century writer. It was the canonised pre-1066 figure of Edward, King and Confessor, from whom seventeenth-century advocates for curtailing royal absolutism sought inspiration. St Edward was seen as a poignant symbol of how Anglo-Saxon kings had ruled their subjects with justice in the 'ancient constitution' of England. As Coke was writing his *Institutes* he found it highly convenient to cite a number of texts on the 'ancient constitution' as it had been fashioned by customs that could be said to derive from time immemorial. What he treated as authoritative sources included a number of apocryphal texts such as *Leges Edwardi Confessoris*, *Modus Tenendi Parliamentum*, and what Pocock calls 'the lavishly fantastic' *Mirror of Justices*. There are, Pocock (1987) observes, 'few pages of his *First* or *Second Institutes* on which one of these works is not cited' (43). William Prynne, a pamphleteer commissioned to expound on the legality of the parliamentary cause during the civil war period in the 1640s, likewise relied extensively on the same sources (Greenberg 2001: 216–17).

Even in Coke's own time some doubted the historicity of these texts. Polydore Vergil expressed doubts that the laws of the last Anglo-Saxon king had been confirmed by the Conqueror and his Norman successors (Pocock 1987: 18–19, 43). Historians now agree that all Coke's 'ancient' texts were latter-day reconstructions. They were not written during the reign of Edward (1042–66) but at least 100 years later and up to 300 years later: 'they were manufactured by clergymen and politicians who back-dated them in order to produce the illusion of antiquity' (Greenberg 2001: 9). Doubts about their authenticity were disregarded by Coke, Prynne and others, who were determined to demonstrate an 'ancient constitution'. Rights and liberties from Anglo-Saxon times, included in coronation oaths by many monarchs, had circumscribed the prerogative powers of the monarch and acknowledged the role of Parliament in the constitution. This undermined royalist claims that the divinely ordained king had absolute powers:

> Coke not only accepts a legal judgment dating a law from time out of mind as historically valid, but he regards such statements as better historical evidence than those made by chroniclers. Where the courts have adjudged an institution immemorial and a historian alleges that it was set up in such a king's reign, Coke leaves little doubt that we are to think the historian wrong, and he urges the historiographers of his own day to consult a lawyer before making any statement about the history of the law.
>
> (Pocock 1987: 40–41)

Coke was adamant that the historical veracity (or otherwise) of the laws of Edward was irrelevant. They were believed to be true, or they were believed in as true principles of an 'ancient constitution', by people taking a leading role in reshaping and inventing an English constitution for the seventeenth century and the future. As J. P. Reid (1993) put it, 'ancient constitutionalism was less history than advocacy, more imagination than scholarship, yet real enough to be the basic tool for both constitutional argumentation and for the defence of collective liberty' (207).

The Role of Magna Carta Then and Now

Advocacy rather than history must undoubtedly be to the fore when assessing Coke's role as a member of the House of Commons who drafted and promoted the passage of the Petition of Right 1627. That Petition required the 'common consent by Act of Parliament' for any payments or taxes, forbade the imprisonment of freemen who refused to pay royal imposts made without parliamentary consent, and prohibited proceedings by martial law. As the eminent Anglo-American scholar Arthur Goodhart noted, Coke made much of Magna Carta in advocating passage of that Petition:

> I know that prerogative is part of the law, but 'Sovereign Power' is no parliamentary word. In my opinion it weakens Magna Charta [*sic*], and all the statutes; . . . Take we heed what we yield unto: Magna Charta is such a fellow, that he will have no 'Sovereign'.

Goodhart then commented:

> It has been said that Coke either intentionally or unintentionally misinterpreted the Charter, . . . What is true is that Coke did not always distinguish between the original Charter and the Charter as it was understood in later centuries, . . . but he was not analyzing the technical provisions of an ancient Charter: he was concerned with the principles of a living constitution.
>
> (1966: 68)

The laws of St Edward and Magna Carta were and are hugely important elements of a myth of an 'ancient' English constitution. The myths represented an understanding of constitutional norms that eventually did indeed come to be 'true' in a way that a modern legal positivist would understand. They were translated into real laws such as the Petition of Right 1627, the Bill of Rights 1688 and the Act of Settlement 1700. Idealised notions of a constitutional monarchy and of an independent judiciary – unsupported at the time court precedents were handed down by judges subservient to the kings who appointed them – eventually became constitutional facts and accepted legal norms. Myths that began as tools of contested legal debate at the beginning of the seventeenth century were embedded in the English constitution by the end of that century. Moreover, the Imperial Laws Application Act 1988 in New Zealand retains English statutes of high constitutional principle as part of the law of New Zealand to this day.

Tensions between history, myth and law in relation to constitutional principles continue into the twenty-first century. This was particularly evident in the celebrations of the 800th anniversary of Magna Carta in 2015. One member of the United Kingdom Supreme Court, Lord Sumption, sought to demystify Magna Carta in no uncertain terms. His stinging broadside aimed at those who invoke the medieval charter sealed at Runnymede in support of modern political agendas included these comments:

> Now I have nothing against the liberty of the subject, the rule of law, the Human Rights Convention, legal aid, democracy, motherhood and apple pie or even international marketing opportunities for lawyers. But I do have a problem with the distortion of history to serve an essentially modern political agenda. Claims like those which I have just cited are high-minded tosh. They represent the worst kind of ahistorical Whiggism.
>
> (2015: 4)

Sumption noted two main schools of thought about Magna Carta. One 'holds the charter to be a major constitutional document, the foundation of the rule of law and the liberty of the subject in England'. The historian's view, on the other hand, 'has tended to emphasise the self-interested motives of the barons and has generally been sceptical about the charter's constitutional significance' (Sumption 2015: 1). An Australian academic described this binary as a contest between 'votaries', who are true believers in Magna Carta as a source of justice and freedom, and 'sceptics', who tend to Krygier's (2016) view that 'The cult of Magna Carta is historical nonsense. No wonder Oliver Cromwell called it "Magna Farta".' (11–16)

Why, then, do so many people regard the Magna Carta as the historical origin of important elements of rule of law, due process and representative parliamentary democracy? Sumption (2015) has a simple answer: 'Magna Carta as we know it was reinvented in the early seventeenth century, largely by one man, the judge and politician Sir Edward

Coke. A man of prodigious learning and bilious disposition . . . ' (14). Sumption strenuously argued against accepting Coke's inventions:

> So when we commemorate Magna Carta, perhaps the first question that we should ask ourselves is this: do we really need the force of myth to sustain our belief in democracy? Do we need to derive our belief in democracy and the rule of law from a group of muscular conservative millionaires from the north of England who thought in French, knew no Latin or English, and died more than three quarters of a millennium ago? I rather hope not.
>
> (2015: 18)

His severe strictures against myths in legal discourse failed to convince other senior members of the British judiciary. The President of the United Kingdom Supreme Court, Lord Neuberger, quoted with approval the sentiments of Lord Bingham:

> The significance of Magna Carta lay not only in what it actually said but, perhaps to an even greater extent, in what later generations claimed and believed it had said. Sometimes the myth is more important than the actuality.
>
> (Bingham 2011: 12)

Neuberger mentioned Sumption's address, but he arrived at very different conclusions to those of his judicial colleague:

> Magna Carta can claim to be the Bible of our constitution, even if its Biblical role is as much based on myth as it is on reality. I would say that, far from being a disgrace to the nation, it represents the United Kingdom's greatest contribution to the world – the rule of law and democratic government. Both these fundamental features of a modern civilised society can be traced back to a shoddy ineffective compromise in a boggy field between a horrible King and his revolting Barons eight centuries ago.
>
> (Neuberger 2015: para. 63)

It is apparent, whether historians like it or not, that judges in the twenty-first century are as capable of finding comfort in convenient invented myths as were parliamentarians of the seventeenth century. How do myths and inventions impact on the role of the Crown in the constitutional arrangements of postcolonial common law jurisdictions which are the objects of our study? What intellectual suppleness is required to account for an indivisible British Crown in the nineteenth century morphing into the multitude of Queen's bodies now to be found in Commonwealth realms? Before discussing that question, a brief constitutional history of New Zealand provides some background for understanding the importance of the seventeenth-century English origins of the system of government, and also the continuing role of Crown prerogative powers in that system.

From Indivisible Imperial Crown to Divisible Constitutional Monarchies

Whilst many Māori hold to a different version of the history and mythology of colonial origins – one recognised and upheld by the Waitangi Tribunal (Waitangi Tribunal 2014) – in terms of imperial law, the territory of New Zealand was annexed to the British Empire in 1840. The English Laws Act 1858, the effect of which continues in force under the Imperial Laws Application Act 1988, stipulated 14 January 1840 as the reception date for the application of English laws in New Zealand, though the Treaty of Waitangi was not first signed until 6 February (Williams 1988). In the Crown colony period the Governor held the full powers of government in a manner somewhat reminiscent of the powers exercised by Stuart kings. Governors such as George Grey relished the power, as historian Keith Sinclair put it, 'to govern as a despot' (Sinclair 1990).

A settler-controlled responsible government was introduced following the imperial parliament's enactment of the New Zealand Constitution Act 1852. Under that Act, from 1856 an elected ministry responsible to the General Assembly exercised most governance powers within the colony. Elected ministers assumed responsibility for all aspects of government during the colonial wars in the 1860s after imperial troops withdrew and Native Affairs was transferred from the governor and the imperial government to become a colonial responsibility (Quentin-Baxter and McLean 2017: 15–22).

The gradual evolution from colonial status to independent nation-state took quite a while. The Colony became the Dominion of New Zealand in 1907 and a member of the League of Nations in 1920. Not until 1946 were government departments instructed to stop using the term 'Dominion' (McIntyre 2002) and the next year the Statute of Westminster 1931 (discussed later) was finally adopted in New Zealand, thus creating a separate Crown in right of New Zealand (McIntyre 2007). New Zealand was the last of the Dominions to cut the imperial apron-strings and even so clung to British connections when enacting the British Nationality and New Zealand Citizenship Act 1948. By comparison, the separate Crown in Canada followed immediately upon the enactment of the 1931 Statute.

The Canadian identity of the Crown was emphasised when the Canadian Citizenship Act 1946 was passed. At Canada's first citizenship ceremony, with great fanfare, individuals from a wide variety of backgrounds were presented with certificates of Canadian citizenship. Among the recipients was Prime Minister Mackenzie King, who received certificate 0001 (Knowles 2000: 66).

The Constitution Act 1986 in New Zealand

After 1947 the parliament of New Zealand was still defined by the 1852 imperial enactment, though its legislative competence was broadened by an Amendment Act in 1973. This swept away the quaint limitation of legislative competence to 'peace, order, and good government'. This was probably a meaningless formula after the imperial Colonial Laws Validity Act 1865 had ceased to apply to New Zealand, following its adoption of the Statute of Westminster. However, for avoidance of doubt about extra-territoriality powers, but not until 1973, the New Zealand Parliament bestowed on itself 'full power to make laws having effect in, or in respect of New Zealand . . . and laws having effect outside New Zealand'.

Eventually, the 1852 imperial act was repealed after Robert Muldoon made another contribution to constitutional law at the end of his tenure as prime minister in 1984. He refused to adopt the advice of incoming, but not yet sworn-in, ministers to devalue the New Zealand dollar (Quentin-Baxter and McLean 2017: 174–76). The new government determined that the constitution should be enacted in New Zealand legislation at last. The Constitution Act 1986, though, is a distinctly bare-bones constitution.

Part 1 of the Act concerns 'The Sovereign'. Of its few sections, section 2 reads:

(1) The Sovereign in right of New Zealand is the head of State of New Zealand, and shall be known by the royal style and titles proclaimed from time to time.
(2) The Governor-General appointed by the Sovereign is the Sovereign's representative in New Zealand.

Section 3 provides:

(1) Every power conferred on the Governor-General by or under any Act is a royal power which is exercisable by the Governor-General on

behalf of the Sovereign, and may accordingly be exercised either by the Sovereign in person or by the Governor-General.

Section 5 covers 'Demise of the Crown':

(1) The death of the Sovereign shall have the effect of transferring all the functions, duties, powers, authorities, rights, privileges, and dignities belonging to the Crown to the Sovereign's successor, as determined in accordance with the enactment of the Parliament of England intituled The Act of Settlement (12 & 13 Will 3, c 2) and any other law relating to the succession to the Throne, but shall otherwise have no effect in law for any purpose.

And that is it. Constitutional conventions developed over the centuries in Westminster-style parliaments since the Glorious Revolution and the Act of Settlement 1700 are noticeable only by their total absence. The 'functions, duties, powers, authorities, rights, privileges, and dignities belonging to the Crown' no doubt includes prerogative powers of the Crown, but they are not defined here.

New Zealand retains perhaps the most 'pure' form of Westminster parliamentary sovereignty anywhere in the world. The Constitution Act 1986 is an ordinary statute without any amending formula granting it protection from amendment or repeal by a simple majority in the House of Representatives. In contrast, the parliaments in Australia and Canada have to operate within the restraints of federal constitutions and judicial review to assess the constitutionality of enacted legislation. As we will discuss further in Chapter 11, constitutional amendments are few and far between in those nations. Meanwhile, this chapter concludes with some comment on the divisible and multiple Crowns that emerged in the Commonwealth following the Statute of Westminster 1931.

The Indivisible Crown, It Turns Out, Is Divisible

Writing at the turn of the twentieth century, F. W. Maitland – often regarded as the father of modern English legal history – was content to quote with approval words from the Tudor lawyer Plowden on the metaphysical indivisibility of the king's bodies. The king, he wrote,

> has a body natural adorned and invested with the estate and dignity royal, and he has not a body natural distinct and divided by itself from the office and dignity royal, but a body natural and a body politic together indivisible, and these two bodies are incorporated in one person and make one

> body and not divers, that is, the body corporate in the body natural *et e contra* the body natural in the body corporate. So that the body natural by the conjunction of the body politic to it (which body politic contains the office, government and majesty royal) is magnified and by the said consolidation hath in it the body politic.
>
> (1901: 135–36)

The indivisible Crown of Tudor England, and of the Whig constitution following the Glorious Revolution, had become an indivisible Crown in which the Queen of the United Kingdom and Her Other Realms and Dominions had also been proclaimed to be Empress of India. As Miles Taylor observed, 'British monarchy was ... woven into the fabric of Empire' (Taylor 2016: 43).

As the twentieth century unfolded, however, a multi-polity Commonwealth of Nations emerged. Whilst most Commonwealth member nations rapidly moved to republican constitutions shortly after political independence from 1947 onwards, our focus is on those nations that remained under the Crown – but no longer an indivisible imperial Crown. Even before the imperial conferences of the 1920s the divisibility of the Crown had been recognised in a number of court decisions 'as part of the evolutionary and devolutionary process' from Empire to Commonwealth (*R* v. *Secretary of State for Foreign and Commonwealth Affairs, Ex parte Indian Association of Alberta* 1982: 928–33). In practice and international law, it was the Balfour Declaration 1926, followed by the Statute of Westminster 1931, that enabled the self-governing dominions of Canada and South Africa and the Irish Free State to obtain full legislative autonomy over their own affairs. With separate personality as independent nations, the formerly indivisible British Crown now comprised several Crowns. Unless abolished by statutory fiat, prerogative powers in each of the separate Crowns continued to be available to clothe government actions with the cloak of legality.

This evolution of the Crown necessarily complicated Plowden and Maitland's understandings of the king's two bodies. Philosopher Giorgio Agamben (1998) argues that the notion of the king's two bodies is a revelation of sovereignty's defining characteristic: its perpetuity. The twinned metaphors of body natural and body politic mean that in states where the body politic dominates, it will endure over the demise of the natural body. Kantorowicz (1997 [1957]) imagined a doubled body, to grasp the sovereign's 'continuous personality', with a 'virtual identity of predecessor and successor' (402). Consequently, this concept of the uninterruptable body politic articulated 'the cipher of the absolute and inhuman character of sovereignty' (Agamben 1998: 62). The concept of the king's two bodies reveals the ritual and theatrical construction of political power. This abstract, transcendental thinking – with one person embodying kingship's dualities of mortal and immortal, abstraction and corporeal, sacred and banal, *gravitas* and *celeritas* (Sahlins 1985) – is probably unparalleled in the secular imagination (Kantorowicz 1997 [1957]: 4).

Yet now we have multiple versions of the Queen's 'two bodies'. Each of the realms over which Elizabeth II reigns as sovereign is a distinct body politic. Some of those polities have federal structures, and the states or provinces are additional separate and discrete Queen's bodies within one realm (McLean 2015; Twomey 2018). Even the non-federal Realm of New Zealand includes separate self-governing states (Cook Islands and Niue) and dependencies (Tokelau and Ross) under the Queen in right of New Zealand (Quentin-Baxter and McLean 2017: 104–6). Clearly, there is just the one physical (very elderly) body of Elizabeth II and one physical (quite elderly) body of her heir apparent, but by stretches of the imagination that medieval thinkers certainly could not have contemplated, there are now a very large number of bodies politic that comprise the other body of the Queen or King.

This necessitates a different perspective on the historical evolution of the Crown from that of leading British scholars. Martin Loughlin identifies three phases of monarchical power in the development of the British Constitution. The first was reached by distinguishing between the public and private aspects of kingship; the second recognised the representative nature of the office of the king – an office held in trust for the common good; the third acknowledged the 'necessity for the institutional differentiation of governmental functions between king's council, king's court, and king-in-Parliament' (Loughlin 2013: 106). Janet McLean insists that Loughlin's chronology does not describe the New Zealand experience either at the point of formal colonisation or in the present day:

> Not only were all three versions of the Crown – personal, moral and institutional – instrumental at the time of the inception of the colony, but different versions of the monarch have also been instrumental in attempts to redress historical grievances between the Crown and Māori. There is a certain internal logic about this and symmetry in the way in which Imperial techniques have played a role in unravelling and redressing the colonial past. The monarch is simultaneously an individual person, an abstract body vested with a moral personality, and is institutionally

> distinct from the ordinary Crown in Parliament. She represents statehood and continuity in ways that government, as we typically understand it, does not do.
>
> (2015: 195–96)

The important roles of the persons of the monarch described by McLean, and the ideological significance attributed by indigenous peoples in Canada and New Zealand to the monarch and to the Crown (often negatively contrasted with the actions of colonial and postcolonial governments), are explored further in Chapter 4. Next, though, we examine another element of Maitland's seminal thinking – his suggestion that reliance on the idea of the 'Crown' is a convenient cover for ignorance – and then we explore the idea of the Crown as a personification of, or metonym for, the modern state.

References

Agamben, Giorgio. 1998. *Homo Sacer: Sovereign Power and Bare Life*, translated by Daniel Heller-Rozaen. Stanford, CA: Stanford University Press.

Baker, John. 2002. *An Introduction to English Legal History*, 4th edn. London: Butterworths.

Barclay, Andrew. 2008. 'The 1661 St Edward's Crown – Refurbished, Recycled or Replaced?' *The Court Historian* 13(2): 149–70.

Bingham, Tom. 2011. *The Rule of Law*. London: Penguin.

Goodhart, Arthur. 1966. *Law of the Land*. Charlottesville: University of Virginia Press.

Greenberg, Janelle. 2001. *The Radical Face of the Ancient Constitution: St Edward's 'Laws' in Early Modern Political Thought*. Cambridge: Cambridge University Press.

Hobsbawm, Eric and Ranger, Terence (eds.) 1983. *The Invention of Tradition*. Cambridge and New York: Cambridge University Press.

Kantorowicz, Ernst H. 1997 [1957]. *The King's Two Bodies: A Study in Mediaeval Political Theology*. Princeton, NJ: Princeton University Press.

Keay, Anna. 2002. 'Toyes and trifles.' *History Today* 52(7): 31–37.

Keir, D. L. 1936. 'The Case of Ship-money.' *Law Quarterly Review* 52(4): 546–74.

Knowles, Valerie. 2000. *Forging Our Legacy: Canadian Citizenship and Immigration, 1900–1977*. Ottawa: Public Works and Government Services Canada.

Kós, Stephen. 2014. 'Constitutional Collision: *Fitzgerald v Muldoon v Wild*.' *Otago Law Review* 13(2): 243–306.

Krygier, Martin. 2016. 'Magna Carta and the Rule of Law Tradition.' In *Papers on Parliament: Magna Carta 800 Symposium Parliament House, Canberra*, edited by Paula Waring, 11–30. Canberra: Department of the Senate.

Loughlin, Martin. 2013. *The British Constitution: A Very Short Introduction.* Oxford: Oxford University Press.

Maitland, Frederic. 1901. 'The Crown as Corporation.' *Law Quarterly Review* 17(2): 131–46.

Malinowski, Bronislaw. 1926. *Myth in Primitive Psychology.* London: Kegan Paul, Trench, Trubner and Co. Ltd.

1944. *A Scientific Theory of Culture and Other Essays.* Chapel Hill: The University of North Carolina Press.

McIntyre, W. David. 2002. *When, If Ever, Did New Zealand Become Independent?* Christchurch: Canterbury History Foundation.

2007. *Dominion of New Zealand: Statesmen and Status, 1907–1945.* Wellington: New Zealand Institute of International Affairs.

McLean, Janet. 2015. 'Crown, Empire and Redressing the Historical Wrongs of Colonisation in New Zealand.' *New Zealand Law Review* 2015(2): 187–212.

Morris, Nigel. 2008. 'The Big Question: Why Doesn't the UK Have a Written Constitution, and Does It Matter?' *The Independent*, 14 February 2008. www.Independent.Co.Uk/News/Uk/Politics/The-Big-Question-Why-Doesnt-The-Uk-Have-A-Written-Constitution-And-Does-It-Matter-781975.Html.

Neuberger, David. 2015. 'Magna Carta: The Bible of the English Constitution or a Disgrace to the English Nation?' Speech, Guildford Cathedral, 8 June 2015. Accessed 7 April 2018 at www.supremecourt.uk/docs/speech-150618.pdf.

Palmer, Geoffrey. 1979. *Unbridled Power: An Interpretation of New Zealand's Constitution and Government*, 2nd edn. Wellington: Oxford University Press.

Palmer, Geoffrey and Andrew Butler. 2016. *A Constitution for Aotearoa New Zealand.* Wellington: Victoria University Press.

2018. *Towards Democratic Renewal: Ideas for Constitutional Change in New Zealand.* Wellington: Victoria University Press.

Palmer, Geoffrey and Matthew Palmer. 2004. *Bridled Power: New Zealand's Constitution and Government*, 4th edn. Melbourne: Oxford University Press.

Pocock, John G. A. 1987. *The Ancient Constitution and the Feudal Law: A Study of English Historical Thought in the Seventeenth Century*, 2nd edn. Cambridge: Cambridge University Press.

Quentin-Baxter, Alison and Janet McLean. 2017. *This Realm of New Zealand: The Sovereign, the Governor-General, the Crown.* Auckland: Auckland University Press.

Reid, John. 1993. 'Law and History.' *Loyola of Los Angeles Law Review* 27: 193–223.

Robertson, Geoffrey. 2010. *The Tyrannicide Brief: The Story of the Man Who Sent Charles I to the Scaffold.* New York: Vintage.

Sahlins, Marshall. 1985. *Islands of History.* Chicago: University of Chicago Press.

Sedley, Stephen. 2017. 'Short Cuts.' *London Review of Books* 39(5): 26–27, 2 March 2017.

Sharman, Campbell. 1994. 'Reforming Executive Power'. In *We, the People: Australian Republican Government*, edited by George Winterton, 113–124. St. Leonards, New South Wales: Allen and Unwin.

Sinclair, Keith. 1990. 'Grey, George'. In *Dictionary of New Zealand Biography*. Accessed 8 March 2018 at teara.govt.nz/en/biographies/1g21/grey-george

Sorel, Georges. 1999 [1908]. *Reflections on Violence*. Cambridge: Cambridge University Press.

Sumption, Jonathan 2015. 'Magna Carta Then and Now: Address to the Friends of the British Library, 9 March 2015.' Accessed 7 January 2017 at www.supremecourt.uk/docs/speech-150309.pdf.

Taylor, Miles. 2016. 'The British Royal Family and the Colonial Empire from the Georgians to Prince George.' In *Crowns and Colonies: European Monarchies and Overseas Empires, Studies in Imperialism*, edited by Robert Aldrich and Cindy McCreery, 27–50. Manchester: Manchester University Press.

Thorne, Samuel (ed.) 1968. *Henry de Bracton: On the Laws and Customs of England, Volume 2*. Cambridge, MA: Harvard University Press.

Twomey, Anne. 2018. *The Veiled Sceptre: Reserve Powers of Heads of State in Westminster Systems*. Cambridge: Cambridge University Press.

Waitangi Tribunal . 2014. *The Report on Stage 1 of the Te Paparahi o Te Raki Inquiry, He Whakaputanga me te Tiriti – The Declaration and the Treaty*, WAI 1040. Wellington: Waitangi Tribunal.

Williams, David V. 1988. 'The Foundations of Colonial Rule in New Zealand.' *New Zealand Universities Law Review* 13(1): 54–67.

3

The Crown as Metonym for the State?

The Human Face of Leviathan

CRIS SHORE

Introduction: The Greatest of Artificial Persons

> There is one term against which I wish to warn you, and that term is 'the crown'. You will certainly read that the crown does this and the crown does that. As a matter of fact we know that the crown does nothing but lie in the Tower of London to be gazed at by sight-seers. No, the crown is a convenient cover for ignorance: it saves us from asking difficult questions. . . . If you are told that the crown has this power or that power, do not be content until you know who legally has the power – is it the king, is it one of his secretaries: is this power a prerogative power or is it the outcome of statute?
>
> F. W. Maitland, 1908: *Constitutional History*

In 1902 the Supreme Court of New South Wales was asked to decide whether goods imported by the state government were liable to customs duty owed to the Commonwealth of Australia. This highlighted the failure of English law to recognise the state as a legal person (or develop a coherent theory of the state). The state government argued that as the goods in question were destined for the service of the state, and therefore the service of the king, they should be exempt from Commonwealth tax. The court agreed, the decision of each of the three judges resting on the notion that the state, as the embodiment of the king, is covered by royal prerogative. During the hearing it was pointed out that if the Commonwealth were granted the right to impose taxes and those taxes were refused, the ensuing legal suit would be one of Crown *versus* the Crown. It was also noted that it made no difference that in Australia Commonwealth and state are distinct entities since the revenue was technically a grant to the sovereign, either by the people of the Commonwealth or by the people of the state. In short, the court proposed that in these matters, there cannot be any legal rights or obligations between the Commonwealth and the states.

In his essay 'The Crown as Representing the State', the legal historian Pitt Cobbett suggested that the explanation for this anomaly lay in the curious evolution of English legal history and its conception of the king 'not merely as the chief source of the executive power, but also as the *sole legal representative* of the State or organised community' (Cobbett 1904: 23–24, emphasis in the original). Like his contemporary Frederick William Maitland, Cobbett highlights 'that curious freak of English law, the corporation sole'[1] (Maitland 1901: 131) and the problems created by the idea of the Crown as the embodiment of the state. According to Maitland, '[t]he greatest of artificial persons, politically speaking, is the State' (131). Yet for Maitland the English legal conception of the Crown as corporation represented an even stranger conceit, one whose origins lie in church property law and medieval cosmology.

Cobbett's reasoning illustrates some of the political and constitutional problems typically associated with the Crown as a legal entity. It also exemplifies how the British Crown was (and perhaps continues to be) closely associated with the immunities and privileges of the state rather than its obligations or duties, and how the notion of the Crown as private person provides a cover for the accumulation of executive power.

In Chapter 2 we charted the genealogy of the modern Crown and its development from medieval absolutism based on the doctrine of the divine right of kings to the idea of a constitutional monarchy within a democracy. This chapter takes that genealogy further by exploring the idea of the Crown as a personification of, or metonym for, the modern state. I also address some of the conceptual and practical problems that arise from that conceit. Taking up wider debates in the social sciences about the difficulties of theorising the state and the now pervasive argument that we should see the modern state not as a 'thing' but as a fluid 'set of practices and processes and their effects' (Trouillot 2001: 131) and an assemblage of competing institutions and discourses (Scott 1994; Steinmetz 1999; Sharma and Gupta 2006), I ask, what exactly *is* the 'state' in those countries where the Crown and constitutional monarchy feature prominently in the political landscape, and where is it located? More specifically, what does the Crown 'do' for our understandings of the state

[1] An office residing in a single person – as distinct from a 'corporation aggregate', which refers to an entity that is greater than the sum of its individual members (see McLean 2012: 133).

and the practices of statecraft? What are the implications of personifying the state in the figure of a king or queen? What are the 'Crown effects' with regards to authority and legitimacy, and what would be lost if the Crown were removed?

To answer these questions I draw on debates concerning the difficulties of studying the state and the dangers of attributing a misplaced concreteness to what some contend is an ephemeral, elusive and largely fictitious phenomenon (Corrigan and Sayer 1985; Abrams 1988). But to give context to these arguments, I begin with some reflections on the competing conceptions of Crown and state in British legal thought.

The question of the modern state has received considerable attention in both legal–historical studies and the social sciences, yet these literatures have tended to work in isolation, rarely speaking to each other. In what follows, I suggest that we might gain greater analytical purchase on the modern state by combining perspectives from legal history and anthropology in a way that brings the Crown into sharper focus. As we illustrate throughout this book, these issues regarding the legal and conceptual distinctions between Crown and state continue to pose challenges, particularly where governments use the residual powers of the sovereign – or Crown prerogative – in ways that are unaccountable to Parliament or public scrutiny.

Conceptions of Crown and State in Legal Thought

In the introduction to their 1999 book, *The Nature of the Crown*, Maurice Sunkin and Sebastian Payne pose three fundamental questions about the Crown as a concept in public law.

> Is the concept of the Crown equivalent to that of the state? Does it symbolise overarching principles such as those of integrity of the law or the public interest, which ought to inform the work of every institution of government? Or, is the Crown simply a cover for the power of the executive?
>
> (Sunkin and Payne 1999: 3)

The contributors to that volume offered numerous different perspectives but drew no firm conclusions. Yet these questions remain important, not least because they go to the heart of debates over constitutional reform. The UK, together with New Zealand and Israel, is often depicted as peculiar among modern states in not having a written constitution – or, to be more precise, a codified constitution. Many writers see this peculiarity as linked to the equally unusual and democratically flawed anomaly of the royal prerogative powers, which are wielded by the executive, often in ways that are outside of any parliamentary statute and unaccountable (Blick 2011: 5). While some claim this gives 'flexibility' to the British constitution, an advantage that codification would undermine (Bogdanor 2009: 14), others complain that it renders the workings of the constitution unhelpfully obscure. As Iain McLean (2010: vii) argues, the main problem with the British system of constitutional monarchy is simply that 'nobody knows what it is'.

Other writers insist that shifting from the current archaic and opaque system of constitutional monarchy to a more transparent and rational republican constitutional order requires not only a written constitution but also substituting the word 'Crown' for that of 'state' (Palmer and Butler 2016). Their reasoning is that the state is a much more rational, coherent and modern concept than the Crown, with all its medieval and feudal associations. But are the concepts of Crown and state synonymous, and to what extent do they map the same semantic fields? Most legal scholars seem to agree that Crown and state are, broadly speaking, the same. For example, Janet McLean defines the Crown as 'the common law's closest approximation to the state' (McLean 2012: 2). Stephen Sedley calls it 'the visible icon which stands for that intangible yet very real entity, the state' (Sedley 2011: 270). Noel Cox says the Crown 'is legally important because it occupies the conceptual place held by the State in those legal systems derived from or influenced by the Roman civil law' (Cox 2002: 237). For Jeff King, it is the 'legal personification of the state or the legal personality through which the powers of the state are exercised' (Interviews, 2016). And for Martin Loughlin it is a 'mechanism for the state' that 'becomes the nearest we get in the British system of government to acting as a symbol of the state' (Interviews, 2016).

In a legal sense, the state can be defined as a 'sovereign and independent entity capable of entering into relations with other states and enjoying international legal personality' (Law 2015: 592), and to be recognised as a state has traditionally entailed having a permanent population, a defined territory and an effective government (592). These features are common to both constitutional monarchies and republican states. However, while there seems to be a consensus among public law scholars that Crown and state are closely related terms that approximate each other, legal historians recognise that they are also substantially different phenomena and that the Crown cannot be regarded as a metonym for the state. As Martin Loughlin summed it up:

> [T]he Crown has, in practice, provided a poor substitute for the idea of the state. The main reason for this is that the monarchical structure of our system of government has frustrated any attempt systematically to unravel the 'public' from the 'private' aspects of the Sovereign's responsibilities; the identification of the Crown as a 'corporation sole' may indeed have been the result of a confusion in our understanding of canon law, but it was a deliberate confusion which was effected for the purpose of ensuring that, though they may be distinct entities, the King could not be separated from his Crown.
>
> (Loughlin 1999: 33)

These limitations on the use of the Crown as a synonym for the state have created particular difficulties for government. Moreover, as Loughlin notes, the idea of the Crown may have actually inhibited the development of a coherent concept of the modern state of the kind that emerged in other European countries. Much of this confusion arose from the idea of the Crown as 'corporation sole', a notion promoted by the eighteenth-century Tory jurist Sir William Blackstone. Loughlin argues that while this resulted from a misunderstanding of common law, it was a deliberate confusion to ensure that the king could not be separated from his 'Crown', even though these may be distinct entities. From a public law perspective this has created a further problem in that '[t]he British state has no legal personality' (Sedley 2015: 209). This means it 'cannot be directly sued for civil wrongs done by it or in its name' (209); only its agents can be sued – an idea that recalls the dictum that "the king can do no wrong'. It is a bizarre fact, as Stephen Sedley wrote, 'that in the twenty-first century the common law still possesses no solid or unitary concept of the state' (Sedley 2015: 210). Some argue that this is because a coherent concept of the state was not really needed in common law (Interviews, King 2016). Still others contend that British legal thought developed its own uniquely flexible and adaptable state tradition (McLean 2012: 310). As McLean argues, in language that recalls Rousseau and Durkheim, 'the Crown often does represent a version of the state – being the "collective will" or "society in a moral guise"' (McLean 2012: 7). However, that notion (which is attributed to the eighteenth-century political philosopher Edmund Burke) raises the obvious question: How can the Crown, conceived as the government apparatus, be responsible for wrong-doing if it also represents the state or society in a moral guise?

This idea of the state as representing the collective will of the people, a concept promoted during the pre-modern period, crystallised in the modern era in the political thought of English philosopher Thomas Hobbes, arguably the first modern theorist of the state. While earlier republican writers had helped to formulate the idea of the state as an impersonal apparatus that could be clearly distinguished from those who exercise its power – building on the medieval theological doctrine of the king's two bodies (Kantorowicz [1957] 1997) – they nevertheless tended to equate the state with its citizens (Loughlin 2000: 129). By contrast, Hobbes rejected the notion that sovereignty lay with the people. Hobbes, it should be noted, strongly opposed the dangerous and deadly republican ideas about liberty put forward by radical and parliamentarian writers in the course of the English Civil War and had been in exile with other monarchist supporters during the interregnum (Pocock 2009; du Gay and Scott 2010: 5). Although he saw the origins of modern government as vested in a contract with the people, for him, that contract entailed subordination and surrender to the power of the sovereign. As Loughlin (2000: 129) notes, Hobbes was 'unusual in viewing the power of the State as a form of alienation rather than delegation'. In his book *Leviathan* (1651), Hobbes proposes the modern idea of the state as an independent, free-standing entity that is both greater than, yet set apart from, the people who constitute and administer it (Geuss 2001). Whereas other theorists saw the state's authority as derived from the people and therefore limited by natural law, Hobbes' organic monster – the great Leviathan – was an impersonal entity more powerful than society itself. Indeed, the frontispiece image of *Leviathan* depicts the state as the giant body of an all-pervasive king or ruler who towers over the people and territory it rules. Inspired by the anamorphic art forms of the Renaissance that were popular in the seventeenth century,[2] the book's cover provides a graphic representation of Hobbes's key themes (see Figure 3.1). The bottom images represent the balance between ecclesiastical authority (on the right) and human/temporal authority (on the left). In the centre stands the figure of the sovereign king, a crowned giant wielding sword and sceptre in each hand. Only on closer scrutiny does it become apparent that the king's body is constituted, both figuratively and literally, by a blurred pastiche of the individual bodies of the citizens, who make up the other party to the social contract. Significantly, their gaze is turned inwards, facing away from the viewer and towards the mighty sovereign (Richardson 2016). This image and iconography succinctly capture Hobbes's notion of the state or sovereign as an artificial person

[2] Anamorphosis is distorted projection or representation that requires the viewer to occupy a specific vantage point or use special devices to reconstitute the image.

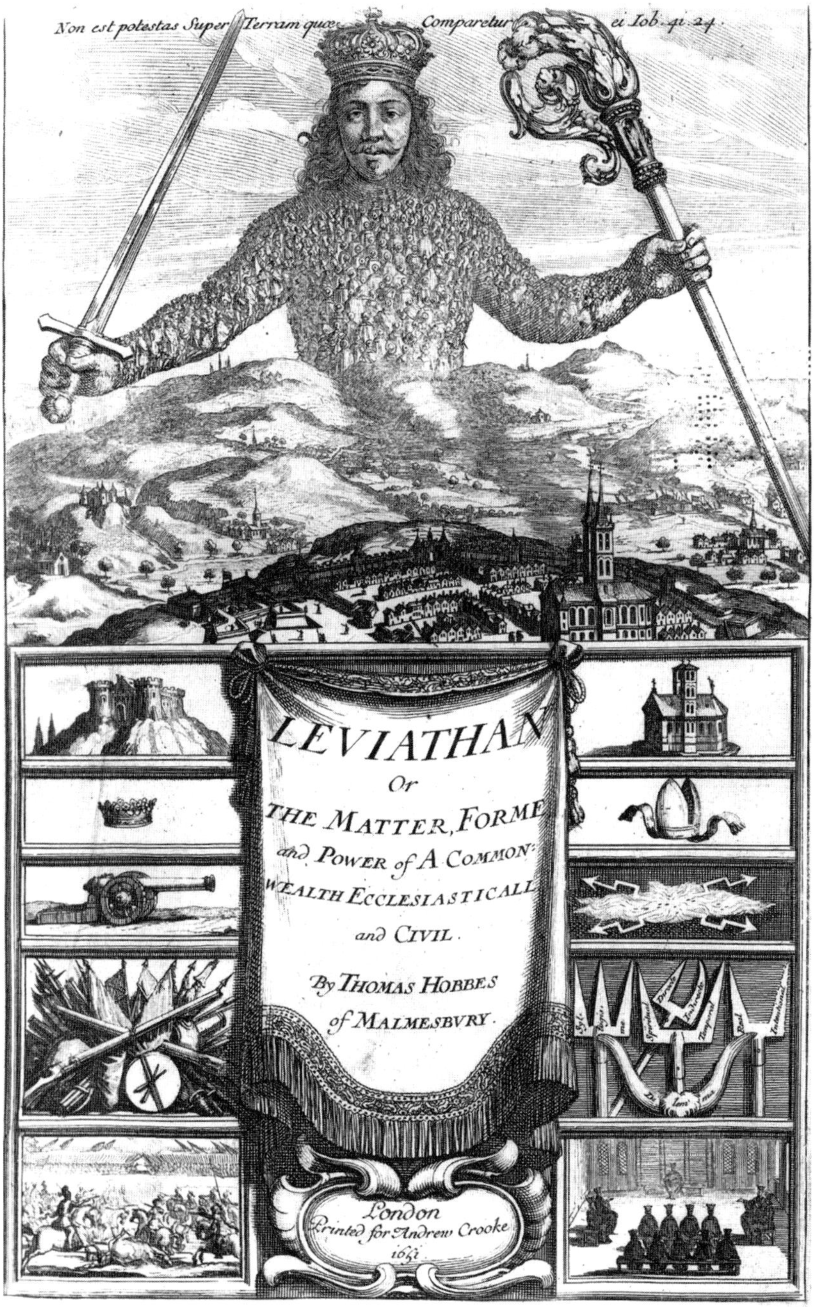

Figure 3.1 Abraham Bosse's frontispiece for Thomas Hobbes's *Leviathan*, published 1651

constructed through voluntary submission of those individuals who accede to its authority; or as Hobbes wrote, '[a] Multitude of men, are made *One* Person, when they are by one man, or one Person, Represented; so that it be done with the consent of every one of that Multitude in particular' (*Leviathan*, I.16.13 [2006: 131]).

The Hobbesian theory of the state – as a moral entity that 'can claim for itself a distinct, overriding, civil authority in its own right' and as 'an abstractly defined set of offices and associated powers' (Geuss 2001: 50) – came to play a significant role in shaping English legal thought, particularly through Blackstone's influential *Commentaries*:

> Blackstone portrays the people, unified through a social contract, as forming the state. The state is a *persona ficta* with a distinct moral personality which is in turn represented by the sovereign which is itself an artificial person. By these fictions, the state as a collective is able to act as if it were 'one man' with 'one uniform will'. Sovereigns may come and go but the state endures.
>
> (McLean 2012: 3)

As legal historians note, this attempt to transform the king's authority into a more impersonal public sphere by grafting a Hobbesian theory of the state as a corporation sole onto the much older papal doctrine of the 'king's two bodies' (the body natural which dies and the body politic which is perpetual) may have created the confusion that continues to haunt contemporary understandings of the Crown (Loughlin 1999; Sedley 2015).

Hobbes's crowned Leviathan epitomises several key themes that have become central to modern theories of the state, from the idea of the state as a body that is greater than the sum of its parts and that transcends the authority of its subjects who, individually and collectively, constitute it, to the notion of the state as something abstract, contingent, contractual and socially constructed, yet nevertheless endowed with agency, autonomy, concreteness and permanence. One of the paradoxes of the modern state, then, is that while it is composed of countless individuals and appears to dominate its citizens, its unity and coherence are dependent precisely upon the actions and activities of those individuals, whether they form part of the state or not.

Anthropological Perspectives on the Crown and the State

While legal theorists and historians have been largely concerned with understanding the origins and development of the state concept in legal thought and public law, anthropologists and social theorists have been more preoccupied with the ontological status of the state and with understanding its power, legitimacy and effects rather than its legal standing and personality. The difficulty with analysing the modern state often lies in the fact that it is not easy to observe empirically, nor is it the tangible, cohesive entity that traditional writings on the subject often assume. Indeed, the variety of different institutional forms that today constitute the state suggest that it seldom acts as a unified or homogenous entity. As Akhil Gupta (1995: 375) noted, what is striking today 'is the degree to which the state has become implicated in the minute texture of everyday life' through its myriad links with schooling, policing, taxation and local administration. It is this diffuseness and ubiquity that renders the state so difficult to perceive.

Michel Foucault (2008: 76–77) famously remarked that one should refrain from theorising the state in the sense that one should refrain from eating 'an indigestible meal'. However, and at the risk of indigestion, it is important to advance some theoretical concepts to make sense of this 'thing' that we call the modern state. Indeed, since the 1990s the concept of the state has undergone a major reconceptualization in both anthropology and political science in ways which, following Foucault, have decentred and problematised what was often treated as an 'unanalysed given', or at best as a 'hostile and invasive presence in local social life' (Herzfeld 1997: 1). In his review of contemporary theories of the state, Bob Jessop observed that there is a remarkable convergence within social science around the idea of the contingency of the state apparatus and state power and concluded that the state 'should be dethroned from its central position in analyses of political power and domination' (Jessop 2001: 149). But how should we 'dethrone the Crown' from our analyses of constitutional monarchies? This question merits further elaboration before I turn to consider how anthropological perspectives on the state might provide analytical purchase on the concept of the Crown, or vice versa.

Following the Hobbesian view of the state as an entity born of voluntary and necessary subjection of citizens to the authority and protection of their sovereign, most post-war political science tended to conceptualise the state either in terms of systems-theory approaches or state-centric approaches, particularly focusing on institutions of coercion and violence (Tilly 1992; Steinmetz 1999: 9; Sharma and Gupta 2006: 8). Max Weber's (1946) classical definition of the state as a body that 'claims the *monopoly of the legitimate use of physical force* within a given territory' helped to reify the idea of the state as a coherent and unitary actor that governs over a particular population and space. The traditional Marxist view of the state as the 'management committee' of the ruling class reinforced this functionalist and teleological idea of the state as an autonomous institution set apart from society with its own interests and goals.[3] Such representations of the state as a bounded, rational actor with supreme authority to coerce and regulate populations within a territory are clearly inadequate for understanding modern state systems (Alonso 1994; Nagengast 1994; Ferguson and Gupta 2002; Sharma and Gupta 2006). Or if we are to think of the state in these terms, we need to adopt much broader conceptions of 'legitimacy', 'regulation' and 'coercion' and ask, how are these effects actually achieved? In short, the state idea is not reducible to 'bodies of armed men' or formal governmental structures: it is also a type of abstraction and, more importantly, an exercise in legitimation (Abrams 1988).

This does not mean that the state has no physical reality or has lost its grip over its citizens. Rather, the problem is that scholars often tend to objectify the state and endow it with a 'misplaced concreteness' (Alonso 1994: 380). This has resulted in a conception of the state as a unified, coherent entity with a clear hegemonic project, rather than a complex and messy set of agents and processes that do not necessarily share a common purpose at all. Against this, as James C. Scott (1994: xi) wrote, 'we cannot simply take it for granted that state elites *have* a "hegemonic project" at all. This must be an empirical question, not a presupposition'. Similarly, Corrigan and Sayer argued long ago that the state should be seen more as a 'message of domination – an ideological artifact attributing unity, morality and independence to the disunited, amoral and dependent workings of the practice of government' (1985: 77). In other words, the state cannot be reduced to an apparatus of power in the service of the dominant: it constitutes the form of collective belief that structures the whole of social life. Or as Pierre Bourdieu put it; 'the jurists who say that the state is a legal fiction . . . are right, and at the same time they do not concretely conceive the social conditions that make this fiction not fictitious but operative – which is what the sociologist has to do (Bourdieu 2014: 31).

What these writers share is a conception of the state based around the idea of the practices of government and the exercise of power, rather than

[3] Although Karl Marx also recognised the state as both ideological and concrete (see Miliband 1969; Poulantzas 1978).

deducing the modern activities of government from the state's assumed essential properties. The idea that the state has a substantive 'essence' also needs questioning. As Carole Nagengast summed it up:

> the state is not just a set of institutions staffed by bureaucrats who serve public interest. It also incorporates cultural and political forms, representations, discourse, practices and activities, and specific technologies and organisations of power that, taken together, help to define public interest, establish meaning, and define and naturalize available social identities.
>
> (Nagengast 1994: 116)

This shifts the focus of analysis to the cultural forms and practices that constitute the state: those everyday state routines, rituals, activities and policies that 'regulate the social making of meaning and of subjects' (Alonso 1994: 380). Sharma and Gupta suggest viewing states as 'culturally embedded and discursively constructed ensembles' that are 'produced through everyday practices and encounters and through public cultural representations and performances' (Sharma and Gupta 2006: 27). As Timothy Mitchell (1999) and Michel-Rolph Trouillot (2001) argue, 'state-like effects' previously produced by the institutions of the state have to an increasing extent been relocated to other institutions such as international NGOs, educational systems, rating agencies, private venture capitalists and global corporations – which have no obvious geographical or spatial fixity and which very often bypass the power of nation-states.

To sum up, the power of the state lies largely in its *cultural* forms and its effects: above all, in its capacity to engender moral regulation and the illusion of its own coherence. To understand the modern state, we therefore need to explore the subtle and more diffuse ways that power and governance work – including the norms and everyday practices that govern conduct and make populations amenable to governing in the first place. This is what Abrams (1988) termed 'politically organised subjection', and what others call 'governmentality' (Foucault 1991; Larner 2000; Lemke 2007): the myriad techniques used by the modern state to individualise and objectify its subjects.

Theories of the State as a Lens for Understanding the Crown?

> What we need, however, is a political philosophy that isn't erected around the problem of sovereignty .... We need to cut off the King's head: in political theory that has still to be done.
>
> Foucault (1980), 'Truth and Power'

As noted in the previous section, most contemporary theories on the modern state tend to adopt a 'governmentality' approach focusing less on the concrete institutions and apparatuses of the state than on the production of what Timothy Mitchell (1999) termed 'state effects'. This entails reconceptualising the state as a fluid, dynamic and contingent set of relations constituted through symbolic devices, government practices and political technologies – including technologies of the self (see Lemke 2007: 43–44; 57). This 'analytics of government' approach shifts the focus from fixed institutions to the complex and often intangible processes of rule and relational understandings of power. This is consistent with Foucault's argument (1980: 121) about the need to 'cut off the king's head' in political analysis and recast the problem of government in terms of norms, legitimisation, hegemony, and what Herman and Chomsky (2002) have termed 'the manufacture of consent'.

But how does this 'dethroning' work in the case of the Crown? What does 'cutting off the king's head' mean, analytically – or even metaphorically – when applied to constitutional monarchy, particularly when that 'head' is symbolically and structurally adorned by a Crown? In the last part of this chapter I address this question by exploring three ways in which modern state theory can offer insights for understanding the political, constitutional and symbolic work of the Crown.

The Illusion of Its Own Coherence

First, the state, like the Crown, plays an important role in maintaining the illusion of its own coherence. It also plays a central role in structuring our political reality and has 'overall responsibility for maintaining the cohesion of the social formation of which it is a part' (Jessop 2001: 167). Yet as Abrams (1988: 59) observed, we still 'take the state for granted as an object of political practice and political analysis while remaining quite spectacularly unclear as to what the state is'. The same can be said for the Crown. Indeed, the ontological status of the Crown has received even less critical scrutiny than that of the state. This has important implications for understanding how constitutional monarchy works as a political system. As Abrams argued:

> The state is not the reality which stands behind the mask of political practice. It is itself the mask which prevents our seeing political practice as it is. . . . There *is* a state-system . . . a palpable nexus of practice and

> institutional structure centred in government and more or less extensive, unified and dominant in any given society. There *is*, too, a state-idea, projected, purveyed and variously believed in in different societies at different times. . . . it starts its life as an implicit construct; it is then reified – as the *res publica*, the public reification, no less – and acquires an overt symbolic identity progressively divorced from practice as an illusory account of practice.
>
> (Abrams 1988: 82)

This shift from the state idea as an implicit, relational and conceptual construct to its reification as an autonomous, unified *res publica* (lit. 'public affair/thing') mirrors the historical development of the Crown outlined in Chapter 2. However, if the state is the mask that obscures the reality of government preventing us from seeing the reality of political practice as it is, what can be said about the Crown, its effects, and the political practices it conceals?

A Powerful Fiction: Socially and Symbolically Constructed

Second, and in answer to that question, both the Crown and the state are powerful fictions. Each is a socially constituted and symbolically constructed entity typically portrayed as a unitary body situated above and beyond society. In the case of the Crown, however, it needs to be seen circulating through society: hence the importance of royal tours, 'homecomings' and the various rituals of monarchy (see Chapter 8). Yet in its more formal ceremonial garb the Crown often appears even more Olympian and detached than the state: the public are invited to stand and gaze in wonder outside the gates of Buckingham Palace to catch a glimpse of their sovereign and the enchanted lives of the royal family (Nairn 1988; Bagehot [1867] 2001). The pomp and ceremony associated with Crown and monarchy are, of course, fundamental to its legitimacy. As Clifford Geertz (1980) argued, the idea of the state is predicated not only on statecraft (i.e. domination, mastery and governance) but also on 'stateliness' and its connotation of pomp and ceremony. Sometimes, as in Geertz's account of nineteenth-century Bali, theatre and spectacle are not simply at the service of the state but are themselves constitutive of state power. Ritual and ceremonial performances, even the most mundane ones, thus help to ground the fiction of the Crown and endow it with a sense of reality.

Personifying State and Crown: Cold-Hearted Monster Versus Warm-Blooded Monarch

Like the state, the Crown has legal personality and often represents itself as technically 'indivisible', even though it is personified by different actors (including ministers, Crown Prosecution Service lawyers, High Court judges and senior military officers) and appears in different guises that shift according to context. Both can also be understood as artificial persons and 'corporations aggregate' (i.e. a separate legal entity formed by several individual persons); yet, as Maitland noted, the Crown is also represented as a real person and as a corporation sole. This has important implications for statecraft. To exercise authority, both the state and the Crown require legitimacy that goes beyond the Weberian principle of legal–rational authority; they also need a measure of public recognition and some degree of loyalty and identification from the population over which they seek to govern. Michael Walzer (1967: 194) captured this point succinctly when he wrote, 'The state is invisible; it must be personified before it can be seen, symbolized before it can be loved, imagined before it can be conceived.' By contrast, the Crown is highly visible and is almost always personified, even if its effects are less visible. Compared to the cold-hearted, remote and abstract state, the Queen and her family are relatively easy to imagine, to symbolise and, for some at least, to love. As a personified sovereign, the Crown offers far more possibilities for the politics of distraction and enchantment (Nairn 1988; Bagehot [1867] 2001). As Walter Bagehot ([1867] 2001) shrewdly observed over a century ago, the idea of a king or queen as head of state provides a wonderful distraction for the public and deflects attention from the more 'efficient' parts of the constitution where political power operates. England, he wrote,

> has whole classes unable to comprehend the idea of a constitution – unable to feel the least attachment to impersonal laws. Most do indeed vaguely know that there are some other institutions besides the Queen, and some rules by which she governs. But a vast number like their minds to dwell more upon her than on anything else, and therefore she is inestimable. A republic has only difficult ideas in government; a constitutional monarchy has an easy idea too; it has a comprehensible element for the vacant many, as well as complex laws and notions for the inquiring few.
>
> (Bagehot [1867] 2001: 37)

Bagehot also highlighted the political effect of having a *family* on the throne: 'It brings down the pride of sovereignty to the level of petty life'.

'No feeling', he added, 'could seem more childish than the enthusiasm of the English at the marriage of the Prince of Wales' (37). Royal rituals, when they are successful, become important foci for expressions of loyalty and patriotism. The monarchy is often far more successful in casting an aura of enchantment than other kinds of state performance. The monarchy provides a powerful figurehead and focus for national cohesion and identity. Queen Elizabeth and the royals are far more personable and seemingly approachable than the cold-hearted monster abstraction of the Leviathan state. As one elderly Māori leader expressed it to us, 'the Crown represents the decent face of Leviathan' (Patel 2016: 168). In this respect, a monarch who both acts as head of state and is the embodiment of the state provides a potent and seductive face for that assemblage of impersonal institutions that we call the State. This idea is cleverly captured by Helen Marshall in an artwork that now hangs in the South Terminal of Gatwick airport (see Figure 3.2). Commissioned by BBC South East to celebrate the Queen's diamond jubilee in 2013, *The People's Monarch* (Figure 3.2) is a massive 38 square metre double-portrait of the Queen at the time of her coronation and 60 years later.[4] Like the cover of Hobbes' *Leviathan*, the image is a mosaic made up of hundreds of tiny figures. However, unlike the inward-looking, anonymous, grey and faceless subjects in Hobbes' image, these individuals are colourful, clearly recognisable as real people, and all facing forwards, many smiling and standing with friends, families and partners. The monarch here is depicted as a warm and engaging figure and someone who embodies or reflects the diversity of contemporary British society.

The argument that the Crown lends a more human face to the state, thereby providing legitimacy and a sense of intimacy and loyalty to what might otherwise be experienced as a remote apparatus of power, is one that monarchists and advocates of constitutional monarchy often made when explaining to us why constitutional monarchy was the 'best of all political systems' for ensuring stability, continuity and good governance. The merit of these claims is a theme we will return to in Chapter 12. What is important to stress here is the important role that affect plays in

[4] BBC South East commissioned the artwork for the Diamond jubilee, inviting viewers and listeners to send in their treasured photos to help create the huge double portrait of the Queen; it is a mammoth collection of people's social history. Thousands sent family portraits, snaps of important occasions in their lives and many used the opportunity to remember loved ones they had lost – all sharing precious memories. The project found that everyone thought long and hard about the image they wanted to represent them and their family in the Jubilee artwork.

Figure 3.2 *The People's Monarch*, Helen Marshall, 2013
(Courtesy of BBC South East)

statecraft, particularly in producing allegiance to state sovereignty and the experiential sense of solidarity among citizens. As Muir and Gupta (2018: S10) point out, 'such commitments and sense of conviviality do not require naive belief in the state, but can thrive, however paradoxically, in conditions of critique, suspicion, and even resistance'. In other words, one does not have to be a true believer in or even a supporter of the Crown in order to be caught up in what many of our informants referred to as 'the magic of monarchy'. If the state, as something 'set apart' from everyday life, can sometimes provide an avenue into the 'sacred', in Durkheim's ([1912] 1965) sense of the term, the Crown can do this in even stronger ways because it is both abstract and detached from the everyday *and* experienced as part of the fabric of society. In this way it opens up a powerful space for a transcendent experience of sovereignty and community. This sense of intimacy and affect is perhaps the Crown's most important and distinctive 'state effect'.

Conclusion: The Greatest of All Artificial Persons?

I began this chapter by asking whether the Crown is a metonym for the state and whether the concepts of Crown and state are functionally equivalent. The answer appears to be both yes and no: yes because the Crown does frequently serve as a conceptual placeholder for the state, but no because the terms Crown and state do not map the same semantic terrain, as will become clearer in this book. Anne Twomey, Professor of Law and arguably Australia's leading expert on the Crown and constitutional reform, estimates that there is about an 80 per cent overlap between these terms (*Twomey, Interviews 2015 – see also Chapter 12*). In other words, 20 per cent of the Crown's powers – including prerogative powers – are *not* covered by the state and lie in what some would call the dead zone of the constitution.

If the Crown has inhibited the development of a coherent state concept in English law (Loughlin 1999: 33; McLean 2012: 2), one reason for this is the personified nature of the Crown in the figure of the monarch. The public/private distinction that developed out of the medieval political theology and the doctrine of the king's two bodies was given an unusual twist in the evolution of the Westminster model of constitutional monarchy. As Maitland noted, the distinctive feature of the English system of government was not so much that the state is personified in the figure of the king, but rather that 'the King is "parsonified"' (Maitland 1901: 131). By this, Maitland meant that English lawyers, following medieval lawyers like Coke, used ecclesiastical property law to frame their understanding of the timeless and corporate nature of the Crown. Hence, a metaphysical conception of the Crown arose that was shaped by that religious-inspired notion of the corporation sole. This strangely unreal 'royal *persona ficta*', as Kantorowicz ([1957] 1997: 4–5) put it, was imagined as immortal ('because legally he can never die'), indivisible and incapable of doing wrong: a body existing in a 'state of superhuman "absolute perfection"'. Catholic and Roman political theologians who saw the world divided between a spiritual realm and an earthly realm further bolstered these ideas.

While legal scholars have explored this theme extensively, little attention has been paid to its implications for public understandings of constitutional monarchy. How do the Crown's subjects perceive the difference between the 'king's two bodies', or the distinction between the Crown as physical person and the Crown as a set of institutions? For example, when judges, ministers and members of the armed forces pledge their oaths of loyalty to Her Majesty the Queen, is that to the office of the Crown or to the person of the Queen herself? Most of our legally trained informants were clear about the distinction and recognised the Crown as a corporation aggregate. However, those from military backgrounds tended to hold a different view. For example, when I put the question to the Queen's Herald Colonel Alistair Bruce, his answer was that the oath of loyalty was sworn to her Majesty the Queen as a living person rather than as the embodiment of a particular office, but added that he saw no clear separation between the two notions.

> I don't think one is separable from the other because you're dedicating yourself to the sovereign. But by doing that you're dedicating yourself to all that she has committed to. And at her coronation she made three very clear oaths. And that is the essence of her being connected to her people. And she's even given a wedding ring; she marries herself to the nation.
>
> (Interviews, Bruce, 2016)

This highlights my earlier point about 'Crown effects' and their capacity to engender feelings of loyalty, community and conviviality. Every country has its symbols of statehood to which state servants must pledge their allegiance, be it to flag, nation or constitution. What the Crown offers its subjects is a focus of allegiance that is neither to some abstract principle or remote authority figure of the kind imagined by Hobbes nor to a particular flesh-and-blood king. Rather, the Crown is at once all of these phenomena. Herein lies its potency as a symbol of statehood, with all its ambiguous, condensed and polysemic meanings. This also explains why it is that for Māori in New Zealand and First Nations peoples in Canada, the Crown assumes such importance in their dealings with the state and provincial governments.

This brings us back to Foucault's admonitions about moving beyond outdated notions of sovereignty in order to properly understand the workings of power. In a lecture he gave at the Collège de France Foucault declared that:

> we have to abandon the model of Leviathan, that model of an artificial man who is at once an automaton, a fabricated man, but also a unitary man who contains all real individuals, whose body is made up of citizens but whose soul is sovereignty. We have to study power outside the model of Leviathan, outside the field delineated by juridical sovereignty and the institution of the State.
>
> (Foucault [1975] 2003: 34)

In response to Foucault, I suggest that we need to do more than this. In the case of the Crown, abandoning the model of Leviathan might not always assist our efforts to understand how state power and authority work. Rather than abandon the conception, we need to pay closer attention to how this artificial man is fabricated. That requires looking beyond the field of juridical sovereignty and state institutions – and beyond what Kantorowicz ([1957] 1997: 5) called 'the allegedly sober and realistic realms of law, politics, and constitution', into the more ephemeral realms of emotion, religion, political enchantment and cultural mystique. While I agree that the Crown, like the state, is an artificial person and a legal fiction, it is nonetheless constituted and embodied by real individuals and has very real effects. In this respect, the Crown is both a metonym for the state and a personification of state sovereignty, yet also something more than the state. Exactly what that 'more than the state' entails is the subject we address in the next section of the book, which examines the complex ways in which the Crown and sovereignty are embodied and personified in the different realms.

References

Abrams, Philip. 1988. 'Notes on the Difficulty of Studying the State (1977).' *Journal of Historical Sociology* 1(1): 58–89.

Alonso, Ana María. 1994. 'The Politics of Space, Time and Substance: State Formation, Nationalism, and Ethnicity.' *Annual Review of Anthropology* 23: 379–405.

Bagehot, Walter. (1867) 2001. *The English Constitution*, edited by Paul Smith. Cambridge: Cambridge University Press.

Blick, Andrew. 2011. 'Codifying – Or Not Codifying – the United Kingdom Constitution: The Existing Constitution.' *Centre for Political and Constitutional Studies*, Series Paper 1. London: King's College. www.parliament.uk/documents/commons-committees/political-and-constitutional-reform/KCLexistingconstitutionMay2012.pdf.

Bogdanor, Vernon. 2009. *The New British Constitution*. London: Hart Publishing.

Bourdieu, Pierre. 2014. *On the State: Lectures at the Collège de France, 1989–1992*, translated by David Fernbach. Bristol: Polity.

Cobbett, Pitt. 1904. '"The Crown" as Representing "the State".' *Commonwealth Law Review* 1: 23–30.

Corrigan, Philip and Sayer, Derek. 1985. *The Great Arch: English State Formation as Cultural Revolution*. Oxford: Basil Blackwell.

Cox, Noel. 2002. 'The Theory of Sovereignty and the Importance of the Crown in the Realms of the Queen.' *Oxford University Commonwealth Law Journal* 2(2): 237–55.

Du Gay, Paul and Alan Scott. 2010. 'State Transformation or Regime Shift? Addressing Some Confusions in the Theory and Sociology of the State.' *Sociologica* 4(2): 1–23.

Durkheim, Emile. (1912) 1965. *The Elementary Forms of the Religious Life*, translated by Joseph Ward Swain. New York: Free Press.

Ferguson, James and Akhil Gupta. 2002. 'Spatializing States: Toward an Ethnography of Neoliberal Governmentality.' *American Ethnologist* 29(4): 981–1002.

Foucault, Michel. 1980. *Power/Knowledge: Selected Interviews and Other Writings 1972–1977*, edited by Colin Gordon. New York: Pantheon.

1991. 'Governmentality.' In *The Foucault Effect: Studies in Governmentality*, edited by Graham Burchell, Colin Gordon and Peter Miller, 87–104. London: Harvester Wheatsheaf.

(1975) 2003. *'Society Must Be Defended': Lectures at the Collège de France, 1975–76*, edited by Mauro Bertani and Alessandro Fontana. Translated by David Macey. London: Macmillan.

(1979) 2008. *The Birth of Biopolitics: Lectures at the Collège de France, 1978–79*, edited by Michel Senellart. Translated by Graham Burchell. Basingstoke: Palgrave MacMillan.

Geertz, Clifford. 1980. *Negara: The Theatre State in Nineteenth-Century Bali*. Princeton, NJ: Princeton University Press.

Geuss, Raymond. 2001. *History and Illusion in Politics*. Cambridge: Cambridge University Press.

Gupta, Akhil. 1995. 'Blurred Boundaries: The Discourse of Corruption, the Culture of Politics, and the Imagined State.' *American Ethnologist* 22(2): 375–402.

Herman, Edward S. and Noam Chomsky. 2002. *Manufacturing Consent: The Political Economy of the Mass Media*. New York: Pantheon.

Herzfeld, Michael. 1997. *Cultural Intimacy: Social Poetics in the Nation-State*. New York and London: Routledge

Hobbes, Thomas. (1651) 2005. *Leviathan*. New York: Continuum.

Jessop, Bob. 2001. 'Bringing the State Back In (Yet Again): Reviews, Revisions, Rejections, and Redirections.' *International Review of Sociology/Revue internationale de sociologie* 11(2): 149–73.

Kantorowicz, Ernst Hartwig. (1957) 1997. *The King's Two Bodies: A Study in Mediaeval Political Theology*. Princeton, NJ: Princeton University Press.

Larner, Wendy. 2000. 'Neo-liberalism: Policy, Ideology, Governmentality.' *Studies in Political Economy* 63(1): 5–25.

Law, Jonathan (ed.). 2015. *A Dictionary of Law*, 8th edn. Oxford: Oxford University Press.

Lemke, Thomas. 2007. 'An Indigestible Meal? Foucault, Governmentality and State Theory.' *Distinktion: Scandinavian Journal of Social Theory* 8(2): 43–64.

Loughlin, Martin. 1999. 'The State, the Crown and the Law.' In *The Nature of the Crown: A Legal and Political Analysis*, edited by Maurice Sunkin and Sebastian Payne, 33–76. Oxford: Clarendon Press.

2000. *Sword and Scales: An Examination of the Relationship between Law and Politics*. London: Hart Publishing.

Maitland, Frederic W. 1901. 'The Crown as Corporation.' *Law Quarterly Review* 17(2): 131–46.

(1908) 2001. *The Constitutional History of England: A Course of Lectures Delivered*. The Lawbook Exchange.

McLean, Iain. 2010. *What's Wrong with the British Constitution?* Oxford: Oxford University Press.

McLean, Janet. 2012. *Searching for the State in British Legal Thought: Competing Conceptions of the Public Sphere*. Cambridge: Cambridge University Press.

Miliband, Ralph. 1969. *The State in Capitalist Society*. London: Quartet Books.

Mitchell, Timothy 1999. 'Society, Economy, and the State Effect,' in *State/Culture*, edited by George Steinmetz, 76–97. Ithaca, NY: Cornell University Press.

Muir, Sarah and Akhil Gupta. 2018. 'Rethinking the Anthropology of Corruption: An Introduction to Supplement 18.' *Current Anthropology* 59(S18): S4–S15.

Nagengast, Carole. 1994. 'Violence, Terror and the Crisis of the State.' *Annual Review of Anthropology* 23: 109–36.

Nairn, Tom. 1988. *The Enchanted Glass: Britain and Its Monarchy*. London: Radius.

Palmer, Geoffrey and Andrew Butler. 2016. *A Constitution for Aotearoa New Zealand*. Wellington: Victoria University Press.

Patel, Aaron Jai. 2016. 'Imagining the Right to Rule: The Crown as a Political Symbol in New Zealand.' MA Thesis. Auckland: The University of Auckland.

Pocock, John G. A. 2009. 'Quentin Skinner: The History of Politics and the Politics of History,' in *Political Thought and History: Essays on Theory and Method*, 123–44. Cambridge: Cambridge University Press.

Poulantzas, Nicos. 1978. *State, Power, Socialism*. London: Verso

Richardson, Janice. 2016. 'Hobbes' Frontispiece: Authorship, Subordination and Contact.' *Law and Critique* 27(1): 63–81.

Scott, James C. 1994. 'Foreword,' in *Everyday Forms of State Formation: Revolution and the Negotiation of Rule in Modern Mexico*, edited by Gilbert M. Joseph and Daniel Nugent, vii–xii. Durham, NC: Duke University Press.

Sedley, Stephen. 2011. *Ashes and Sparks: Essays on Law and Justice*. Cambridge: Cambridge University Press.

2015. *Lions under the Throne: Essays on the History of English Public Law*. Cambridge: Cambridge University Press.

Sharma, Aradhana and Akhil Gupta. 2006. 'Introduction: Rethinking Theories of the State in an Age of Globalization.' in *The Anthropology of the State: A Reader*, edited by Aradhana Sharma and Akhil Gupta, 1–41. Oxford: Wiley-Blackwell.

Steinmetz, George (ed.). 1999. *State/Culture: State-Formation after the Cultural Turn*. Ithaca, NY, and London: Cornell University Press.

Sunkin, Maurice and Sebastian Payne (eds.). 1999. *The Nature of the Crown: A Legal and Political Analysis*. Oxford: Clarendon Press.

Tilly, Charles. 1992. *Coercion, Capital, and European States AD 990–1992*. Oxford: Blackwell.

Trouillot, Michel-Rolph. 2001. 'The Anthropology of the State in the Age of Globalization: Close Encounters of the Deceptive Kind.' *Current Anthropology* 42(1): 125–38.

Walzer, Michael. 1967. 'On the Role of Symbolism in Political Thought.' *Political Science Quarterly* 82(2): 191–204.

Weber, Max. 1946. 'Politics as a Vocation,' in *From Max Weber: Essays in Sociology*, edited by H. H. Gerth and C. Wright Mills, 77–128. New York: Oxford University Press.

4

Indigenous Peoples and the Crown

The Sacred Duty

SALLY RAUDON

Waitangi, 1963

In February 1963 Sir Turi Carroll, 72 years old, travelled to Waitangi, a settlement in the Bay of Islands in New Zealand's sub-tropical north, from his farm on the isolated East Coast. Active in local politics throughout his life, he had focused on Māori welfare through land, health, education and veterans' issues, the latter directly inspired by his own Māori Battalion service in the Great War. The previous year, he had been knighted for these efforts and was elected president of the New Zealand Māori Council, a statutory body which replaced the non-official Dominion Council of Tribal Executives in 1962. Carroll's family was steeped in politics: his uncle Sir James Carroll was the first Māori to hold cabinet portfolios and had twice been acting prime minister. Carroll had always worked to benefit Māori with skills acquired from both Māori (indigenous New Zealander) and Pākehā (European New Zealander) worlds. He was happiest on the East Coast, comfortable with conservative values and rural people. But today, he was off to welcome Queen Elizabeth at Waitangi. They had met previously during her first New Zealand visit in 1954, at Carroll's investiture as an OBE (Officer of the Order of the British Empire). Then there had been little opportunity for *kōrero* (conversation). This time, Carroll would be giving the speech of his life.

Some twenty thousand other New Zealanders had descended on Waitangi to see the Queen. As this was four times more than the anticipated numbers, the government hurriedly dispatched the army to erect field kitchens and pitch some two hundred tents to shelter the impromptu town from the late summer heat. About a quarter of the crowd were Māori, enthusiastically fulfilling their responsibilities to welcome the royal visitors, and determined to support Carroll.

Chapters 2 and 3 discussed how the British Crown transformed into the various Crowns of Australia, Canada and New Zealand, each with distinctive characteristics and practices, and how settler governments employed the Crown's conceptual imprecision to acquire political legitimacy through a state-like veneer of coherence and independence. Here, we examine how New Zealand Māori, Canadian First Nations peoples and Australian Aboriginal and Torres Straits Islanders (Indigenous Australians) perceived the Crown, then and now.

We ask, how have indigenous perspectives shaped the Crown's role in postcolonial settler societies, and what is at stake when indigenous peoples emphasise their relationship with the Crown? Why are Queen and Crown so important for indigenous peoples, and when are appeals directed to the Crown rather than the government or the state? We examine how these relationships have developed in New Zealand and Canada where the 'honour of the Crown' is a familiar trope, and in Australia where the Crown has little relevance for Indigenous Australians. To begin, we return to Waitangi on 6 February 1963.

Then, as now, Waitangi was rich in the origin myths of modern bicultural New Zealand. In 1840, Crown agents of Queen Victoria had begun signing the Treaty of Waitangi ('the Treaty') with Māori *rangatira* (chiefs) on the Treaty House grounds. When Queen Elizabeth sailed into Waitangi to begin her second New Zealand visit, on the 123rd anniversary of the Treaty signing, Carroll was waiting. The Queen and Prince Philip – in white naval dress uniform with sword, sash and medals – were welcomed formally with a *wero* (ceremonial challenge) by Lieutenant Colonel Arapeta Awatere of the famed 28th Māori Battalion, and a 'thunderous' *haka* (ceremonial posture dance) (*Te Ao Hou* 1963: 23). Before a richly carved *whare rūnanga* (meeting house) built in 1940, Queen Elizabeth greeted each of sixty Māori dignitaries, many draped in *korowai* (cloaks) made of kiwi feathers to indicate their high status (see Figure 4.1). With these formalities concluded, the speeches began.

Carroll was no agitator, and his speech seems measured, even conciliatory, by the standards of radical Māori protest today. But he was also resolute. At a time when government policy stressed racial integration, he called for recognition for Māori as equal citizens, with full protection of Māori rights; for the Treaty to be embodied in New Zealand statute; and for these matters to be commemorated by marking 6 February as the new national holiday of Waitangi Day. Carroll

Figure 4.1 Queen Elizabeth and Prince Philip greet Māori elders at the Waitangi Treaty Grounds, 6 February 1963
(Courtesy of Ans Westra; Te Papa Tongarewa)

underscored his authority to raise these issues by affirming the relationship between Māori and the Crown:

> Your Majesty's presence once again underlines for us the deep significance of the compact that was freely agreed to on this very spot by the representative of Queen Victoria, your illustrious great-great-grandmother, and by the ancestors of so many of us gathered here today . . . We gladly offer today, on this anniversary of the signing of the Treaty of Waitangi, to renew the spirit of that compact and, above all, to reaffirm our loyalty to the Crown.
>
> (Te Ao Hou 1963: 24)

In response, Queen Elizabeth's first few words in Te Reo (the Māori language) received boisterous cheers from the crowd. She reiterated her pleasure at being present on this 'hallowed ground' on this auspicious date:

> I want to renew those pledges and to assure my Maori people that the obligations entered into at Waitangi go *far deeper than any legal provision* in any formal document *[applause, roars of approval]*. Whatever may have happened in the past and whatever the future may bring, it remains *the sacred duty of the Crown* today, as in 1840, to stand by the spirit of the Treaty of Waitangi, and to ensure that the trust of the Maori people is never betrayed.
>
> (Te Ao Hou 1963: 28; my emphasis).

By adopting the language of sacred obligations, Elizabeth's speechwriters had played on idioms of local understanding that they hoped would resonate – which they surely did, as the Queen had to pause until the cheering subsided. Queen Elizabeth stood in New Zealand as its sovereign and ultimate source of legal and political authority, and simultaneously claimed that the Crown's duties to Māori surpassed even these grave responsibilities.

This exchange between Carroll and Queen Elizabeth signalled that the relationship between Māori and the Crown was measurably different from that between the Crown and other New Zealand citizens. This bond held rich significance for both parties, with ritual declarations of renewed vows bound by ancestral ties of fealty and protection. But what did Queen Elizabeth mean by declaring that commitments made in her ancestor's name exceeded that of any legal document? She asserted that the Crown's responsibilities 'go far deeper than any legal provision', and, moreover, that it is the Crown's 'sacred duty' to stand by its Treaty obligations of 1840. Both parties mention the Treaty's 'spirit' as if it had an independent vitality (a notion later articulated in New Zealand law as 'the Treaty principles' in 1987). For both parties in 1963 the Treaty not only existed as a formal document, it also embodied concepts of honour, virtue, integrity and trust.

These speeches suggest that the Crown as an institution belongs to a higher order to that of the state or government, one capable of more sophisticated understandings and relationships. This perception marks the Crown as a source of moral power, a final arbiter to petition when all other avenues have been exhausted – a position that Elizabeth herself asserted. However, appealing to the Crown for justice carries an apparent contradiction for indigenous peoples because it positions the Queen as both oppressor and protector: the source of colonial authority is also the one called upon to intercede against it.

The Dispossessing Crown as a Source of Redress

In Canada, New Zealand and Australia, indigenous land rights have been both quintessentially inalienable and especially vulnerable to cancellation (Secher 2014). Each former colony was founded on appropriating indigenous peoples' land and rights, but each took different legal approaches to extinguishing and then replacing indigenous sovereignty and property systems with that of the Crown (McHugh and Ford 2012). In Canada and New Zealand, imperial and then colonial governments used the Crown instrumentally to enter into treaties and sign promissory documents. These included the Treaty of Waitangi in New Zealand in 1840 and the Royal Proclamation 1763 (British North America) and numerous treaties and compacts of alliance in Canada. These agreements entirely failed to protect indigenous peoples against settler dispossession and were grievously breached numerous times in both countries.

In Canada and New Zealand, subsequent indigenous claims for rights and redress have proceeded within the legal frameworks employed in the original wrong, meaning they are inevitably founded on certain Western-centric understandings of property rights and dispossession which see land as commoditised property rather than a sacred life force (McCormack 2011; Lea 2012: 191). Treaty guarantees continue to shape how indigenous peoples present themselves to the Crown within the neoliberal political, legal and economic structures of contemporary societies (McCormack 2011; cf. Comaroff and Comaroff 2009). Though treaties with the Crown were tools of colonial dispossession, they also provide the basis for formal claims to redress in contemporary reconciliation processes.

'We Talk about the Crown because Māori Talk about the Crown'

Today, talk about the Crown is ubiquitous throughout New Zealand, and nowhere more so than in *te ao Māori* (the Māori world). In our fieldwork, people often suggested that the Crown is deeply anchored in New Zealanders' thinking because of the Treaty of Waitangi. Before the 1970s the discourse of the Crown was largely restricted to official state arenas and the courts. References to the Treaty were almost always framed in terms of the 'spirit of the Treaty'. Māori leaders such as Carroll and Sir Āpirana Ngata, aiming to expand the scope of Māori claims for rights, insisted that the Treaty's spirit was what mattered, not the narrow, legally defined obligations that it triggered. It suited New Zealand governments to describe the Crown's commitments to Māori as moral or political compacts, as these were unenforceable by courts and so did not impose any precise obligations on governments – and left Māori without enforceable legal options.

The Crown re-emerged as a concept in New Zealand during the 1970s and 1980s, particularly within government circles, and largely in response to Māori discourse about the Crown and the Treaty (Hayward 1995; O'Malley, Stirling, and Penetito 2010; Wheen and Hayward 2012). As historian Richard Hill described:

> I think the increasing use of the term the Crown came in the wake of government policy that was responding to the so-called Māori renaissance in the 1980s. Once state officials started talking to Māori more, and Māori talked often about their partnership with the Crown since 1840, it seems the government started to accommodate this perspective.
>
> (Hill, cited in Shore and Kawharu 2014: 23)

It is an irony of colonial history that the relationship between the Crown and Māori has now been inverted: in the nineteenth century the Crown, though espousing a protective role, provided a cloak of authority for colonial policies to dispossess Māori of their land; today, it is Māori efforts to find redress for those wrongs which ensure the continuing prominence of the Crown in the settlement of historic grievances. As one senior minister said: 'We talk about the Crown because Māori talk about the Crown' (Finlayson, Interviews, 2014).

The Treaty itself was incorporated into New Zealand law as a schedule to the Treaty of Waitangi Act 1975, as Carroll had called for. This established the Waitangi Tribunal, a permanent commission of inquiry that makes recommendations to the government on claims brought by Māori about Crown breaches of the Treaty. The notion of the Treaty as a 'living document' was enshrined into legal obligations owed by the Crown to Māori when the Court of Appeal gave a broad interpretation of the 'principles of the Treaty of Waitangi' in the State-Owned Enterprises Act 1986. As the court's President explained:

> The duty of the Crown is not merely passive but extends to active protection of Maori people in the use of their lands and waters to the fullest extent practicable. That duty is not a light one and is infinitely more than a formality.
>
> (*New Zealand Māori Council* v. *Attorney-General* [1987]: 642)

Clearly, treaties between imperial governments and indigenous peoples can acquire the status of founding documents. Today, the Treaty and its principles provide the foundations for a wide range of bicultural public policy guidelines (Gover and Hancock 2002). Taking account of Treaty principles has been imposed by law throughout New Zealand society and affirmed in the bureaucratic processes of public-sector organisations, social agencies and community groups.

Today, New Zealand's national day is Waitangi Day, fulfilling another of Carroll's resolutions. It does not celebrate the nationhood of the postcolonial settler majority Pākehā population but instead focuses on the Māori–Pākehā partnership brokered by the Crown – and Māori still utilise it to highlight unresolved grievances (McAllister 2012). The Treaty remains 'a contemporary basis for negotiation and participation in national life' (McAllister 2012: 190), and its spirit seems likely to endure in New Zealand political life (Ward 1999: 79). Renewed attention to the Treaty during the 1980s consequently gave the Crown greater currency in New Zealand political discourse and, significantly, the majority settler population has followed the minority indigenous one in this practice.

Indigenous Conceptions of the Crown

So what do Māori mean when they talk about the Crown? Meanings within Māori discourse fall broadly into the Crown's ability to be personified, to assert kinship and ancestral ties of reciprocal obligation, to personify a moral actor which can accept accountability, and to elevate the Treaty partnership so that Māori appear not to deal directly with government (McLean 2015).

Queen Elizabeth personally embodies the political abstraction of the Crown, and the Crown as Queen resonates within Māori discourse. Māori activist and academic Margaret Mutu was emphatic when asked what the Crown signified: 'It's Queen Elizabeth the Second . . . exactly as it was set out in Te Tiriti o Waitangi [the Treaty of Waitangi] . . . it was Queen Victoria. The Queen of England.' For political authority to be inherited by bloodline is familiar and legitimate within hierarchical Polynesian societies; the royal family's hereditary practices accord with Māori practices of *whakapapa* (valuing genealogical knowledge) and tribal hierarchy. Mutu outlined how power is constituted in Māori worldview:

> For us, power and authority is really simple – it derives from the gods, and you get it through genealogy and you're passed it down . . . to even have authority, we must be able to show our genealogical links to a place . . . you see, it's all genealogical.
>
> (Interviews, 2014)

This conception resonates with ideas about divine kingship and the notion that authority derives from the land that is ruled (Frazer 1922). Crucially, both parties recognise and valorise their chiefly lineage and the obligations which flow from this.

Personification allows for reciprocal kinship and genealogical ties between the parties. When Carroll greeted Queen Elizabeth, he reiterated that his ancestors had forged agreements with the representative of her ancestor, Queen Victoria. These ancestors were embodied by the speakers themselves at the very place of this decisive action, making past and present visible, and gave the ceremony a genealogical weight to enrich its commemorative density: why all the talk of ancestors if not to recognise their presence? This mutual recognition founded on agreements between respective ancestors is often repeated by royal visitors and Māori hosts.

Similar quasi-kinship relationships were crucial in early imperial contacts with First Nations in Canada as former British Columbia lieutenant governor, and First Nations leader, Steven Point reflected. Colonial agents identified themselves to First Nations peoples as representing 'your father in England or your mother in England', with instructions about what this father or mother hoped they would do, while assuring them that this parent worked to shield First Nations peoples from the excesses of the settlers. With indigenous peoples being decimated by infectious diseases carried by settlers and subject to forced dispossession of lands, the idea of a powerful overseas protector anxious about indigenous welfare made sense. As Point described it, 'someone that was kind of like a big chief . . . somewhere, far away, this big, big person, right? That there was this queen that was going to look after us' (Interviews, 2016). Critics have described the paternalistic relationship between the Queen and indigenous peoples as 'an instrument of Imperial statecraft' (McLean 2015: 211), but it was more than this, with both parties seeking common ground through common idioms with which to establish relations; and it has provided a useful tool for addressing the wrongs of these actions. The faraway Queen took on the mantle of the honest broker between settlers and indigenous peoples.

Further, embodying the Crown in the form of the Queen means allowing affective bonds with her personally. People's engagement with monarchy can take on relational, personalised dimensions, which are not due to political abstractions. Aboriginal Gumbaynggir activist, writer, actor and academic Gary Foley argued that while most Indigenous Australians regard the Crown as 'a non-event', insignificant and irrelevant, many hold a different sensibility towards Queen Elizabeth; as he stated, for example, 'My grandmother loved the Queen. There was a (portrait of the) Queen in my grandmother's lounge room till the day she died' (Interviews, 2015). This was common for Australians of the mid-twentieth century, across ethnic and class groups, because royal memorabilia was a central prop for performing Australian identity in the early and mid-twentieth century. While dismissing the Crown as an institution, Foley intimated that his own personal dealings with Queen Elizabeth had been meaningful and encouraging: 'On certain occasions, within the limits of her protocols, she has expressed what I believe [are] genuine concerns about Aboriginal things ... She's quietly indicated support for certain things at times' (Interviews, 2015).

The Crown as Partner

When Carroll spoke of his ancestors as Treaty signatories he evoked a sense of equivalence between himself and Queen Elizabeth to support his assertions about the Treaty's spiritual compact. If the Crown is the ultimate source of political and legal authority, then partnering with it enhances one's status. If the Crown is superior to, and independent from, the government of the day, then the signatories are likewise elevated. Similarly, if the Crown sits above party politics, then agreements with it will likewise be preserved through independence. Entering a partnership with the Crown allows indigenous peoples agency within the colonisation narrative; Carroll pointedly noted that the Treaty was 'freely agreed to' (*Te Ao Hou* 1963: 24). This sense of agency links directly with contemporary political claims for *tino rangatiratanga* (absolute sovereignty, which the Māori-language version of the Treaty reserves for Māori).

However, the Treaty partnership between Māori and the Crown remains controversial in New Zealand as it implies Māori have a special status, which some contend is divisive and incongruous with democratic citizenship (Rata 2005). Others equate it with ethnic nationalism (Rata 2005), and still others with racism. For example, politician Don Brash and Canterbury academic David Round argue that the Treaty partnership has created a separate and racially determined category of New Zealand citizenship, with Māori given a privileged status through the Treaty, whilst the non-Māori majority are merely the Crown's subjects (Round 1998; Brash 2004). Others maintain that even if this notion of 'privilege' were true, it has not rectified the structural violence and ongoing institutional racism that colonial dispossession inflicted on Māori. This tension within democratic liberal values points to a major challenge faced by governments in settler states when seeking to redress claims made by indigenous minorities (Gover 2016: 366): compared with other citizens, indigenous peoples may well have measurably different and discrete moral and legal rights, including rights to land and resources that have been improperly extinguished.

Why do indigenous peoples place so much reliance on the Crown, when many other citizens consider it an embarrassing anachronism or an awkward and impotent vestige of colonial force? Māori petitioners have a long history of travelling to London seeking audiences with the monarch to complain that the colonial government had breached the Treaty of Waitangi. *Kīngitanga* (the Māori King Movement), for example, took petitions to London in 1884 and 1914 led by the Māori king. Even if formal meetings with British royalty occurred, all Māori petitioners were firmly told to take up their Treaty issues with the government in Wellington rather than expect any practical help from the monarch (Mahuta, Interviews, 2013; O'Malley 2016; Belgrave 2017). Yet the affective element of their Treaty with the Crown continued and continues to inform a desire by many Māori leaders, as Carroll put it, to renew the spirit of that compact with the person of the sovereign, and especially so in her presence. The Constitutional Advisory Panel in 2013 found that Māori continue to strongly support the Treaty of Waitangi as fundamental to how the nation should be governed (Constitutional Advisory Panel 2013: 32). It follows that proposals for a republican constitution will likely be strongly resisted because Treaty rights may well be eroded if the government or the state replaced the Crown as Treaty partner. Of course, while not all Māori oppose republicanism (Mahuta, Interviews, 2013; Godfery 2018), they are currently a minority within Māoridom.

The Royal Proclamation 1763

Looking to the monarch in England and invoking the Crown is also important in Canada. For example, many First Nations leaders vigorously protested patriation of the Canadian constitution in 1982 when the British North America Act 1867, originally passed by the British imperial parliament, was transformed into the Constitution Acts 1867 to 1982, making it autochthonous to Canada. Their protests, which included travelling en masse to Ottawa in hired trains (called the 'Constitution Express'), were not targeted towards Canadian governments alone. From Alberta, New

Brunswick and Nova Scotia, association and union leaders travelled to London to support a case heard by the Court of Appeal in England. Their lawyers argued that indigenous nations of British North America remained entitled to direct access to the imperial Crown that had issued the Royal Proclamation in 1763. Without the assent of these indigenous nations, the UK Parliament ought not to pass the Canada Act 1982 to give effect to a request submitted by the Senate and House of Commons of Canada. The English court was unmoved. If the Crown was thought to be indivisible in 1763, it was certainly not so in 1982. The Queen in right of Canada, advised by her Canadian ministers, would decide when and if the constitution should be patriated to Canada (*R* v. *Secretary of State for Foreign and Commonwealth Affairs, Ex parte Indian Association of Alberta* [1982]).

Significantly, this court case in England was initiated by First Nations representatives from different provinces. The histories of Crown and indigenous relationships vary considerably within the provinces of what became Canada. The provinces within what was New France (Québec and the Maritime Provinces) were areas of fur-trading and then colonisation without formalised treaty transactions. From 1701, British traders and colonisers opted to enter into numerous alliances and treaties of friendship and trade prior to confederation in 1867. In Upper Canada (now Ontario) the Crown developed special responsibilities towards the 'Six Nations' who were military allies of the British in the war of rebellion in thirteen British colonies – better known as the American War of Independence. An agreement between Queen Anne and an indigenous delegation to England in 1710 resulted in a dedicated Chapel Royal celebrating their friendship and loyalty to the Crown. Having moved north with Empire Loyalists from Fort Hunter, New York, a Mohawk Chapel Royal was built anew in Brantford in 1785 (Tidridge, Interviews, 2017). Layered onto this was a different history of the indigenous nations who were parties to the eleven 'numbered treaties' signed in the post-confederation period from 1871 to 1921. In return for various promises and guarantees, those treaties enabled colonial settlement of much of Ontario, Manitoba, Saskatchewan, Alberta, the Northwest Territories and part of British Columbia (though most of British Columbia saw no treaties at all). Yet, as the 1982 litigation illustrates, the Royal Proclamation 1763, issued after the Treaty of Paris and which ceded New France to the British, has been invoked as a beacon of hope for indigenous peoples from all provinces of Canada when they seek to hold the Crown to account – though not without acknowledging the ambiguity of relying on a Crown document when asserting First Nations' sovereignty claims (Borrows 1997; Borrows and Coyle 2017). The last five paragraphs of the Royal Proclamation recognised indigenous rights to possess territories beyond existing colonial boundaries, and these lands, it said, were reserved for the Indians. Indeed the Proclamation is often labelled the 'Indian Magna Carta' (Miller 2013) in the same way that the Treaty of Waitangi is referred to as the 'Māori Magna Carta' (Williams 2017).

A Minority in Their Own Lands

What is it, then, that Māori and First Nations peoples believe is enabled by appealing to the Crown? What propositions and submissions are facilitated by invoking the Crown that references to states or governments could not achieve? The argument of this book is that the Crown is a shapeshifting and multifaceted historical actor, and so it is not a surprise that it is now being called upon to deliver just redress to descendants of the dispossessed.

Many indigenous interviewees stressed that, when democratic institutions claim full authority over indigenous peoples who have become a minority within their own lands, there must be a morally legitimate way to challenge the tyranny of the democratic majority, or resist proposals that an elected government wants to pursue. In Canada and New Zealand, courts in modern times have crafted principles requiring governments to uphold the Crown's honour by acting in good faith in a relationship with indigenous peoples that is akin to a fiduciary duty. On numerous occasions governments have had to rethink policy decisions and sometimes abandon proposals that might otherwise have been pushed through regardless of indigenous objections because the Crown has a duty to consult and accommodate indigenous concerns (*NZ Māori Council* v. *Attorney-General* [1989]; *Haida Nation* v. *British Columbia* [2004]). Further, the enduring Crown can be held accountable *today*, which sidesteps the difficulty of holding past governments accountable when all the actors of those governments are long dead. From the government's perspective, the Crown's durability also creates a conceptual space that has allowed governments to do or say things which may otherwise be unpalatable, such as admit wrongs, offer apologies and provide redress that in part at least may atone for the devastating impacts of colonisation (Hayward 1995; McLean 2008, 2015; see also Chapter 1). However, in Australia, things are rather different.

The Australian Counter-Example

Having led an inquiry into the Native Title Act 1993 (Australian Law Reform Commission 2015), law professor Lee Godden is well positioned to reflect on the Australian Crown's distinguishing aspects. As she noted:

> People use the Crown in a very instrumental way in Australia, so you talk about Crown land, you talk about the Crown in right of state ... But we don't generally ... pick up the notion of a Crown in a personified way as having obligations and responsibilities ... for example in relation to the honour of the Crown in Canada, or the way the [New Zealand] Crown is understood to have particular obligations under the Treaty of Waitangi. So it's a very narrow way in which the Crown is understood here in Australia, by comparison I think to other Commonwealth countries. And yes, I think it's bureaucratic in its orientation, as opposed to having moral dimensions.
>
> (Interviews, 2015)

By bureaucratic and instrumental Godden means that the Crown's primary social role is concerned with procedures as means for pursuing certain ends, rather than participating in broader reciprocal relations as the Crowns of other Commonwealth settler states do. Godden expressed, in legal terms, an appreciation that where a symbol's operation becomes too easily recognised and narrowly defined, it cannot undertake broader symbolic work.

By contrast, the Crowns of Canada and New Zealand respond to their obligations to indigenous peoples, including rights to land and resources, to accommodate, to varying degrees, indigenous interests and customary law (Gover 2016). In both cases, responsibilities towards indigenous peoples became infused with moral and political duties, and these Crowns have broad roles in the social worlds of those states (Behrendt 2000, 2002; Slattery 2005; McLean 2008, 2015; McHugh 2009, 2011; Gover 2016). The 'honour of the Crown' is shorthand for these processes, which characterise the Crown's expanded roles in Canada and New Zealand (Saunders 2014).

In Australia, by contrast, relations between Indigenous people and the Crown have been relegated to property litigation (disputes over ownership and management of land, water and resources) and anti-discrimination rights (Behrendt 2000, 2002; Australian Law Reform Commission 2015; Gover 2016). The Crown's role focuses on ensuring that the law has been correctly applied or complied with and does not encompass moral, relational and political obligations to Indigenous Australians (Gover 2016).

The legal instrumentality of the Australian Crown has implications beyond Indigenous Australians. In New Zealand and Canada, relationships between indigenous peoples and the Crown have helped make the Crown a significant moral actor, which effectively ensured it remains conceptually relevant. In Australia, without these relationships, the Crown lacks currency and, as we argue in Chapter 6, is not visible in everyday Australian social life.

The relative paucity of Indigenous Australian views represented so far illustrates that their advocacy is not framed in honour of the Crown terms, as indigenous claims are in New Zealand and Canada, where the Crown has been reinvigorated as useful to both indigenous peoples and governments. An important demographic fact is that Indigenous Australians comprise only 2.8 per cent of the population (Australian Bureau of Statistics 2015), with derisorily small representation in parliament. Though still a minority, a much larger proportion of the New Zealand population – some 15 per cent (Statistics New Zealand 2017) – identify as Māori. Like Indigenous Australians, Māori are grossly overrepresented in social deprivation statistics, including imprisonment rates and poor mental health, housing and education outcomes. Yet in 2018, in the New Zealand House of Representatives comprising 120 MPs there are 26 MPs of Māori descent – including the leader and/or deputy leader of all five political parties in Parliament.

Australia has held several national consultation processes about constitutional recognition for Indigenous Australians, including an Expert Panel on Recognising Aboriginal and Torres Strait Islander Peoples in the Constitution (2012); the Joint Select Committee on Constitutional Recognition of Aboriginal and Torres Strait Islander Peoples (2015); and the Referendum Council (2017) (Dodson 2012; Davis and Williams 2015). A major outcome was the Uluru Statement from the Heart (Referendum Council 2017) calling for the establishment of an indigenous 'Voice to Parliament'. Progressives joined Indigenous Australian commentators in condemning the recognition project as repugnant tokenism unless accompanied by substantive measures to address the serious structural violence suffered in Aboriginal communities. Indigenous Australian and law professor Megan Davis summed up the relevance of the debate for indigenous communities: 'If they [Australian voters] choose not to recognise us, it won't affect us. Whether we have recognition or not, we know we're here. We'll continue doing what we're doing without your recognition, just as we have been for the last 250 years' (Interviews, 2015). Conservatives, however, worried that the proposal would undermine social cohesion by establishing separate categories of citizenship for Indigenous Australians. Former Prime Minister Malcolm Turnbull promptly rejected the proposal because '[o]ur democracy is built on the foundation of all Australian citizens having equal civic rights' (Turnbull 2017). The Crown, though referenced in the Uluru Statement, played no role whatsoever in these constitutional reform debates.

The Australian Crown's Absence

Aboriginal epistemology begins with the land. It permeates Indigenous Australian experiences and interpretations of life (Myers 1986; McKenna 2004; Strang 2005) through traditional knowledge of time, space and relationships associated with particular places (Milton 2002). Quite simply, 'there is no aspect of traditional Aboriginal life that does not contain the land as a central medium' (Strang 2005: 46–48). The land is not an asset which can be owned or divided. This worldview was fundamentally incompatible with that of settlers and convicts who arrived in Australia under the Crown's protection.

When Governor Phillip arrived at Sydney Cove in 1788, he carried instructions from George III: 'You are to endeavour, by every means possible, to open an Intercourse with the Natives, and conciliate their affections, enjoining Our Subjects to live in amity and kindness with them' (George III 1787: 52). Phillip was instructed to punish transgressors. The reality fell short of these aspirations, and the Crown made no formal treaties with Indigenous Australians. Aboriginals were seen as wandering the land and inhabiting it not as occupying or possessing it in ways recognised by the British Imperial Crown agents. They saw lands that were vacant 'wastelands' over which no property rights existed, and so concluded that none needed to be extinguished prior to settlers moving in and occupying the continent: this is now known as the doctrine of *terra nullius*. Indigenous Australians experienced invasion and dispossession without even the figment of consensual deeds or treaties to facilitate and legitimate the invasion (Hirst 1983; Reynolds 1987; Wolfe 1999; Attwood 2005; Bashford and Macintyre 2013). When challenged, the mass expropriation of territory and property rights was legally justified by reference to the eighteenth-century commentaries on English law by Oxford professor William Blackstone:

> Plantations, or colonies in distant countries, are either such where the lands are claimed by right of occupancy only, by finding them desart and uncultivated, and peopling them from the mother country; or where, when already cultivated, they have been either gained by conquest, or ceded to us by treaties. And both these rights are founded upon the law of nature, or at least upon that of nations. But there is a difference between these two species of colonies, with respect to the laws by which they are bound. For it is held, that if an uninhabited country be discovered and planted by English subjects, all the English laws are immediately there in force. For as the law is the birthright of every subject, so wherever they go they carry their laws with them.
>
> (1765: 104–5)

The Australian High Court finally rejected this Blackstonian doctrine in 1992 and recognised the continuing existence of Indigenous Australian native title customary rights to Crown lands (*Mabo* v. *Queensland (No 2)* [1992]). Like 'Crown land', *Mabo* refers to both the thing itself and a certain form of law shaped by colonial history. The ruling stated that the Crown had *acquired* sovereignty, giving it radical title to lands. Crucially, it recognised that Aboriginal and Torres Strait Islanders' pre-existing rights and interests in land survived the Crown's assertion of sovereignty, effectively acknowledging traditional law and custom as an additional source of Australian law which does not originate from the Crown (Brennan, Gunn, and Williams 2004: 325). No Australian, New Zealand or Canadian court has accepted that indigenous sovereignty survived imperial acquisition. Indeed, 'whenever aboriginal sovereignty has been raised in the courts the judicial response has been sharp and immediately dismissive' (McHugh 2000: 205, citing *Berkett* v. *Tauranga District Court* [1992] and *Walker* v. *New South Wales* [1994]).

Indigenous scholars reverse the question: if indigenous sovereignty was never explicitly surrendered, then how can the Crown claim radical title (Christie 2015)? As John Borrows (2015) stated: 'Some kind of legal vacuum must be imagined in order to create the Crown's radical title' (703). But the pre-colonisation existence of First Nations remains invisible and courts accept the Crown's claims. Recognising native title operating within common law paradigms is palatable for courts and governments, but recognising prior and ongoing indigenous sovereignty is another matter altogether.

Māori as Crown Partner: The Crown's Duties

Since the Treaty Principles were articulated in 1987, New Zealand courts and governments have elaborated the concept of a Treaty *partnership* between Māori and the Crown. In 2017 the courts took a further step. Following Canadian precedents, the Supreme Court made a decisive finding that there can be an enforceable fiduciary duty owed by the Crown to the collective descendants of the original customary title holders to land when the facts disclose a direct breach of an obligation undertaken by the Crown. The judges noted that where the Crown wears many hats and represents many interests it may not owe specific fiduciary duties to individuals or groups, but only that governmental obligations are owed to all. So, the court's decision cannot be taken to suggest that there is a general fiduciary duty at large owed by the Crown to Māori. However, if a direct breach can be proved then this is no longer a matter of unenforceable moral and political duties but a breach of an enforceable legal duty (*Wakatū* v. *Attorney-General* [2017]).

Fiduciary duties represent the highest possible standards of care and the duty to act in the best interests of the other party. For the relationship between the Crown and indigenous peoples to be 'trust-like' means that it should not be adversarial (although it has been so, and in practice still may be). It invests the relationship with virtuous ideals, such that the Crown and its institutions are legally obliged to act with integrity, sincerity, trustworthiness and the burden of doing right in the best interests of indigenous peoples.

The Crown's honour and its fiduciary responsibility are not new ideas, as a 'Crown with duties of sincerity, fair dealing and honour can be found in the colonial documents' including treaties themselves (McLean 2015: 211). While legal scholars have scrutinised the emergence, operation and implications of these descriptors, what is more interesting is the conceptual framework underpinning these phrases. While partnership implies equality if not equivalence, the notion of fiduciary duty directs obligations of care from one party to another, suggesting that one party holds greater power than the other.

The relationship between Māori and the Crown has been honed by decades of Treaty jurisprudence in which the partnership concept attaches legal force to Treaty obligations and paralegal duties. Documents such as Waitangi Tribunal reports and judicial rulings articulate the Crown's obligations as ongoing, evolving and dynamic; a recurring theme is the notion that the Treaty possesses a spirit and even organic vitality. Echoing Queen Elizabeth's words, a 1983 Waitangi Tribunal report stated that the Treaty's 'wairua or spirit is something more than a literal construction of the actual words used can provide. The spirit of the Treaty transcends the sum total of its component written words and puts literal or narrow interpretations out of place' (1983: 49). Cooke, president of the Court of Appeal, emphasised that 'what matters is the spirit' because the Treaty is best understood as 'an embryo, rather than a fully developed and integrated set of ideas' (*NZ Māori Council* v. *Attorney-General* [1987]: 667). Deliberately rudimentary and open-ended, these abstract values are articulated as broad principles for how the Crown shall conduct itself morally towards Māori. This broad role gives parties scope to manoeuvre to make or fulfil claims, and indigenous peoples may call on the Crown to fulfil its obligations on diverse aspects of citizenship, such as healthcare, fishery quota, veteran rights, justice, education, conservation and others. The constant quest to have the Crown fulfil its partnership obligations provides never-ending opportunities for it to renew its role and significance. Fiduciary duties and honour place a heavy burden on the Crown to translate into action what Queen Elizabeth termed its 'sacred duty'.

Canada's Constitutional Imperative: Honour and Fiduciary Duty

In Canada, the decision of *Guerin* v. *The Queen* (1984) transformed the Crown's moral and political obligations to First Nations Canadians into legal commitments described as 'trust-like'. This was the leading case that the New Zealand Supreme Court cited and approved in the Wakatū case. Since 1984 in Canada, the Supreme Court has ruled (*R* v. *Sparrow* [1990]) that the enactment of section 35, Constitution Act 1982, imposes obligations on Canada's provincial and federal governments that have enhanced the significance of the Crown's fiduciary relationship. Indigenous rights must be given an appropriate priority and any restriction on those rights must be justified. The Crown's obligation to honour has become a constitutional principle (Gover 2016: 355–56). The courts tolerate no undermining of the Canadian Crown's sovereignty over Canadian land but acknowledge that this was not consensual, and continuing assertions of the Crown's rights carry a debt of honour to First Nations Canadians: the Crown must do whatever is reasonable to reconcile differences with indigenous peoples. These obligations are framed as the Crown's duties to consult and accommodate.

As lawyer Bruce McIvor described, these duties are enshrined in the Constitution. 'It's a constitutional imperative,' he said. 'This duty to consult, and honour of the Crown, is upstream of any statutory obligations . . . You don't get anything higher than that . . . it's overarching' (Interviews, 2016). These constitutional obligations continue developing as case law, with expanded understandings less about procedural obligations than attempts to shape those who represent the Crown. Those acting for the Crown must demonstrate that 'everything you did encouraged and supported reconciliation' with indigenous peoples, adds McIvor, as one way of 'holding the Crown to a higher standard'. Jurist Lance Finch, formerly Chief Justice of British Columbia, stated:

> I'm honestly not sure where the honour of the Crown idea came from. The best I can make out, it's sort of the sequel to the Crown's making treaties with people, whether they're indigenous people or foreign countries, and they're bound to honour their agreements. They've given their word and they're expected to live up to it. And somehow that notion . . . has been transposed into areas where there is no agreement at all . . . [we've] settled on the honour of the Crown as that fundamental bedrock these other duties stem from. And I have to say, I think the honour of the Crown is a pretty elastic, evolving concept.
>
> (Interview, 2016)

Finch suggests that the honour of the Crown evolved from an attempt to fill a conceptual void, and the concept has been seized on by the Supreme Court of Canada as fundamental, becoming a valuable asset to judicial deliberations since 1982. So the trains to Ottawa, and the failed attempt in an English court to prevent patriation of the constitution in 1982, were not ultimately without reward. The belated inclusion of section 35 in the constitution as eventually enacted would not have happened without the political and legal pressure that First Nations leaders exerted on Canadian governments.

Conclusion

Indigenous peoples' recognition of and regard for the Crown is central to the way it has been constituted in postcolonial settler societies. In New Zealand and Canada Māori and First Nations tribes have harnessed the Crown's conceptual vagueness, charging it with moral obligations in order to remedy treaty breaches and pursue their rights. Their insistence on using the discourse of the Crown has played a crucial role in establishing the Crown as a social fact in New Zealand and Canada. This discourse is almost entirely absent in Australia.

The Crown's ambiguity allows for multiple, even contradictory, interpretations, enabling it to play the roles of oppressor and protector simultaneously. In New Zealand and Canada, the Crown's multiple identities enable it to undertake relational and moral duties through accepting accountability, offering partnership or honour, and being capable of personification, framed in terms of kinship, ancestors, reciprocity and hierarchy. It would be unable to bear these functions if it were more instrumentally defined. Consequently, the Crown remains useful to governments because it can perform tasks and make statements that a government might prefer to avoid. The figure of an elevated moral entity, epitomised by the Queen, has aided indigenous peoples by providing a partial mechanism for redress.

The Crown was the historical mechanism of indigenous peoples' colonisation, yet paradoxically only the Crown can undo the consequential damage. As a key symbol of colonisation, the Crown is frequently a metaphor for the discrepancy between how things *are* and how they could or *ought* to be. When indigenous peoples identify and specify the Crown, it makes the wrongs of colonisation visible today by implying a causal connection between past and current suffering, and invokes a moral demand for a difference between the present and the future.

In Australia, by contrast, the relationship between Indigenous Australians and the Crown is far less significant. Despite Governor Phillip's instructions, no special intimacy emerged between local indigenous peoples and the sovereign, and no treaties or promissory documents were developed. Indeed until 1992 Australia was regarded as *terra nullius* open to British settlement without treating in any way with those who had occupied the continent for tens of thousands of years prior to 1788. It is difficult to imagine an occasion when Indigenous Australians might have eagerly vouchsafed themselves as sovereign subjects or Queen Elizabeth claiming them as my 'Aboriginal people'. Devoid of treaties and the relationship burdens they impose, a narrower, more instrumental and less personalised understanding of the Crown has prevailed. The Australian Crown lacks a duty of honour, which is one of its distinguishing characteristics as a moral actor in New Zealand and Canada. In these countries the Crown's moral obligation to indigenous peoples is said to go beyond legal prescription and assumes an almost sacred character, which explains why indigenous appeals for rights and redress are so often directed to the Crown, rather than the government or the state.

How indigenous peoples deploy the Crown concept to stake out high moral ground, and how the state uses the cloak of the Crown to fulfil its obligations, is only one part of the story. Equally important is how state actors themselves use the Crown. As we will argue in the next chapter, if the Crown is a valuable resource for indigenous peoples, it can also be harnessed for strategic purposes by the state.

References

Attwood, Bain. 2005. *Telling the Truth about Aboriginal History*. Sydney: Allen and Unwin.

Australian Bureau of Statistics. 2015. Accessed 8 April 2018 at www.abs.gov.au/ausstats/abs@.nsf/mf/3238.0.

Australian Law Reform Commission. 2015. *Connection to Country: Review of the Native Title Act 1993 (Cth) (ALRC Report 126)*. 4 June 2015. Sydney: Australian Government, Australian Law Reform Commission. Accessed 10 January 2016 at www.alrc.gov.au/publications/alrc126

Bashford, Alison and Stuart Macintyre. 2013. *The Cambridge History of Australia*. Cambridge and Port Melbourne, Victoria: Cambridge University Press.

Blackstone, William. 1765. *Commentaries on the Laws of England*. Oxford: Clarendon Press.

Behrendt, Larissa. 2000. Bargaining on More Than Good Will: Recognising a Fiduciary Obligation in Native Title. *Issues Paper: Land, Rights, Laws: Issues of Native Title* 2(4). Canberra: Native Title Research Unit, Australian Institute of Aboriginal and Torres Strait Islander Studies.

2002. 'Responsibility in Governance: Implied Rights, Fiduciary Obligation and Indigenous Peoples.' *Australian Journal of Public Administration* 61(2): 106–18.

Belgrave, Michael. 2017. *Dancing with the King: The Rise and Fall of the King Country, 1864–1885*. Auckland: Auckland University Press.

Borrows, John. 1997. 'Wampum at Niagara: The Royal Procalamation, Canadian Legal History, and Self-Government.' In *Aboriginal and Treaty Rights in Canada: Essays on Law, Equality, and Respect for Difference*, edited by Michael Asch, 155–72. Vancouver: University of British Columbia Press, 1997.

2015. 'The Durability of *terra nullius*: Tsilhqot'in Nation v British Columbia.' *University of British Columbia Law Review* 48(3): 701–42.

Borrows, John and Michael Coyle. 2017. *The Right Relationship: Reimagining the Implementation of Historical Treaties*. Toronto: University of Toronto Press.

Brash, Don. 2004. Nationhood, Orewa Rotary Club. Website. Accessed on 5 April 2018 at www.scoop.co.nz/stories/PA0401/S00220.htm.

Brennan, Sean, Brenda Gunn and George Williams. 2004. '"Sovereignty" and Its Relevance to Treaty-Making between Indigenous Peoples and Australian Governments.' *Sydney Law Review* 26(3): 307–52.

Christie, Gordon. 2015. 'Who Makes Decisions Over Aboriginal Title Lands?' *University of British Columbia Law Review* 48(3): 743–92.

Comaroff, John and Jean Comaroff. 2009. *Ethnicity, Inc.* Chicago: University of Chicago Press.

Constitutional Advisory Panel. 2013. *New Zealand's Constitution: A Report on a Conversation*. Wellington: Ministry of Justice.

Davis, Megan and George Williams. 2015. *Everything You Need to Know about the Referendum to Recognise Indigenous Australians*. Sydney: NewSouth Publishing.

Dodson, Mick. 2012. Constitutional Recognition of Indigenous Australians. open-research-repository.anu.edu.au/bitstream/1885/9453/1/Dodson_ConstitutionalRecognition2012.pdf.

Ford, Lisa and Tim Rowse (eds.). 2012. *Between Indigenous and Settler Governance*. Abingdon, Oxon and New York: Routledge.

Frazer, James George. 1922. *The Golden Bough*. New York: Macmillan.

George III. 1787. 'Instructions to Governor Phillip. 23 April 1787.' *Historical Records of New South Wales* 1(2).

Godfery, Morgan. 2018. *The Crown: Is It Still 'White' and 'English-Speaking'? The Round Table: The Commonwealth Journal of International Affairs*. 107(4): 493–506.

Gover, Kirsty. 2012. 'Indigenous Jurisdiction as a Provocation of Settler State Political Theory: The Significance of Human Boundaries.' In *Between Indigenous and Settler Governance*, edited by L. Ford and T. Rowse, 187–99. Abingdon: Routledge.

2016. 'The Honour of the Crowns: State-Indigenous Fiduciary Relationships and Australian Exceptionalism.' *Sydney Law Review* 38: 339–68.

Gover, Kirsty and Frances Hancock. 2002. *He Tirohanga ō Kawa ki te Tiriti o Waitangi: A Guide to the Principles of the Treaty of Waitangi*. Wellington: Te Puni Kokiri.

Hayward, Janine. 1995. In Search of a Treaty Partner. Unpublished PhD Thesis. University of Auckland.

Her Majesty's Royal Chapel of the Mohawks. 2018. *Her Majesty's Royal Chapel of the Mohawks: Where Royalty and Nations Unify*. About the chapel. Website. mohawkchapel.ca/about/.

Hill, Richard. 2004. *State Authority, Indigenous Autonomy: Crown-Māori Relations in New Zealand/Aotearoa 1900–1950*. Wellington: Victoria University Press.

Hirst, John. 1983. *Convict Society and Its Enemies: A History of Early New South Wales*. Sydney: George Allen & Unwin.

Lea, Tess. 2012. 'Contemporary Anthropologies of Indigenous Australia.' *Annual Review of Anthropology* 41: 187–202.

McAllister, Patrick. 2012. *National Days and the Politics of Indigenous and Local Identities in Australia and New Zealand*. Durham, NC: Carolina Academic Press.

McCormack, Fiona. 2011. 'Levels of Indigeneity: The Maori and Neoliberalism.' *Journal of the Royal Anthropological Institute* 17(2): 281–300.

McHugh, Paul. 2000. 'Sovereignty This Century: Māori and the Common Law Constitution.' *Victoria University of Wellington Law Review* 31(1): 1–28.

2009. 'Sovereignty in Australasia: Comparatively Different Histories.' *Legal History* 13(1): 57–92.

2011. *Aboriginal Title: The Modern Jurisprudence of Tribal Land Rights*. Oxford: Oxford University Press.

McHugh, Paul and Lisa Ford. 2012. 'Settler Sovereignty and the Shapeshifting Crown.' In *Between Indigenous and Settler Governance*, edited by L. Ford and T. Rowse, 23–34. New York and Abingdon, Oxon: Routledge.

McKenna, Mark. 2004. *This Country: A Reconciled Republic?* Sydney: University of New South Wales Press.

McLean, Janet. 2008. '"Crown Him with Many Crowns": The Crown and the Treaty of Waitangi.' *New Zealand Journal of Public and International Law* 6(1): 34–58.

2015. 'Crown, Empire and Redressing the Historical Wrongs of Colonisation in New Zealand.' *New Zealand Law Review* 26(2): 187–212.

Miller, J. R. 2013. The Royal Proclamation – 'the Indians' Magna Carta'? *Active History*. History and Policy. 30 September. activehistory.ca/2013/09/the-royal-proclamation-the-indians-magna-carta/.

Milton, Kay. 2002. *Environmentalism and Cultural Theory: Exploring the Role of Anthropology in Environmental Discourse*. Abingdon, Oxon: Routledge.

Myers, Fred. 1986. *Pintupi Country, Pintupi Self: Sentiment, Place, and Politics among Western Desert Aborigines*. Berkeley and Los Angeles: University of California Press.

O'Malley, Vincent. 2016. *The Great War for New Zealand: Waikato 1800–2000*. Wellington: Bridget Williams Books.

O'Malley, Vincent, Bruce Stirling and Wally Penetito. 2010. *The Treaty of Waitangi Companion: Māori and Pākehā from Tasman to Today*. Auckland: Auckland University Press.

Rata, Elizabeth. 2005. 'Rethinking Biculturalism.' *Anthropological Theory* 5(3): 267–84.

Referendum Council. 2017. Uluru Statement from the Heart. Website. www.referendumcouncil.org.au/sites/default/files/2017-05/Uluru_Statement_From_The_Heart_0.PDF.

Reynolds, Henry. 1987. *The Law of the Land*. Melbourne: Penguin.

Round, David. 1998. *Truth or Treaty? Commonsense Questions about the Treaty of Waitangi*. Christchurch: University of Canterbury Press.

Royal Proclamation. 1763 (British North America). Accessed 7 April 2018 at atindigenousfoundations.arts.ubc.ca/royal_proclamation_1763/ [Website includes a facsimile of the original Proclamation].

Saunders, Cheryl. 2014. 'The Concept of the Crown.' *Melbourne University Law Review*. 38(3): 873–96.

Secher, Ulla. 2014. *Aboriginal Customary Law: A Source of Common Law Title to Land*. Oxford: Hart Publishing.

Shore, Cris and Margaret Kawharu. 2014. 'The Crown in New Zealand: Anthropological Perspectives on an Imagined Sovereign.' *Sites*. 11(1): 17–38.

Slattery, Brian. 2005. 'Aboriginal Rights and the Honour of the Crown.' *Supreme Court Law Review* 29: 433–45.

Statistics New Zealand. 2017. Māori Population Estimates: Mean Year Ended 31 December 2016. archive.stats.govt.nz/browse_for_stats/population/estimates_and_projections/MaoriPopulationEstimates_HOTPMYe31Dec16.aspx.

Strang, Veronica. 2005. 'Knowing Me, Knowing You: Aboriginal and European Concepts of Nature as Self and Other.' *Worldviews: Global Religions, Culture, and Ecology* 9(1): 25–56.

Te Ao Hou. 1963. 'Queen Elizabeth Visits Waitangi.' *Te Ao Hou: the Māori Magazine, Special Royal Visit Issue*. March (42): 23–29. [Digital archive] Accessed 5 May 2017 at teaohou.natlib.govt.nz/journals/teaohou/thumbnails/Mao42TeA.html.

Turnbull, Malcolm. 2017. Response to Referendum Council's report on Constitutional Recognition. *Malcolm Turnbull Prime Minister of Australia*. Media releases. October 26. www.malcolmturnbull.com.au/media/response-to-referendum-councils-report-on-constitutional-recognition.

Waitangi Tribunal. 1983. *Report of the Waitangi Tribunal on the Motunui–Waitara Claim (Wai 6)*. Wellington, Waitangi Tribunal.

Ward, Alan. 2015. *An Unsettled History: Treaty Claims in New Zealand Today*. Wellington: Bridget Williams Books.

Wheen, Nicola and Janine Hayward (eds.). 2012. *Treaty of Waitangi Settlements*. Wellington: Bridget Williams Books.

Williams, David V. 2017. 'Myths and History: The Treaty of Waitangi as "the Magna Charta of New Zealand".' In *Magna Carta and New Zealand*, edited by Stephen Winter and Chris Jones. Cham: Palgrave Macmillan.

Wolfe, Patrick. 1999. *Settler Colonialism and the Transformation of Anthropology: The Politics and Poetics of an Ethnographic Event*. London: Cassell.

PART II

The Crown as an Embodied Entity

5

The Rituals of Crown and State in New Zealand

JAI PATEL

Governors-general in New Zealand represent the sovereign as the head of state when the sovereign is not in the country and are appointed by the sovereign as advised by the prime minister. In 2011, Lieutenant General Sir Jeremiah (Jerry) Mateparae was sworn in as New Zealand's twentieth governor-general. Mateparae was formerly the chief of defence and the second Māori person to hold the office of governor-general. The formalities began as his black Jaguar, uniquely adorned with a crown emblem in place of a registration plate, drew into the forecourt of Parliament under police escort in front of an eagerly waiting crowd. Accompanied by his delegation, Mateparae stepped out and began to cross the space towards the assembled audience. Wearing an exquisite *korowai* (a Māori feather cloak reserved for people of high status) that almost dragged at his ankles, he was approached by a stern-faced Māori warrior, who twirled his *taiaha* (spear) and bellowed as he advanced in a martial fashion. The warrior paused and crouched, pointing his *taiaha* at the new arrivals, as he laid down the *taki* (usually a feather, leaf or twig), a symbol of the *wero* (challenge) he is making to the visitor. Mateparae walked slowly and bent down to pick up the *taki*, under the watchful eye of the warrior (Figure 5.1). Raising it for all to see, signalling his peaceful intentions, he was motioned forward as the *karanga* (welcoming call) began, and harmonious ranks of women and men performed the *haka pōwhiri* (welcoming dance and song).

In New Zealand, the swearing-in ceremony of the governor-general incorporates elements of the Māori welcoming procedure known as a *pōwhiri*, a ritual by which a host *tāngata whenua* (people of the land – in this case, local *iwi* [tribe]) welcome the *manuhiri* (visitors) to their *marae* (meeting house). The *wero* was traditionally a means by which *iwi* came to know each other's intentions in meeting; through the *karanga*, a spiritual rope is woven to allow the *manuhiri* safe passage onto the *marae*; the *haka pōwhiri* is then sung to metaphorically pull the

Figure 5.1 Lieutenant General Sir Jerry Mateparae picks up the *rakau tapu* (sacred symbol of peace) as a warrior performs the wawae (cleansing movements) during his swearing-in ceremony as New Zealand's 20th governor-general in Wellington; 31 August 2011
(Department of Prime Minister and Cabinet)

waka (canoe) of the *manuhiri* onto the *marae*, giving *mana* (spiritual power, authority) to the *tāngata whenua* and their *tūpuna* (ancestors) (Barlow 1994).

Mateparae was then met by the prime minister and the herald of arms – a state official who advises on heraldic matters and accompanies the sovereign or governors-general during state events. He walked along the forecourt, draped with the colour and livery of national and regal flags, and peopled by the Royal Guards and military musicians. As the *haka pōwhiri* drew to a close, Mateparae was escorted to a large stage to stand with the clerk of the Executive Council (who coordinates with the Office of the Governor-General) and the chief justice (the head of the judiciary) in front of esteemed guests, politicians, members of the armed forces and a small gathering of the public. The clerk then read the Royal Commission, a document signed by the Queen which formally appointed Mateparae, before the chief justice administered the Oath of Allegiance. With his right hand on the Bible, Mateparae declared, in both English and te reo Māori (the Māori language), his loyalty to Queen Elizabeth the Second, Queen of New Zealand, and to her successors.

Having made his commitments, Mateparae stood, and a moment of silence ensued. Slowly and methodically, the clerk and the herald removed Mateparae's *korowai* and replaced it with a large gold necklace with a glistening cross-shaped medallion, known as the chains of office. Though Mateparae wore plenty of military medals and ribbons that he had earned during his distinguished military career, he now also wore a symbol of the highest honour and rank in his society – the chains of office represent the office of the governor-general, the sovereign's representative in the realm. As the physical weight of the chains hung around his neck, so too did the authority and responsibility that he now possessed. Addressed as 'Your Excellency', the new governor-general then signed the proclamation of his ascendance and inspected the Royal Guard. After Prime Minister John Key and Mateparae each spoke to the audience and stood with onlookers to sing the national anthem 'God Defend New Zealand', the delegation moved into Parliament Buildings for a reception event behind closed doors.

During his speech, Key told the audience that the governor-general 'is a constitutional linchpin that ensures the smooth functioning of our system of government. [Governors-general] sign legislation, appoint ministers, attend executive councils ... These functions on behalf of the Queen and on the advice of ministers are essential, but often unseen.' But what exactly does it mean to be a 'constitutional linchpin'? How does one represent the Queen if one acts upon the advice of responsible ministers? What functions are deemed 'essential' to the government's 'smooth functioning'? Was this event one of those essential functions, or just a courteous recognition of an esteemed figurehead?

What Key did not mention is that one of the governor-general's essential roles is the ritual construction of political and sovereign authority. Duties such as giving royal assent to legislation, attending Executive Council meetings, and appointing ministers, public servants and judges are undoubtedly important. However, it is ritual performances that establish the governor-general's authority to undertake these duties in the first place; ritual is at the heart of what it means to be a 'constitutional linchpin'. It was not enough for politicians, state officials or even the Queen herself to simply appoint a new governor-general in writing or by proclamation. Instead, Mateparae – who began as a regular, though accomplished, citizen – had to pass through a rite of passage (van Gennep 1960; Turner 1969) from which he emerged as 'His Excellency'.

It was only through this process of ritual movement and formal liturgies that Mateparae could truly be transformed into an honourable representative of the Queen and an embodiment of sovereignty.

This chapter examines ceremonies of constitutional monarchy through the lens of ritual. Anthropologists have long drawn connections between kingship systems and ritual, and this chapter brings contemporary constitutional monarchies into this discussion. Following a brief review of this literature, I describe the role of governors-general and the distinction between what they do as 'reigning' and what the government of the day does as 'ruling'. I then illustrate what reigning means in practice and show how the Crown is ritually constructed through an interpretation of the state opening of Parliament, which takes place after a new government is elected.

Whereas previous chapters have shown how the Crown can mean different things according to context (including the state, government or executive power), I argue here that the Crown takes on quite unique meanings during rituals that involve the Queen's representative. I show how the Crown often stands for the sovereign and her representative, in distinction to branches of government or the executive. According to the *Cabinet Manual* (the guiding document for political practice), 'the office of Governor-General is apolitical. By convention, the Governor-General avoids becoming involved in the party politics of government, despite having an integral role in the formal processes of government' (Cabinet Office 2017 paragraph 1.14). It is in these state rituals which involve the governor-general that the apolitical nature of the Crown is constructed. While the Crown is understood to be the ultimate and perpetual bearer of sovereignty in New Zealand, it is ritually separated from the domain of everyday politics and governance. It is also during these rituals, however, that the governing apparatus and its actors draw on the specific form of authority that the Crown possesses.

Lastly, I also illustrate how Westminster state rituals have been transformed in New Zealand. As the vignette at the beginning of this chapter shows, they incorporate ritual elements from *te ao Māori* (the Māori world), to the point where there are rituals within rituals. They are syncretic ritual practices. State rituals in New Zealand, then, are invented traditions (Hobsbawm and Ranger 1983), not only evoking notions of biculturalism (a political ideology that has had increasing significant policy ramifications since the 1970s – discussed later) but also constructing the Crown as standing in a particular relationship with Māori and possessing a certain form of sovereign authority enshrined in the Treaty of Waitangi (the Treaty). I argue that the bicultural and syncretic nature of state rituals demonstrates the cultural specificity of sovereignty, and the degree to which the Crown has become domesticated or localised as part of New Zealand society and culture.

Sovereign Authority and the Ritual Process

In our interview with Sir Anand Satyanand, New Zealand's nineteenth governor-general, he recalled his experiences of preparing for his own swearing-in ceremony, when his staff were going over the proceedings of the day. After being told he would inspect a military guard before receiving the chains of office, he told his staff, 'I just have an anxiety . . . at the point of reaching the tri-service guard, I am an unfrocked member of the public, I do not have any legal right to inspect a guard of military people . . . why can't I inspect the guard after I have been sworn in?' He laughed as he recollected the frantic logistical negotiations that followed. While he had raised a minor legal issue, Satyanand was drawing attention to the affective nature of the ritual: he quipped, 'You don't do it [inspect the guard] until you're baptised!' For Satyanand, the swearing-in was not just a formality, it was a meaningful act that bestowed upon him powers and authority he did not previously possess.

I take ritual to be standardised, repetitive and typically solemn actions expressed through symbolic acts, often referring to deep time or tradition. Where Turner famously defined rituals as 'prescribed formal behaviour . . . having reference to beliefs in mystical beings or powers' (Turner 1967: 19), I follow Moore and Myerhoff (1977) in their assertion that rituals can be secular in nature. For instance, anthropologists have long drawn connections between the constitution of political structures and ritual performance (see Abélès 1988; Kertzer 1988; Comaroff and Comaroff 1993; Little 1995; McLeod 1999, Stepputat 2004; Cook and Hardin 2013).

The swearing-in has many hallmarks of a ritual: it follows a strict and choreographed plan, giving legitimacy to the appointment; the governor-general-to-be is guided through the process by ritual experts, like the herald of arms; drawing on ideas of tradition, it is repeated every five years when a new governor-general is appointed; it deploys material symbols, like the chains of office and the *korowai*; it is communicative, making a statement about what sovereignty is and who does and does not possess it. Lastly, because it is a particular type of ritual, a rite of passage, the swearing-in is transformative. It takes a person from their previous status and bestows upon them the highest constitutional standing in the land. Anthropologists Victor Turner (1969) and Arnold van Gennep ([1909] 1960) wrote extensively about rites of passage, rituals that typically entail three distinct phases. The first phase is separation, in which individuals or initiands are removed from their daily life and normal status; the next phase is one of liminality, the unsettled ambiguous state when one is in between identities; and finally comes the phase of incorporation, in which one re-enters society with a new identity and status.

Anthropologist Meyer Fortes (1967) claimed that an office holder is not fully empowered to act until they have been through an installation ritual. He argued that a recurring theme is that the office is an immortal property and exists independently of the person who temporarily occupies it; he suggests that '[h]eirlooms, relics and regalia are vehicles of the continuity of office ... Possession of them thus frequently becomes the indispensable condition for consummating the attainment of office' (Fortes 1967: 16). This point is illustrated by the crown in the coronation of the Queen, or the chains of office of the governor-general. They symbolise the perpetuity of the state while making it tangible. The St Edward's Crown, for instance, was carried in front of the Queen-to-be, taking ritual precedence. The bestowing of the governor-general with the chains of office is the most significant expressive moment of their swearing-in and marks their departure from liminality; by wearing the chains of office, the citizen Jerry Mateparae becomes the governor-general of New Zealand and is truly transformed into the embodiment of sovereignty.

Rituals have long been central to how monarchs construct their authority, and this has been of enduring interest to anthropologists (Frazer 1922; Hocart [1936] 1970; Feely-Harnik 1985; de Heusch 1997; Scubla 2002; Graeber and Sahlins 2017). Kingship is founded on separating the monarch from society through rituals. Quigley explains that 'a monarch may only be addressed in an extraordinarily formalized way, must live in a kind of dwelling that no-one else would live in, and must, on occasion, wear clothes that clearly serve some purpose other than covering or protection' (2005: 4). In New Zealand, governors-general are distinguished from the public on a regular basis. During the swearing-in ceremony, the *korowai* singles out the governor-general as a person of higher status. There is even a tradition, evident at times to this day, where people will avoid turning their back on the governor-general, instead preferring to walk away from 'their Excellency' forward-facing.

Governors-general live in the prestigious Government House, with five-star service that is allegedly unrivalled in any hotel or restaurant in the country. One moment that amused me during my field work was when I was on a tour of Government House, and Mateparae arrived home early from a state visit – a staff member approached our group quite frantically warning 'His Excellency is here!' I was quickly hurried out the back door.

If one aspect of monarchical ritual separates the sovereign from the citizenry, another dimension is the somewhat paradoxical connection that it creates between a monarch and their subjects (Quigley 2005). During his speech at the swearing in of Mateparae, Prime Minister John Key told the audience that governors-general 'inspire young New Zealanders. They acknowledge the highest achievements of our people. They share in sorrow in difficult times.' During his own speech, Mateparae said that he relished the opportunity to meet, celebrate and support the people of New Zealand. Satyanand, his predecessor, explained to us that one of the governor-general's tasks 'is to be connected with the community, to encourage people in their efforts, to see people in the country putting their best foot forward'. They enact this connection primarily through patronage and touring; each governor-general is the patron of dozens of organisations, hosts dinners and opens schools and new facilities; in all, a governor-general will attend more events than there are days in the year.

The most important element of monarchical ritual, and the focus of this chapter, is the role it plays in constructing sovereign authority, especially in the context of constitutional monarchy, where the sovereign is no longer entitled to direct governance of the state. The understanding that constitutional monarchy means that sovereigns 'reign rather than rule' dates back to the Restoration. Anthropologist Lucien Scubla distinguishes between the two by arguing that 'to reign does not mean to govern or to give orders, but to guarantee the order of the world and of the society by observing ritual prescriptions' (Scubla 2005: 40). According to Scubla, reigning is performed primarily through ritual that provides stability and perpetuity to the banal world of ruling. In his review of the literature on kingship, Declan Quigley goes on to argue that 'it is a mistake to perceive this [reigning] as "mere pomp and ceremony" in the sense of a superstructural gloss on materialist realities, or icing on the cake. It *is* the cake' (Quigley 2005: 5–6). Clifford Geertz made a similar argument in discussing Bagehot's characterisation ([1867] 2001: 7) of the efficient (or ruling) and dignified (or ceremonial) aspects of government: to Geertz, it is a mistake to view the dignified as serving the efficient, as 'artifices, more or less cunning, more or less illusional, designed to facilitate the prosier aims of rule' (1980: 122). Rather, from Geertz's perspective, monarchical ritual, like a coronation, constructs a particular form of power itself and constitutes political relationships. State ceremonies, like the swearing-in of the governor-general or the Opening of Parliament (as explored later), are the most visible illustrations of this dimension of monarchical ritual in New Zealand. Most notably, they construct the relationship between those that reign and those that rule.

'The Queen Reigns but the Government Rules'

Political authority in New Zealand is not merely derived from the support of the electorate; it needs a symbolic head to represent the perpetuity of the state itself. Our informants often expressed this, citing the constitutional maxim that 'the Queen reigns but the Government rules, so long as it has the support of the House of Representatives'. This statement highlights the ambiguity at the heart of constitutional monarchies of the Westminster system that has arisen out of a history of Parliament incrementally encroaching on the sovereign's powers. Sir Kenneth Keith, former Supreme Court Judge, explains this maxim in the *Cabinet Manual*:

> This basic equation and the democratic character of the main conventions appear clearly in relation to the powers of the Queen and Governor-General under the law. Thus they may appoint Ministers and other holders of important offices ... they may dismiss them ... they may summon and dissolve Parliaments, they may assent – or not – to Bills passed through the House ... The Queen and the Governor-General are free to take those steps as a matter of law. But, as a matter of convention, they do so only on the advice of the Prime Minister or Ministers who have the support of the House of Representatives – that is, on the advice of those who are elected by the New Zealand voters.
>
> (Cabinet Office 2017: 3)

The maxim ensures that while the Queen and the Governor-General are the ultimate holders of sovereign authority, their actions are ultimately accountable to the democratic process. It would be constitutionally inappropriate, if not taboo, for the sovereign or governor-general to act in an overtly political way, or even to speak out on political issues, without being advised to do so. For instance, Mateparae was publicly criticised in 2015 for his suggestion that members of the *iwi* Ngāpuhi work to get their Treaty settlement with the Crown completed (*The Northern Advocate* 2015). There is also a popular tale that we heard from multiple participants of former governor-general Dame Catherine Tizard signing legislation with a different coloured ink when she disagreed in principle with them. However, while Keith helps us understand the democratic constraints on the sovereign, or what the sovereign is not able to do, he sheds less light on what reigning itself constitutes.

This became clearer during our discussion with Satyanand, who represented the sovereign for five years. He described the opening of Parliament to us as 'part of the caravan moving forward', evoking the image of an ongoing cycle that ends with the governor-general dissolving Parliament at the completion of its term and issuing a writ to the Electoral Commission to conduct the next election. In this manner, the opening can be seen as a calendrical rite which gives 'socially meaningful definitions to the passage of time' (Bell 2009: 102). Parliament is opened and closed using potent monarchical symbolism, inscribing continuity and traditional legitimacy onto successive governments. These cyclical rituals mark the political calendar, 'moving the caravan forward' while bestowing permanence, due process and sovereign jurisdiction on party politics of the day. As Satyanand put it:

> If you strip away all the panoply to do with the Queen and the history and so forth and say, 'What is actually important? What is the vital thing that the governor-general has to do or the Queen has to do?' . . . I think it is at that time of the general election, saying 'I appoint you prime minister'. It is what Dame Catherine Tizard called 'passing the parcel of power' . . . There has to be someone to pass the parcel of power.

In short, what makes the office most significant is the ability to delegate political authority to a newly elected government. This is an embodied process; the governor-general has to be physically present and speak the prescribed words. The person who 'passes the parcel' must be authorised to do so, and it is during the swearing-in ceremony that governors-general acquire this capacity.

Political practice in New Zealand therefore requires two distinct but co-constituting forms of authority: those that rule – the members of Parliament (MPs) and executive government who hold office on account of the democratic mandate obtained through general elections – and those that reign, the Queen and the governor-general, who possess sovereign authority. It is in state ritual – the opening of Parliament, the swearing-in of the Executive Council, the confirmation of the Speaker and giving the royal assent – where these domains not only come into contact but are mutually constituted. During state rituals, the boundary between the domain of reigning and that of ruling is consistently affirmed. The Crown, as sovereign, refers to something quite different to the state, the people, the government or the executive.

This boundary-making was illustrated when I met Miranda Thomson, the education coordinator for the Parliamentary Service, who offered to show me through Parliament's educational facility. The walls are plastered in pictures and posters, and the room itself is a miniature version of the House of Representatives where visiting students debate mock bills. Ushering me through a side door into the office area, she pointed to the dress-up material and lanyards that students wear, denoting their mock roles. Each political party had its own fruit symbol, and the Speaker, clerk and serjeant-at-arms lanyards had little crowns on them. Pointing to a picture of the Queen on the wall, she said:

> It is funny because the general manager of Parliamentary Service came up once [into the office area] and he said, 'Oh, why have you got the Queen up in here?' And I said, 'Well, that is the [mock] House. I cannot have a picture of the Queen in there: you should know that!'

The sovereign and their representative, the governor-general, are forbidden entry to the House, harking back to King Charles I's forced entry into the House of Commons in 1642. This epitomised the struggle, which concerned the extent of the sovereign's powers, between the King and Parliament in the years leading up to the outbreak of the English Civil War. The story goes that Charles I went to the House to arrest 'the Five members' for treason but found the doors were barred (Carlton 1995: 232–33). After Charles's guards managed to force their way in and he sat in the Speaker's chair, the Speaker, William Lenthall, refused to tell him the whereabouts of the members, who, with ample warning, had fled. In this moment, it is said, the House secured its independence from the sovereign, and since then no sovereign has been back inside. While Thomson's reference to such practices was made in jest, the importance of the legislature's separation from the sovereign is re-enacted time and time again through vivid state ceremonies, a ritual separation that remains relevant to the exercise of power in New Zealand today.

Opening Parliament in the Name of Her Majesty

The opening of Parliament, which happens every three years, 'is one of the few times when the Crown and the House of Representatives come together as Parliament, in a display of pomp and ceremony' (New Zealand Parliament 2014). It is split into two parts, the first of which is the Commission Opening of Parliament. This ceremony begins with the arrival of Her Majesty's commissioners (the chief justice, the chief High Court judge and the president of the Court of Appeal), dressed in their red robes and white wigs, who are welcomed by the *tāngata whenua* and guided into Parliament by the Usher of the Black Rod. Following ritual prescription, the commissioners visit the House on behalf of the governor-general, who is, as a representative of the sovereign, not permitted to enter.

The chief justice then tells the newly elected politicians that the commissioners are present on the authority of the governor-general to 'do all things in her Majesty's name necessary to be performed'. The letters patent, by which the commissioners are authorised by the Queen to open Parliament, are then read by the clerk of the House, before the chief justice reads the governor-general's proclamation summoning the House to meet with him the following day.

After the commissioners leave the chamber, the clerk of the House, as authorised by the governor-general, administers the oaths for the members of the new Parliament. According to the Standing Orders of Parliament, 'no member may sit or vote in the House before taking the Oath of Allegiance or making an Affirmation of Allegiance to the Crown' (New Zealand Parliament 2008). In this part of the ritual, the Crown symbolises the monarch as the Oath of Allegiance is made to the Queen. These formalities are taken very seriously: for instance, in 2011 Hone Harawira, a democratically elected MP, was barred from sitting in the House because he pledged allegiance to the Treaty rather than to the Crown (Watkins 2011). Other MPs yelled 'shame' and 'no respect' as he walked out in protest. This incident highlighted the depth of emotion that the observance of ritual, or the failure to follow ritual procedure, can elicit.

After members swear their oaths, the Speaker of the House is elected. The Speaker chairs parliamentary sessions and 'embodies the House in its relationship with the Crown' (New Zealand Parliament 2009). Until the seventeenth century, the Speaker usually acted as an agent of the sovereign in parliament; more recently, the Speaker has acted as the voice of the House to the sovereign (New Zealand Parliament 2009). In 2011, Alexander Lockwood Smith, an MP with the National Party, was elected Speaker, and then dragged by two fellow members to the Speaker's chair, in a ritual re-enactment of the Speaker-elect's traditional reluctance to accept the role. Several British Speakers were executed in the period between 1300 and 1500: during this time, the Speaker was often blamed by the monarch if they did not like House of Commons decisions (UK Parliament 2018). As he took his new seat at the centre of the House, Speaker-elect Lockwood Smith told the members:

> The standard was set by a Speaker at Westminster many, many years ago, when in 1642, Charles the First forced his way in [to the House of Commons]. . . . [The Speaker] sent him packing with the words, 'May it please your Majesty, I have neither eyes to see, nor tongue to speak in this House, but as this House is pleased to direct me, whose servant I am'. And to me that is the key: that as Speaker I am the servant of this House.

These words appealed to the tradition surrounding the role of the Speaker and the relationship between Parliament and the Crown. Lockwood Smith's commitment to Lentham's 'standard' and staged reluctance express the value of the separation of powers and the danger in giving those that reign the right to rule. It is through such gestures and statements that the Crown and Parliament are constructed as separate yet co-constitutive entities with their own forms of authority.

At this point, Lockwood Smith was only Speaker-elect; he was technically in a liminal stage of his rite of passage to become the Speaker. Though he had obtained authority through his appointment process, he required the sovereign authority of the Crown to complete his transformation. This takes place through the confirmation of the Speaker, enacted in a setting that is symbolically dense with references to the monarchy. He was led out of Parliament to Government House (the residence of the governor-general) by the serjeant-at-arms who carried the mace in the crook of his arm, representing that Lockwood Smith did not yet possess the complete authority of the Speaker. It is significant that the Speaker-elect must go to Government House while the rest of the ritual process takes place at Parliament Buildings. This part of the installation ritual, involving the sovereign's representative to the Speaker-elect, takes place in a space wholly associated with the monarchy. What is more, it is conducted before a huge portrait of the Queen, its gilt frame adorned with a crown.

The mace (Figure 5.2) is officially a symbol of the authority of the House. However, it also has more complex and subtle allusions to the authority of the sovereign or Crown. It is a material object, made potent through social action. During subsequent sittings of the House, the mace sits on a table in the centre of Parliament, affirming that the House has it on the sovereign's authority to act. While members of Parliament are

Figure 5.2 Each parliamentary mace is topped by a crown, modelled on this ceremonial mace at the Palace of Westminster
(Dan Kitwood/Getty Images)

present on the authority of a democratic process and the sovereign may not interfere with governance, members may only act with the blessing of the Crown. Less figuratively, the top of the mace even takes the form of a crown and is embellished with the Queen's royal cypher, the letters ER (Elizabeth Regina, or queen in Latin), expressing the authority which the mace itself represents. In fact, maces in medieval Europe were weapons wielded by royal bodyguards to protect the sovereign.

At his confirmation, Lockwood Smith wore the formal dress of the Speaker: a black cloak, red robe and white wig. He stood before the governor-general, Mateparae, accompanied by the serjeant-at-arms holding the mace in his arm, and with an audience of cabinet ministers, MPs and representatives of the judiciary. His Excellency then confirmed the House's choice and guaranteed the House's rights and privileges. David McGee (2005) explains that this guarantee 'echoes of days of conflict and suspicion between the Crown and Parliament' (141). Mateparae similarly explained that the ceremony is 'steeped in history' and told the Speaker that 'today's ceremony is a direct consequence of the will of New Zealanders', and 'your colleagues have given you the singular responsibility to represent the House to the Crown and to New Zealanders'. After the acceptance of the new Speaker by the sovereign's representative, the serjeant-at-arms shifts the mace to his shoulder. This signals that the House, led by the Speaker, now has the sovereign authority, as well as the democratic authority, to act. While official explanations of the mace emphasise the authority of the House, the symbolic power of the sovereign is central to the process of its legitimisation.

On the day following the Commission Opening and the confirmation of the Speaker, the governor-general comes to Parliament for what is known as the state opening. At the state opening in 2008, columns of armed forces lined up outside Parliament on the forecourt as Satyanand, then governor-general, arrived under police convoy in the Crown car. Across the harbour at Point Jerningham, the battery fired a twenty-one gun salute, announcing his arrival. The governor-general's flag was also raised, symbolising his presence – usually only the national flag flies over Parliament. The governor-general's flag flies over Government House when the governor-general is home and from the Crown car when travelling. It also flies from Parliament when the governor-general attends weekly Executive Council meetings.

The official commentator for the occasion explained that the public is notified in this way, with flags and gunfire, 'to reassure us that it is all happening in the approved way and with due legal and constitutional authority'. He described the opening as 'an important ceremony, conducted according to old practice and with a very strong sense of history'. If it did not occur, he said, 'we would have cause for concern'. His words suggest that the ritual is not a mere legal requirement; rather, it is affective and expresses the notion of constitutionally exercised power, in the Queen's name.

The *tāngata whenua* began the *pōwhiri* as the Royal Guard opened the car doors and Satyanand stepped out of the car. He then approached the herald and the Black Rod, who led him to the steps of Parliament, where he met the chiefs of the Defence Force and stood for the royal salute as trumpets blared. As the trumpeting faded, the congregation sang the national anthem, before His Excellency inspected the troops. The repetition (from the governor-general's swearing-in) of these ritual procedures reproduces the authority of the sovereign's representative. It is not enough that governors-general be welcomed by the *tāngata whenua* or presented arms a single time. Rather, their authority must be reiterated, re-enacted, especially in cases like this where their symbolic references have meaning in the context of others, namely, the democratic authority of the members of Parliament.

Satyanand then entered Parliament, walking up the red carpet to the Legislative Council room, before taking his seat on the throne – a gold-framed, red-cushioned seat with a crown embroidered on the backrest. Members of the judiciary and the Defence Force were also present, making the state opening one of the few occasions when all the branches of state are represented together, with the governor-general at its centre. His Excellency then asked: 'Black Rod, please summon the House of Representatives'. However, the Black Rod found the doors of the House barred. This ritual locking of the door 'symbolises the reluctance of the MPs to be dominated by the Crown' (New Zealand Parliament 2014) – a reference to the events of 1642. The Black Rod then banged on the door three times, upon which the serjeant-at-arms ordered the doors unlocked and authorised the Black Rod to enter. He then reported to the Speaker: 'Mr Speaker, His Excellency the Governor-General requests the immediate attendance of this House in the council chamber'. The serjeant then picked up the mace and led the Speaker and the members to the Legislative Council chamber to take their seats. Once seated, their exits were roped off, symbolically forcing them to attend and to listen, although it was Satyanand's performance and not his words that were significant. The speech, following convention, covered the policy programme that Her Majesty's government would set out over the coming term. Its content was of little surprise given that the National Party had run on the very same policy issues during the election campaign the previous year.

There is a complex process of signification here. On one hand, the governor-general's presence and performance bestow legitimacy on the actions of the government. Satyanand began the speech by addressing the members: 'It is a privilege for me to exercise the prerogative of Her Majesty the Queen and open the 49th Parliament' (*New Zealand Herald* 2008). Called the Speech from the Throne, this speech is, according to the official commentator, 'a way of letting the House know that the prime minister and his cabinet has the authority of the Crown to proceed with its business'. The government is Her Majesty's government. On the other hand, the speech signifies that governance also requires democratic authority. The speech is written by the prime minister, who physically hands it to the governor-general, before all eyes after everyone is seated, thus constituting the Crown as the sovereign, but one that is told what to do. Satyanand's speech made constant references to 'the good of the people' and the 'will of the electorate': for example, Key had written, 'It is they, our fellow New Zealanders, that my government will ever seek to serve'. The governor-general's speech thus combines the Queen's sovereign authority with democratic authority, making clear not only that politicians have the legitimacy of constitutional tradition but also that the sovereign and her representative do not govern.

After the speech is read, the governor-general leaves Parliament, and the proceedings of the House resume later in the day. The state opening is perhaps the most vivid political ritual in New Zealand. It marks time by dividing one term of government from the next. It follows a formalised schedule that changes little from year to year. The members know the governor-general will come, yet they need to be instructed to attend. What the governor-general says comes as no surprise, yet it must be said. The opening of Parliament, like other state rituals, acts to construct political authority. It involves a delegation of traditional authority while also reaffirming the sovereign's right to reign. The sovereign's role is not established once and for all but is continually reproduced through rituals.

A Syncretic Crown

The rituals that I have outlined are by no means understood, or even witnessed, by the majority of New Zealanders. Rather, they are performances of the state, for the state, by which political actors receive a particular account of what they mean. While these rituals may have other interpretations, I am particularly interested in official accounts, spoken by experts and expressed by key ritual actors – that is, how power represents itself. Keesing (2012) argued that rituals do not necessarily evoke shared meanings; instead, understanding often has an uneven distribution, influenced by a person's access to knowledge, social capital and specific interests. However, he also suggests that rituals can provoke emotional states in their participants and audiences without their meanings being grasped by all. Apprehending a normative interpretation of state rituals in New Zealand is further complicated by the fact that they are syncretic, containing ritual elements from *te ao Māori*. While rituals like the opening of Parliament have their origins in the English Westminster tradition, they have been thoroughly transformed through the colonial experience.

These transformations make state rituals in New Zealand slightly different to the 'invented traditions' described by Hobsbawm and Ranger (1983). They have emerged in just the last few decades, with the now seemingly mandatory inclusion of the *pōwhiri* and *haka pōwhiri* of the *tāngata whenua* only featured from 1984 (New Zealand Parliament 2008). Invented traditions are often seen as symbolic strategies to legitimise social hierarchies, especially during periods of rapid social change when existing forms of tradition no longer make sense (Hobsbawm 1983: 4). Colonisation in New Zealand established the norm of imitating or replicating Westminster traditions in the political world, offering little space for recognising or enacting indigenous political principles. The replication of Westminster political traditions began to make less sense, however, with the challenges made in the 1970s by Māori activists and academics to the Crown's sovereignty and the place of the Treaty.

It was during this period that the notion of biculturalism gained currency (Pearson 2000: 101–2). Biculturalism envisions a nation-state in which both Māori and Pākehā (New Zealand European, or non-Māori) worldviews, values and needs are attended to in the public sector and in government. While this began as a policy directive, biculturalism has also had important symbolic ramifications. Today, te reo Māori is an official state language; Aotearoa (literally long white cloud, an indigenous name for New Zealand) is increasingly used as a signifier of the country; public institutions commonly have names in te reo; and there are an increasing number of co-governance or indigenous governance systems in place. Māori ceremonies, like the *pōwhiri*, have become relatively commonplace and have been incorporated into both private and public spheres.

The combination of Māori ritual elements with Westminster state rituals reflects this paradigm of biculturalism. It recognises the Treaty and the place of Māori as *tāngata whenua*. Most importantly, it adds a local meaning to the construction of the Crown which celebrates the relationship between the Crown and Māori (although the power relations between each party are evidently not equal in the political sense). The fact that two previous governors-general were Māori adds another layer to this symbolic association, revealing how the Crown not only transcends political divides but race and ethnicity too – it sits above everyday life, while encompassing all its subjects.

Conclusion

State rituals invest the constitutional arrangements with significance that is fundamental to political action. They are not 'mere ceremonies' or secondary to the political process but central to the exercise of power and to the legitimation of the institutions of the state. They also symbolise key values that are essential to the operation of the state, including due process, sovereignty and continuity. They are not simply reflections of where power lies nor a mechanism for disguising the real exercise of power. Instead, political ritual constitutes power. Governors-general do not sit on the throne and open Parliament because they are the *de facto* head of state and representative of the sovereign; rather, their doing so is what constitutes their authority regarding, and relationship with, the realm of everyday politics. It is through their enactment that the governing apparatus establishes its authority to govern. As the state opening of Parliament shows, political rituals construct legitimate government by bringing together two symbolic forms of authority, one sovereign and one democratic, which can be imagined as flowing from the sovereign's body natural and the electorate, respectively. At the same time, these rituals constitute two separate domains, the ruling and reigning, dignified and efficient.

The Crown is central to this performative work. In ritual settings it is more closely tied to the person of the Queen and the governor-general; that is, to the monarch's body natural instead of the body politic. It is understood as distinct from Parliament, as something from which the House must assert its independence. In these particular political rituals, the Crown is not the government, the state or the executive; rather, it is imagined as emanating from the sovereign rather than the electorate. As Satyanand put it, the Crown is 'Queen Inc. . . . it is a mechanism to do the things that the Queen would do'. In this way then, the ritual embodiment of the Crown is a further source of the Crown's ambiguity, of the difficulty of defining just what it means or is.

Finally, I have argued that the bicultural and syncretic nature of state rituals in New Zealand adds a further dimension to the Crown's meaning. It constructs the Crown as possessing a form of authority that stems from the Treaty and is local in quality. These rituals illustrate the amorphous quality of the Crown as a flexible and adaptable political symbol that takes up meanings appropriate to its political and social environment. In the next chapter, we examine how the Crown has been invented in a way culturally specific to Australia.

References

Abélès, Marc. 1988. 'Modern Political Ritual: Ethnography of an Inauguration and a Pilgrimage by President Mitterrand.' *Current Anthropology* 29(3): 391–404.

Bagehot, Walter. (1867) 2001. *The English Constitution*, edited by Paul Smith. Cambridge: Oxford University Press.

Barlow, Cleve. 1994. *Tikanga Whakaaro: Key Concepts in Māori Culture*. New York: Oxford University Press.

Bell, Catherine. 2009. *Ritual: Perspectives and Dimensions*. Oxford: Oxford University Press.

Cabinet Office. 2017. *Cabinet Manual*. Wellington: Cabinet Office, Department of the Prime Minster and Cabinet.

Carlton, Charles. 1995. *Charles I: The Personal Monarch*. 2nd edn. New York: Routledge.

Comaroff, Jean and John Comaroff (eds.). 1993. *Modernity and Its Malcontents: Ritual and Power in Postcolonial Africa*. Chicago: University of Chicago Press.

Cook, Susan and Rebecca Hardin. 2013. 'Performing Royalty in Contemporary Africa.' *Cultural Anthropology* 28(2): 227–51.

Feeley-Harnik, Gillian. 1985. 'Issues in Divine Kingship.' *Annual Review of Anthropology* 14: 273–313.

Fortes, Meyer. 1967. 'Of Installation Ceremonies.' *Proceedings of the Royal Anthropological Institute of Great Britain and Ireland* 1967: 5–20.

Frazer, James George. 1922. *The Golden Bough: A Study in Magic and Religion*. New York: Macmillan.

Geertz, Clifford. 1980. *Negara: The Theatre State in Nineteenth-Century Bali*. Princeton, NJ: Princeton University Press.

Graeber, David and Marshall Sahlins. 2017. *On Kings*. Chicago: HAU Books.

de Heusch, Luc. 1997. 'The Symbolic Mechanisms of Sacred Kingship: Rediscovering Frazer.' *The Journal of the Royal Anthropological Institute* 3(2): 213–32.

Hobsbawm, Eric. 1983. 'Introduction: Inventing Traditions.' In *The Invention of Tradition*, edited by Eric Hobsbawm and Terence Ranger, 1–14. Cambridge: Cambridge University Press.

Hobsbawm, Eric and Terence Ranger (eds). 1983. *The Invention of Tradition.* Cambridge: Cambridge University Press.

Hocart, Arthur M. (1936) 1970. *Kings and Councillors: An Essay in the Comparative Anatomy of Human Society.* Chicago: University of Chicago Press.

Keesing, Roger. 2012. 'On Not Understanding Symbols: Toward an Anthropology of Incomprehension.' *HAU: Journal of Ethnographic Theory* 2(2): 406–30.

Kertzer, David I. 1988. *Ritual, Politics & Power.* New Haven, CT: Yale University Press.

Little, Paul E. 1995. 'Ritual, Power and Ethnography at the Rio Earth Summit.' *Critique of Anthropology* 15(3): 265–88.

McGee, David. 2005. *Parliamentary Practice in New Zealand.* 3rd edn. Wellington: Dunmore Publishing Limited.

McLeod, James. 1999. 'The Sociodrama of Presidential Politics: Rhetoric, Ritual, and Power in the Era of Teledemocracy.' *American Anthropologist* 101(2): 359–73.

Moore, Sally F. and Barbara G. Myerhoff (eds.). 1977. *Secular Ritual.* Assen, Netherlands: Van Gorcum.

New Zealand Herald. 2008. John Key's Speech from the Throne. 9 December. Accessed 14 December 2015 at www.nzherald.co.nz/nz/news/article.cfm?c_id=1&objectid=10547208.

The Northern Advocate. 2015. Pressure Goes on Ngapuhi to Get on with Settlement. 5 February. Accessed 18 July 2017 at www.nzherald.co.nz/northern-advocate/news/article.cfm?c_id=1503450&objectid=11396999.

New Zealand Parliament. 2008. Opening of Parliament Ceremonies on 8 and 9 December 2008. Accessed 8 December 2015 at www.parliament.nz/en-nz/features/00NZPHomeNews0512200081/opening-of-parliament-ceremonies-on-8-and-9-december-2008.

2009. The Speaker in History. Accessed 6 January 2018 at www.parliament.nz/en/visit-and-learn/how-parliament-works/fact-sheets/the-speaker-in-history/.

2014. Roles and Regalia at the Opening of Parliament. Accessed 8 December 2012 at www.parliament.nz/en-nz/features/00NZPHomeNews201410131/roles-and-regalia-at-the-opening-of-parliament.

Pearson, David. 2000. 'The Ties That Unwind: Civic and Ethnic Imaginings in New Zealand.' *Nations and Nationalism* 6(1): 91–110.

Quigley, Declan. 2005. 'Introduction: The Character of Kingship.' In *The Character of Kingship*, edited by Declan Quigley, 1–23. Oxford: Berg.

Scubla, Lucien. 2002. 'Hocart and the Royal Road to Anthropological Understanding.' *Social Anthropology* 10(3): 359–76.

2005. 'Sacred King, Sacrificial Victim, Surrogate Victim or Frazer, Hocart, Girard.' In *The Character of Kingship*, edited by Declan Quigley, 39–62. Oxford: Berg.

Stepputat, Finn. 2004. 'Marching for Progress: Rituals of Citizenship, State and Belonging in a High Andes District.' *Bulletin of Latin American Research* 23(2): 244–59.

Turner, Victor. 1967. *The Forest of Symbols: Aspects of Ndembu Ritual*. Ithaca, NY: Cornell University Press.

1969. *The Ritual Process: Structure and Anti-structure*. Harmondsworth: Penguin.

UK Parliament. 2018. History of the Speakership. Accessed 5 January 2018 at www.parliament.uk/business/commons/the-speaker/the-role-of-the-speaker/history-of-the-speakership/.

van Gennep, Arnold. (1909) 1960. *The Rites of Passage*. London: Routledge and Kegan Paul.

Watkins, Tracy. 2011. Speaker Refuses to Swear Harawira in. *Stuff*. July 14. Accessed 2 February 2016 at www.stuff.co.nz/national/politics/5284635/Speaker-refuses-to-swear-Harawira-in.

6

Locating the Crown in Australia

The Swag of Camp Gallipoli

SALLY RAUDON

The previous chapter showed how state rituals in New Zealand operate to endow authority and legitimacy to a constitutional system in which the Crown takes centre stage. As we have shown, the Crown in New Zealand is taken to mean Parliament, the executive, the judiciary and more. In Australia, by contrast, the Crown is not an everyday term of use, although it remains ubiquitous and taken for granted. Despite this, the Australian Crown's changing and continually reinvented meanings play an important role in sustaining everyday forms of nationalism, or what Michael Billig calls banal nationalism (1995). I illustrate this with an ethnographic analysis of an unusual example from the Anzac[1] Centenary of 2015.

On Anzac Day 2015, I stood in a crowd of approximately 30,000 people packed into Sydney's Martin Place (Murphy 2015). The service opened with a song I had not sung before: 'God Save the Queen', the royal and British national anthem, and New Zealand's second anthem. We sang this before the anthems of Australia or New Zealand, the countries whose independent identities Anzac Day purportedly celebrates. No one remarked on this or seemed to find it surprising. Anzac's ties with the British Crown, it seemed, run deep.

Anzac ceremonies have become increasingly important civic rituals, in which the presence of the Crown, although rarely openly noted, is pivotal. The symbolic use of the Crown in Anzac contexts conforms to what many interviewees described as increasingly visible and explicit forms of Australian nationalism and militarism. By nationalism, I mean both a mode of political imagination and an ideology which says that being Australian is something distinctive and knowable against which

[1] The acronym comes from the Australian and New Zealand Army Corps (ANZAC), which first fought at Gallipoli against the Ottoman Empire during the First World War.

other identities can be measured (Anderson 1983). Nationalism is not only reproduced through state rituals, grand public events and official monuments, it is also – and perhaps more effectively – cultivated through mundane yet subliminal exercises, objects and events (Billig 1995). In this instance, the Crown is located in Australian social life in commonplace yet curiously unrecognised ways which speak to broader themes of Australian history and nationhood.

Throughout this chapter, I ask: how is the Crown symbolically implicated in notions of Australian citizenship, service and sacrifice? Given that many Australians dismiss the Crown as a colonial relic and politically irrelevance, why is its presence so common in what has become, *de facto*, Australia's national day (Bridge 2009)? I address these questions by demonstrating how the Crown's chameleon-like character (Twomey 2006) remains central to the Anzac – and consequently, Australian national – imaginary.

The Australian Crown's Distinctive Context

The Crown's role is far more subdued in Australia than it is in New Zealand, Canada or the UK. People rarely mentioned it or saw its relevance in their everyday lives. Even among those experts I met whose work brought them into direct contact with the institutions of the Crown – the judiciary, politicians and senior public servants who are responsible for curating or representing it, or enacting its agency – many thought of it as 'merely symbolic', an ornament to actual political authority (cf. Geertz 1980).

Despite this pervasive sense of the Crown's insignificance, it lies at the heart of the Australian Constitution (1901), and Crown imagery is ubiquitous wherever political authority is claimed (McKenna 2010). What distinguishes the use of the Crown in Australia from other contexts in this study is its unremarked yet ubiquitous presence and its minimised efficacy, despite its very real powers and its obvious manifestation in significant and complex socio-political contexts. The Crown has been central throughout Australian history, as both a decisive actor and as the object of attention when its authority has been called into question. Examples abound in the complex and disputed history of Australian colonisation. Under colonisation the British Crown took possession of Australian territories. The understanding that Australian territories had been wastelands not occupied by civilised people before colonisation (a doctrine which became known as *terra nullius*) legitimised Crown sovereignty. This doctrine was overturned by the *Mabo* decision in 1992 (see Chapter 4). In the Eureka Stockade (1854), Ballarat gold miners revolted against the British colonial authority. With federation (1901) Australian states became a Commonwealth under the Crown. During the constitutional crisis (1975) the governor-general, John Kerr, dismissed the Whitlam Labor government, crystallising Labor's republican policy and galvanising the Australian Republican Movement (Winterton 1986). In the 1999 republic referendum, the fiercely contested proposal that Australia should become a republic was ultimately defeated by sustained opposition from monarchist organisations and a split in the republican ranks over whether the head of state should be popularly elected (Warhurst and Mackerras 2002). In each instance, the Crown legitimates the state while being perceived as sitting above and apart from it. This enabling disjunction holds equally true for instances when the Crown and Anzac memorialisation are periodically united in contemporary political myth-making.

Anzac Day: History of a Political Ritual

The Anzac campaign at Gallipoli Cove, Turkey, in 1915 holds a singular place in the Australian imagination. The rituals and taboos around traditional and contemporary Anzac commemorations yield rich clues about Australian life (Inglis 1965; Thomson 2003; Seal 2004; Bridge 2009) and the Crown's significance to it. The Crown's role in Anzac symbolism, and the meanings of Anzac, have shifted significantly since 1915.

In the First World War Australians officially fought for king, country and loyalty to empire (as Australia remained a dominion of the British Empire until it adopted the Statute of Westminster in 1942), with the Crown displayed distinctively and prominently on uniforms and regalia. Although the Anzac campaign itself was a catastrophic defeat, accounts of the distinctive attitudes demonstrated by Australian troops quickly took hold in the public imagination, infusing the loss with significance and purpose (Cryle 2016; see Bean 1933). These values were immediately subjects of public discussion (Inglis 1965). When the Australian War Museum opened in 1941 (during the Second World War) Anzac values were formally itemised and illustrated in the windows of the Hall of Memories as resource, candour, devotion, curiosity, independence, comradeship, ancestry, patriotism, chivalry, loyalty, coolness, control, audacity, endurance and decision (Australian War Memorial 2017).

From the beginning, Anzac Day's observance and meanings were politically contested. The first Anzac commemorations were held during the war and officially promoted to motivate troop recruitment and the home front as much as to memorialise losses. As casualties increased, volunteering declined in the increasingly war-weary and divided population. Returned soldiers were often ambivalent about commemorating Gallipoli's carnage and resented how the government exploited Anzac events to boost the fast-fading appetite for war and circumvent civic expressions of grief (Cryle 2016). But many communities valued Anzac events as a way to publicly mourn their substantial losses and articulate a consoling sense of purpose for survivors and the bereaved. Initially, Anzac Day did little to promote national unity, as state governments, ex-servicemen, bereaved families, Protestant and Catholic churches, and labour and temperance unions struggled to control its meanings and performance.

Community conflict about Anzac Day persisted well into the 1920s, as servicemen still suffering physically and mentally struggled to reintegrate into civilian life. Although the government's servility to empire was stoutly resented by many who held the British responsible for Gallipoli, the resilient Crown remained symbolically attached on insignia and memorials. When Edward, Prince of Wales, toured in 1920, he spent hours inspecting returned troops, thanking them for their service, and unveiling mournful memorials in decimated communities (Connors 2015: 49). In recognition for this and his own war service, he earned the nickname the 'Digger Prince'[2] (Connors 2015: 49). Anzac's imperial and nationalist meanings were not necessarily contradictory.

Anzac Day was formalised throughout Australia after a decade of lobbying. At the State Premiers' Conference of 1921, delegates agreed that it would be observed on 25 April each year. It took until 1927 for all Australian states to observe Anzac Day as a form of public holiday. The status of Anzac was further secured by the Protection of Word "Anzac" Act (1920), which was designed to ensure that the word could not be trivialised or exploited commercially: permission for use could only be granted by the federal government. However, whatever meanings the government tried to impose on the commemorations, Anzac Day's observance, structure and significance remained largely driven by the actions and interpretations of the public (Bridge 2009). By 1929 the day's familiar structure had developed: the dawn service of wreath laying,

[2] Digger is Australian slang for soldier, a term popularised in the First World War.

observed silence, hymn, flag lowering, military salute and bugle solo, followed by the servicemen's march (Seal 2004; Bridge 2009).

Initially, the Second World War boosted Anzac Day's popularity as its meanings broadened to include new veterans. Yet in the following decades Anzac Day again became marked by ambivalence and acrimony. The Returned and Services League (RSL) ran the commemorations, but veterans themselves were frequently judged as old-fashioned, often drunk and glorifying war (Kapferer 2012: 155–57). Attendance dwindled during the deeply unpopular Vietnam War, and as the government once again conscripted soldiers, Anzac Day became a focus for peace, feminist and indigenous protests. Anzac values and events became objects of scholarly focus during these years of protest, analysed as Australia's 'civil religion' (Inglis 1965) and critiqued for its perceived distortions and jingoism (Serle 1967). In the 1970s and early 1980s Anzac Day was widely expected to fade away as First World War veterans themselves died out.

Brendan Nelson, the director of the Australian War Memorial and former minister of defence in John Howard's government, said, 'In the 1970s there were existential questions about the future of Anzac day', and many newspaper editorials claimed, 'Anzac Day's not likely to survive' (Interviews, 2015). Writer Peter Rees said that when he was at school he would never have imagined how attitudes towards Anzac Day would change: 'My generation in the sixties regarded the diggers quite poorly. They would get pissed, falling over at Town Hall, spewing up – it was pretty awful to see. So we didn't like Anzac Day' (Interviews, 2015). Former Australian Republican Movement president and political scientist John Warhurst agreed that people talked 'about the death of Anzac Day' (Interviews, 2015).

Yet Anzac Day staged a curious revival in the late 1980s, transforming itself from a veterans' day to a patriotic festival of far broader relevance. This revitalisation was prompted by demographic changes (including immigrants keen to prove their citizenship) and by nationalism driven by bicentenary celebrations (1988). Following Prime Minister Bob Hawke's hosting of Anzac veterans at Gallipoli for the 75th anniversary of the battle (1990), the battlefield became a standard port of call for prime ministers; Prime Minister John Howard visited on 25 April in 2000 and 2005. As actual veteran numbers declined, relatives began marching in their place, often wearing the deceased's medals. In what John Warhurst described as 'the surprising resurgence of Gallipoli interest among young Australians' (Interviews, 2015), spending Anzac Day at

Gallipoli became a secular pilgrimage for young middle-class Australians and New Zealanders (McKenna and Ward 2007; West 2008). Even those whose visits formed part of official duties recognised that Gallipoli had become sacred ground for Australians. One senior public servant said that Australian governor-general Peter Cosgrove, who spent the Anzac Day centenary at Lone Pine in Gallipoli, saw this as the defining moment of his tenure (Interviews, 2015). Anzac Day's politically championed revival demonstrates how traditions are invented (Hobsbawm and Ranger 1983) in order to endow them with the gravitas of the past and lend legitimacy to current power structures.

Anzac commemorations have increased in significance and popularity to become, in effect, Australia's national day (Thomson 2003; Bridge 2009). It is the one day of the year with which 'all Australians are required to have a relationship, positive or negative' (Seal 2004: vii). Australia Day (January 26), the official national day, celebrates the First Fleet of British ships arriving at Sydney Harbour. Australia Day is enthusiastically supported by recent immigrant populations. However, celebrating colonisation sits uncomfortably with some Australians, and it has also become the focus of indigenous protests framed as 'Invasion Day.' To resolve this tension many people described Australia Day in terms of beer and barbeques, a day off to spend with friends and family. 'It's a nice day, sure, but it doesn't really mean anything. Anzac Day's when you stop and think about what it means to be Australian', explained one (anonymous, Interviews, 2015). As John Warhurst stated, 'Anzac Day is perhaps seen as something that 95 percent of Australians can agree on, whereas we can't agree on Australia Day – it has a sort of racism aspect to it which we can't get around' (Interviews, 2015). Brendan Nelson echoed this view, adding, 'Australia Day for indigenous people represents the devastating impact on them and their culture of the First Fleet arriving. And then there are a lot of Australians who couldn't even tell you what happened on the 26th of January 1788. But Anzac Day is a completely different matter' (Interviews, 2015).

Today Anzac services and parades attract enormous crowds. 'It's caught the imagination of people in a way which is mind-blowing, really,' said Warhurst (Interviews, 2015). Anthropologist Mitch Low said, 'There's kind of a seriousness to it that takes you by surprise' (Interviews, 2015). Speaking of the Anzac Day 2015 service in Canberra, Brendan Nelson stated that some 128,700 people had attended the dawn service hosted by the War Memorial:

> These people come out in the cold and the dark. There's no free food or drink. There's no movie star or young royal to see. Why are they doing it? . . . My own feeling is there's a sense of coming together to recommit ourselves to one another, our nation, and the ideals to which we aspire as human beings . . . as the 'God, King and Country' framework has broken down through the course of my lifetime, there's a sense of looking for and finding meaning in what it means to be an Australian.
>
> (Interviews, 2015)

Many interviewees shared these observations. People who dismissed the Crown as 'merely symbolic' would tell me how meaningful Anzac Day was, how lovely the ceremonies were and how important it was to have young children attend dawn services. However, I also spoke with people who were ambivalent about the place of Anzac in contemporary Australian life. Republican and historian Mark McKenna saw Anzac Day's popularity as a passing phase (Interviews, 2015). One senior public servant described as 'appalling' and 'loathsome' young people 'patriotically shrouding themselves in flags with stylised Union Jacks on their faces' (Interviews, 2015).

Former Liberal Party leader Fred Chaney explained how Anzac's meanings and practices had changed over his lifetime, culminating in an uncomfortable distance between his own patriotism and what Anzac represents today:

> As the son of an ex-president of the RSL and attender of dawn services since my very early years, and as someone who lost a grandfather in the First World War and father missing in action in the Second, I'm deeply respectful of ex-servicemen . . . I am a patriot. I love this country. I adore it. I think it is the most wonderful country in the world, you know, I really do. I'm all in favour of patriotism, I'm all in favour of being grateful for those who died for us, and I march – I did just last Anzac Day, I marched with the Aboriginal servicemen at their invitation, carried their banner. I marched in my father's place after he died. I think fostering a sense of community, fostering a sense of shared purpose, is absolutely right . . .
>
> But the phrase 'patriotism is the last refuge of scoundrels' does come to my mind when I think of the money that's being spent on popularising and commemorating this. All of the old diggers from the First World War that I've ever met *loathed* war, spoke strongly against war, and unfortunately they're all dead now. But I think there's a very strong jingoistic element in what's being done. Now that's a very unpopular view – it would be offensive to so many people.
>
> Anzac Day fits into what I, on my bad days, would call bread and circuses.
>
> (Interviews, 2015)

In 2015, after a terror threat, conservative Prime Minister Tony Abbott (former leader of Australians for Constitutional Monarchy) urged citizens to attend Anzac celebrations in 'defiance' as a means of supporting 'our country, our values and our armed forces' (Ireland 2015). Some felt this exploited security fears for nationalist political purposes; even so, the centenary Anzac commemorations set attendance records (Murphy 2015). Legal academic Lee Godden stated that Anzac commemorations have been reinvigorated in 'a general turn to a much more conservative political approach that's taken place over the last couple of decades . . . in Australian public life [there is] quite an aggressive nationalism behind the idea of the Crown, and I think that plays out in the way in which Australian troops serve overseas and the commemoration of Anzac' (Interviews, 2015). Unsurprisingly, former defence minister Brendan Nelson saw the situation far more positively:

> In the last 16 years, young Australians especially have seen our Defence Force busy. They've been in Iraq, Afghanistan, the Solomon Islands, East Timor, peacekeeping operations . . . our Defence Force is deployed by our government to serve our national interest, to protect Australia, but it's also deployed in a way which is consistent with our values. The military . . . gives Australians a greater sense of who we are and in what we believe and what's important to us. It's regarded as a force for good.
>
> (Interviews, 2015)

A sweeping inversion of Anzac's original meanings thus took place in 2015, standing in sharp contrast with the first community Anzac services which had been held in tension with the government's military ambitions amid widespread suspicion of warmongering and chauvinistic patriotism.

As several interviewees observed, Anzac Day remains often understood as celebrating 'the moment when Australia became Australia'. Historian Ken Inglis (1965, 1999) proposed that Anzac rites functioned as the high day of Australia's 'civil religion' because sacred characteristics surrounding the attitudes and practices associated with it had developed. Certainly, it shares elements of religious ritual: solemn dawn rites, invocations of ancestors, themes of sacrifice and birth. Interviewees believed that Anzac Day's revered place in Australian identity had become above question or criticism – in other words, taboo. People illustrated this by recalling that a sports journalist who posted pacifist statements on social media on Anzac Day 2015 lost his job and was publicly shamed by senior politicians – including future prime minister Malcolm Turnbull (Meade 2015).

Those who noted the strong social prohibitions surrounding the sacredness of Anzac Day also criticised the excessive nationalism it attracted. Historian Geoffrey Serle coined the term Anzackery (1967) to critique the myth-building jingoism associated with Anzac celebrations, especially the narrative that Australia was 'born' at Gallipoli in 1915. For some, wearing the flag as a cloak – as seen in both Camp Gallipoli advertisements (Figures 6.3 and 6.4) – exemplified Anzackery. Interviewees were uneasy when they perceived distortions to Anzac's meanings but believed that social convention would curtail public criticism. After a century, the 'spirit of Anzac' has been broadened to fully accommodate the state's military and populist priorities.

'Just Like the Diggers Did': Behind the Sandbags at Camp Gallipoli

On 24 April 2015 I joined some 5,000 people at a themed military history camp in Sydney to experience an atmosphere of commemorative Anzac density. Called Camp Gallipoli, it was established to be an annual nationwide event launched to help people 'commemorate ANZAC Day as participants, rather than spectators' (Camp Gallipoli Foundation 2014). Those behind the Camp Gallipoli charity stated they wanted to 'help preserve and foster the unique spirit of ANZAC' (Camp Gallipoli Foundation 2015a) because the 'spirit of ANZAC' is in the DNA of every Aussie' (Camp Gallipoli Foundation 2015b).

The charity received a A$2.5 million grant from the Department of Veterans Affairs and public support from the government and the Australian War Memorial. It formed a partnership with the RSL and secured associations with schools and education programmes. Prominent retired federal politicians served on its board, including former South Australian premier Graham Ingerson as deputy chair. Those behind Camp Gallipoli believed that Australians carry latent within them Anzac's values, which they can access by phenomenological immersion. People bought A$120 tickets to sleep in swags (low single-person tents) on a field and rise in the dark for the Anzac Day dawn service, a religious remembrance ceremony of Anzac hymns, music and requiem. Camp Gallipoli was held the night before and on Anzac Day in the capital cities of most Australian states. Some 40,000 Australians attended Camp Gallipoli's 2015 events around Australia.[3]

[3] Camp Gallipoli also launched in New Zealand in 2015 and 2016, but it was withdrawn due to low ticket sales; this conforms to observations that national days are performed differently in each country (McAllister 2012).

Following a powerful storm, Camp Gallipoli Sydney had been relocated from Centennial Park to drier grounds at Moore Park's Entertainment Quarter, a retail precinct near Fox Studios. People entered the camp stadium past a busy, well-stocked merchandise stand where swags (A$349), apparel and accessories such as scarves and hats were sold alongside 'dog tags' engraved with a dead soldier's ID number. At the entrance was the Camp Gallipoli flame, which burned throughout the event, emulating the Eternal Flame which burns permanently at the Australian War Memorial to represent the nation's perpetual gratitude for the Anzac heroism of its war dead. To get to the swag ground, I passed through a sandbag 'bunker' near the 'mess', where I presented ID to receive 'rations'. Enormous screens projected profiled images of servicemen in their distinctive lemon-squeezer hats. Every turn revealed another piece of staging in the military camp theatre, rich with displays of soldiers in still images, projections, logos, documentaries and feature films.

The crowd was mostly white families with children. Young adults in small groups (those I met were mostly early-career professionals) took selfies of themselves in the bunkers. Children raced about playing tag or tracing the air with glow sticks. On the field, couples bickered quietly as they attempted to pitch their swags. Some enthusiasts decorated guy ropes with flags and koalas. Men retreated to the edges of the arena to watch sports on their phones. Later that night, people could watch a movie on a huge outdoor screen (*The Water Diviner* (2014), a historical drama movie based on the aftermath of Gallipoli). In the auditorium, families solemnly watched live and recorded interviews as war heroes and celebrities described what Anzac Day meant to them. They sang along cheerily with school choirs performing Australian standards such as 'Waltzing Matilda' and 'I Still Call Australia Home'. Later, a small crowd danced and chanted with the rock band's Anzac-themed chorus, 'Never forget! Never forget!'.

During the band's intermission, the host interviewed a well-known rugby league player who was 'going to take the spirit of Anzac onto the field' in an Anzac Day match. The player said solemnly, 'We are going into battle tomorrow. It's not exactly like what the Anzacs went through, but we want to do them proud.' He was enthusiastically cheered. The military language is deliberate: league players are icons of Australian manhood and nationhood, especially in the eastern states, and the player was reiterating the tacit fusion of rough sports with Anzac heroism that is celebrated in Australia. Later that day I watched part of a game on television which made the nexus between sports and militarism more visceral: whenever a team scored, serving soldiers in light armoured vehicles at the edge of the field celebrated by firing blanks. The ability to align one's purpose with the Anzacs, to sacrifice for a higher purpose and to take pleasure in virtuous nostalgia is highly valued.

'100 Years of Anzac Spirit'

Camp Gallipoli is a reinvigorated Anzac ritual, developed to give people alternative ways to perform the origin myth of how Australia came to be. It drew people together physically, cognitively and emotionally. The crowd, props, role-play, rhetoric, special food, music and other performances gave the event a festival-like atmosphere, typical of the ways in which ordinary life is periodically interrupted by ritual (Leach 1961). As they recalled the Anzac narrative and queued for the mess or rose at 4:00 am for the dawn service, people could experience what Camp Gallipoli promoted as the 'spirit of Anzac'. Anthropologists call this 'collective effervescence' (Durkheim 2015), the intoxicating sense of unity that arises from participating in a crowd, and communitas (Turner 1967), the temporary disassembling of regular social order when people of all ranks and classes come together in a ritual levelling of society.

The ability to experience 'just like the diggers' – albeit in safety with relative comfort and entertainment – was what Camp Gallipoli had sold its customers. Yet in many ways, as we sat and watched performances and television interviews, campers remained observers rather than participants. This undermined the goal of better comprehending the deprivation and sacrifice of Anzac soldiers through bodily practice, and some were sensitive to the irony. One young man at the mess said cheerfully, 'Eating eggplant moussaka and watching Russell Crowe on the big screen, just like the diggers did'. Of course, disrespect for organised authority and laconic sarcasm are themselves demonstrations of Anzac values.

Many people clearly found Camp Gallipoli purposeful and moving, as well as entertaining. National holidays are often 'a pastiche of solemn feelings, moral ideals, personal fun, and recreation' (Schwartz 2008: 103). In Australia, Anzac Day is marked by contrasts between the solemn dawn service and the boisterous parade that follows; historically it was characterised by drinking, gambling and 'ratbaggery and larrikinism' (Bridge 2009), the local term for boisterous and objectionable behaviour. When I asked people why they had come, several found my question bewildering because it was self-evident. They said things like, 'It's so special to be here'; 'Just all these people coming together'; 'I'm just thinking about what the diggers went through'; 'My granddad served, so . . .'; and 'It's important to teach the kids'. What the 'spirit of Anzac' actually is, and why it matters, has been naturalised such that it elides perception, making its effects difficult to recognise, or at least discuss.

People also described their participation as fulfilling obligations to personal or national ancestors. One woman told me, 'It's a small thing to do, after what the diggers did for us.' The modest temporary inconveniences of swag camping gave participants a way to forge experiential connections with the Anzacs. Narratives of hardship, heroism, fear and great suffering were reiterated through the night in documentaries and murals, frequently affirming the heroic Anzac values of egalitarianism and practicality (Kapferer [1988] 2012). Indexing Camp Gallipoli against these narratives was important. Several times I heard parents admonishing children for their complaints with, 'This is nothing compared to what the diggers went through!' By offering a physical experience of related but not equivalent sacrifice, Camp Gallipoli helped people perform and inscribe collective memory through individual bodies, and related this experience to something ineffable.

Hidden in Plain Sight

But what of the Crown's presence at Camp Gallipoli? Images of crowns were on every piece of merchandise, documentation and promotion I saw. Camp Gallipoli's logo is dominated by a graphical crown: it is the central element, supporting and linking the others. On the top left of the crown is a red poppy and on the top right are two rosemary sprigs (Figures 6.1 and 6.2).

Red poppies and rosemary are symbols of remembrance for Allied veterans, and they grow abundantly in places particularly associated with their deaths: rosemary on the cliffs of Gallipoli in Turkey and red poppies in the fields of northern France and Belgium. Australians often wear rosemary sprigs and imitation poppies on and around the date of Anzac Day to signify remembrance. Below the crown the lettering is in a serif font, which again suggests an appreciation of tradition: sans-serif fonts were not prevalent at the time of the First World War. In advertisements, the phrase 'Spirit of Anzac' appeared below the name 'Camp Gallipoli', indicating that Camp Gallipoli promises transcendence. Each of the logo's visual elements would have been recognisable to Australians at any time over the last century, as the logo has been carefully designed to suggest the authority of heritage (Figures 6.1 and 6.2).

Figure 6.1 Camp Gallipoli logo
(Camp Gallipoli Foundation)

When I asked people at Camp Gallipoli about the crown in the logo – which many were wearing on T-shirts they had just purchased – they said things like, 'I don't know', 'I hadn't really noticed it', 'It'll just be for RSL or Legacy I reckon' (both veterans associations), or 'Yeah, there *is* a crown, I didn't see it! There's the poppy though, and rosemary – that's about the vets.' It seemed as though the image of the crown evaded perception: more than unrecognised, it seemed somehow invisible.

Camp Gallipoli's general manager, David Watson, told me how the crown came to be included in the logo. He said that this crown is a graphical representation of George V's crown,[4] used because he was

[4] In fact, this is a representation of the Tudor Crown, also known as the King's or Imperial Crown. The Tudor Crown is an artist's representation not modelled on an actual crown. It was commonly used in heraldry and military badges throughout the Commonwealth between 1902 to 1953 to visually symbolise both the monarch and the government's authority. Queen Elizabeth requested that the Tudor Crown be replaced by a representation of St Edward's crown, the crown used to coronate a new monarch. The Tudor Crown was historically significant to the royal insignia during the First World War.

Figure 6.2 Camp Gallipoli T-shirt and 'dog tag', 2015
(Sally Raudon)

Australia's monarch during the First World War. He added that organisations like the (actively conservative and monarchist) RSL often used this emblem. They simply wanted to associate Camp Gallipoli with the heritage and significance of the Crown and the respect it commands to

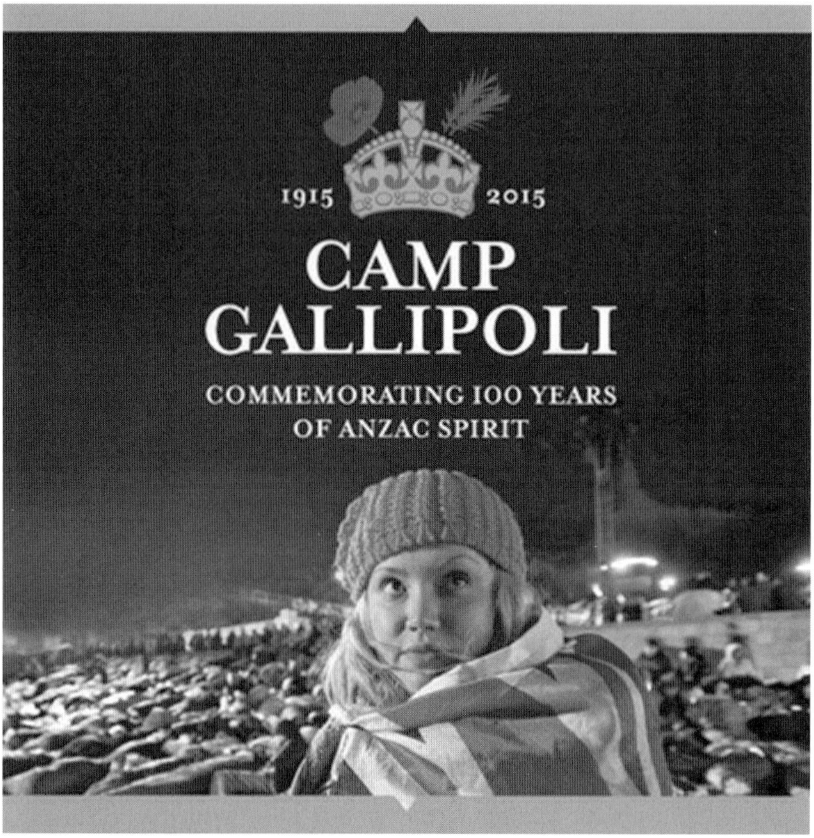

Figure 6.3 Camp Gallipoli advertisement, 2015
(Camp Gallipoli Foundation)

veterans' associations – which had endorsed Camp Gallipoli and were set to receive its profits.

The logo was central to advertising Camp Gallipoli. The most widely used design was that in Figure 6.3. The crown and logo sit above a young white woman. She is foregrounded and draped in a large Australian flag, as though wrapping herself in it for protection. Her pale blonde hair is untidily windblown, suggesting authenticity, as though she is outdoors in the elements and not in a studio. She has pulled the flag high around her neck so that it is also across her left cheek. All that can be seen of the flag is the Union Jack. This seems deliberate, because the Union Jack – the British flag – makes up only the upper-left quarter of the Australian flag, with the remaining three-quarters blue with the stars of the Southern Cross and the federation star. The Union Jack's prominence emphasises Australia's enduring links to Britain; by displaying only the Union Jack, the image orients the viewer towards a historicism and worldview which prioritises Australia's relationship with Britain over other ties. The red of the heraldic crosses of St George and St Patrick in the Union Jack echoes the red poppy. The young woman appears warmly dressed against the night, wearing a knitted hat, also red. Its coarsely ribbed knitting suggests traditional handicrafts and practicality. The dome shape of her hat matches that of the crown directly above her.

The photograph is lit from the viewer's left, washing over the many slumbering bodies in the darkness. It makes the woman seem unusually pale, accentuating her blonde hair and the whites of her very wide eyes. Her gaze is directed upwards. She seems watchful and expectant, rather than alarmed or fearful. Her left eyebrow is raised, indicating that her attention has been captured, but the viewer cannot see what she sees.

In the background is a featureless mass of people, supine and shrouded in brightly coloured sleeping bags. Their prostration and stillness evokes the dead of a battlefield. Embodying collective memories often demands physical and cognitive participation (Connerton 1989), and participation at Camp Gallipoli is a muted form of re-enactment.

Camp Gallipoli's focus is made clear in the text included in the design: '1915–2015, Camp Gallipoli, Commemorating 100 years of Anzac Spirit.' The goal of honouring a spirit resonates with the woman's upward gaze: united with the people, protected by British ties, standing beneath the perpetual Crown and the venerated ancestors, she can focus on higher concerns. At Camp Gallipoli, a kind of domestic pilgrimage, the mystery of Anzac may come within one's grasp. Exactly what the 'Anzac spirit' is remains ambiguous, leaving people free to infer the diverse and inarguable interpretations that community solidarity seems to require.

Compare this with the second advertisement, which I saw comparatively infrequently. The common design elements allow us to infer how the organisers wished to represent Camp Gallipoli and what they believed would have popular appeal. Both feature young white females, alone, eyes gazing upwards, protectively wrapped in an Australian flag which foregrounds the Union Jack. That both figures are evidently white is instructive. Ghassan Hage argued (1998: 121) that in Australia, the dominant white majority exists as an unmarked national collective while others, including Indigenous Australians and non-European migrants, are compared with, and usually considered below, this norm. The

Figure 6.4 Second Camp Gallipoli advertisement
(Camp Gallipoli Foundation)

dominant group 'imagines the nation as "theirs"' (85), and therefore their belonging can be assumed. The woman in the advertisement belongs to Australia, and the nation belongs to her – though this version of Australianness makes particular claims on British heritage. Indeed, the participants at Camp Gallipoli Sydney were mostly white, suggesting that Camp Gallipoli's version of belonging resonates especially with white Australia. The Australian population remains significantly white, thanks in part to the country's notorious historical White Australia immigration policies. In 2016, at least 85 per cent of Australians had European ancestry, the overwhelming majority of which was Anglo-Celtic. The 2016 census results suggest that the population is becoming more diverse, with people born overseas, or who had at least one parent born overseas, making up almost half (49 per cent) of the entire population – with approximately 40 per cent of those born overseas coming from Asian countries (Australian Bureau of Statistics 2016). Further, Sydney has a greater ethnic diversity than any other Australian location.

The choice of females was also deliberate and significant; every advertisement I saw, whether online, in social media or in posters, used female figures. Were they supposed to tacitly represent the women and children on whose behalf the diggers allegedly fought? The experience of Anzac soldiering was an overwhelmingly male one, both in fact and in myth. The semantic domain of these images reveals a call for citizens to be faithful to nationalistic Anzac myths of Australianness (especially the gendered values of mateship and egalitarianism), racial hegemony, patriotism and militarism (Kapferer [1988] 2012). Scholars have analysed both monarchist and republican groups as gendered, with republican symbolism often perceived as determinedly, independently, self-sufficiently masculine, while monarchist imagery often asserts the 'feminine' comforts of powerful protection (Lake 1994; Bulbeck 1996). The image of the lone young female conforms to this apparent monarchist trope, mediated by its relationship with the British Crown.

Camp Gallipoli was a celebration of national identity that was explicitly state-sponsored. The government had endorsed the project through grants, public statements and permission to use the word Anzac in its marketing, because Camp Gallipoli's public goals aligned with government ambitions for Anzac Day. Although some had derided Camp Gallipoli as Anzackery, it accorded with what many participants described to me as the valorisation of Anzac Day. However, after two years of operation Camp Gallipoli was revealed as a commercial enterprise. The government withdrew its charitable status amid media reports that veterans' associations had received none of the promised monies from these events (Vedelago and Houston 2016). Veterans' groups severed their official relationships with the organisation. Even so, it had articulated a profoundly political project of having citizens perform, through consumption and embodiment, values that were readily endorsed by the state. Within the camp the Crown had been invisible in plain sight, unnoticed and unremarked, yet all the same lending an aura of heritage and perpetual honour to this new spin on an old ritual. The Crown's relevance persists even, or perhaps especially, when it goes unnoticed.

Refreshed Memories and Reanimated Meanings

The Crown underpinned the Anzacs in 1915, and remarkably, a century later, it was again central to contemporary Anzac rituals. However, today's Anzac ceremonies invert the meanings which characterised the first Anzac services, which were driven by citizens themselves, suspicious of the state and jingoism, ambivalent towards war, dissenting and demotic. Today, its symbolism has been radically rearranged and is far more closely associated with militarisation and patriotism. This was true at Camp Gallipoli, which was commercially offered but aligned with state ambitions. Some interviewees speculated about the relationship between the Crown and Anzac. Historian and republican Mark McKenna mused: 'We could go out on a limb and say that the irrationality of the Crown has been replaced by the irrationality of Anzac, in the sense that they're both myths for nation-defining' (Interviews, 2015). Despite contemporary antipathy towards empire and strong republican sentiment, the Crown remains essential if unrecognised in this most Australian of festivals.

As a distinctive newly invented Anzac ritual, Camp Gallipoli hones collective memory (cf. Halbwachs 1992). Its evocations help bring the past into the present for participants, enabling them to celebrate what Paul Connerton (1989) has elsewhere termed the 'continuous communal history' (17), in this case between the heroic soldiers who died at Gallipoli and today's Australians. The memorialisation asserts that all Australians can be heirs of the immortal Anzacs. Just as the Crown was strategically mobilised to help Australians reconcile themselves with the suffering and bereavements of war, today it skilfully links hegemonic ideals both to a cosmic order and back again to prosaic daily human experience (Cannadine 1992: 17). As the Crown gains legitimacy and moral authority from the sacrifices Australians made serving under it, so its presence sacralises national occasions like Anzac Day, transforming the otherwise futile loss of life on foreign soil into the productive defence of Australian soil – and perhaps, placing it in Australia's past. While Anzac Day rhetorically emphasises egalitarianism, its practices refer to distinctly hierarchical social forms including colonial conquest, military service and monarchy as expressions of an inclusive nationalism and naturalised militarism.

This state-aligned cultural nationalism seeks to bind Australians together through reciprocal obligations of the national family – and its ancestors, those exemplar citizens, the Anzacs. It minimises ethnic nationalism in an era when Australian governments stress the importance of multiculturalism. Like most nationalisms, it emphasises transcendent unity, and Camp Gallipoli rhetorically asserted its ability to unify Australians. But overwhelmingly, those who represented the Australian Crown were white, as were those at Camp Gallipoli, reinforcing Hage's (1998: 179) point that here, 'the visible and public side of power remains essentially Anglo-White'. Said one senior republican, 'If Anzac Day's going to survive and prosper, it has to be not exclusive, and certainly not racially exclusive. It has to be inclusive, and the danger is it's just a celebration of what remains of British Australia.' Those who emphasised to me the Crown's capacity to unite different peoples, such as at Anzac Day, were usually personally unlikely to be at risk of exclusion.

United under the Crown?

A few days after Camp Gallipoli I was back in Canberra. Behind the Australian War Memorial, about five minutes up Mt Ainslie, is a rocky outcrop facing the city. It feels deliberately informal after the memorial's austere architecture (the courtyard of which is lined by twenty-six stone gargoyles of native animals – and an Indigenous Australian man and woman). Above a few steps is a plaque, and nearby there is evidence of smoking ceremonies. The plaque reads, 'Remembering the Aboriginal people who served in the Australian forces'. This honours the service in both world wars of Aboriginal and Torres Strait Island soldiers. Though their enlistment was technically forbidden, they did so leaving desperately unequal circumstances, fought as British subjects, then returned to searing inequality – all many decades before they were entitled to the citizenship and voting rights accorded to other British subjects in Australia. There is no Crown here. The memorial is a dignified but insistent claim for recognising difference in Australian national identity, and that not all Australians feel unified by the Anzac legend and the Crown that underpins it.

Yet Anzac's extraordinary contemporary popularity testifies to its unifying efficacy: many found Camp Gallipoli's invitation to be joined under it appealing, and paid handsomely to participate. Attending an Anzac Day ceremony is how many Australians demonstrate pride in their citizenship. Anzac provides a forum to articulate what makes a good Australian, and its ceremonies are increasingly occasions for integrating recently arrived immigrant populations. Philosopher and monarchist Damien Freeman recognised that for previous Australian generations, 'the Crown had been a symbol of unity, and I'd suggest that Anzac provides that now' (Interviews, 2015). Significantly, the Crown remains visible, even if unseen, in Anzac rituals, and its rich symbolism still touches a nerve among the Australian public.

So what might this mean for future plans for an Australian republic? Many republican arguments revolve around issues of identity and symbolism rather than monarchy's political deficiencies. For those who would see the Crown removed from the constitution, just how to fill the symbolic void left when it vacates remains a significant problem. As writer Peter Rees observed, 'Anzac is a unifying force. And the republican cause has really failed to address that' (Interviews, 2015).

The Crown's hidden-in-plain-sight character within Anzac commemorations is only one example of how this imperial and colonial symbol has come to stand for ideas which are profoundly national and domestic.

In the Australian example, the processes of mythical construction are openly acknowledged and celebrated through the Anzac legends. As we show in Chapter 7, in other countries the Crown's 'patriation' as it is termed (a notably gendered and familial term) relies on more subtle efforts by governments and lobbyists to furnish the symbol with home-grown qualities. Further, the extent to which the Crown is perceived as indigenised or still signals colonialism is often articulated by local indigenous peoples themselves.

References

Anderson, Benedict. (1983) 2006. *Imagined Communities: Reflections on the Origin and Spread of Nationalism*. London: Verso.

Australian Bureau of Statistics. 2016. Cultural diversity in Australia, 2016. *Census of Population and Housing: Reflecting Australia – Stories from the Census, 2016*. www.abs.gov.au/ausstats/abs@.nsf/Lookup/by%20Subject/2071.0~2016~Main%20Features~Cultural%20Diversity%20Article~60.

Australian War Memorial. 2017. Hall of Memory – Stained-Glass Windows. *Australian War Memorial*. Website. Accessed 30 May 2017 at www.awm.gov.au/visit/visitor-information/features/hall-of-memory/windows

Bean, C. E. W. 1933. *Official History of Australia in the War of 1914–1918, Vol. 1: The Story of ANZAC from the Outbreak of War to the End of the First Phase of the Gallipoli Campaign, May 4, 1915*. Sydney: Angus & Robertson.

Billig, Michael. 1995. *Banal Nationalism*. London and Thousand Oaks, CA: SAGE.

Bridge, Carl. 2009. 'Anzac Day.' In *The Oxford Companion to Australian Military History*, edited by Peter Dennis. Oxford Reference Online. Oxford: Oxford University Press.

Bulbeck, Chilla. 1996. '"His and Hers Australias": National Genders.' *Journal of Australian Studies* 20(47): 43–56.

Camp Gallipoli Foundation. 2014. Camp Gallipoli Launches in NZ for Anzac Centenary Year. *Scoop Independent News*. Website. 11 December 2014. Accessed 10 January 2016 at www.scoop.co.nz/stories/CU1412/S00262/camp-gallipoli-launches-in-nz-for-anzac-centenary-year.htm.

2015a. Camp Gallipoli Forms Partnership with RSA for ANZAC Day. *Scoop Independent News*. Website. 25 January 2015. Accessed 10 January 2016 at www.scoop.co.nz/stories/CU1501/S00288/camp-gallipoli-forms-partnership-with-rsa-for-anzac-day.htm.

2015b. About Camp Gallipoli. *Camp Gallipoli Foundation*. Accessed 10 January 2016 at www.campgallipoli.com.au.

Cannadine, David. 1992. 'Introduction: Divine Rites of Kings.' In *Rituals of Royalty: Power and Ceremonial in Traditional Societies*, edited by D. Cannadine and S. Price, 1–19. Cambridge: Cambridge University Press.

Connerton, Paul. 1989. *How Societies Remember*. Cambridge: Cambridge University Press.

Connors, Jane. 2015. *Royal Visits to Australia*. Canberra: National Library of Australia.

Cryle, Mark. 2016. Making 'the One Day of the Year': A Genealogy of Anzac Day to 1918. Unpublished PhD thesis. The University of Queensland.

Durkheim, Émile. 1915. *The Elementary Forms of Religious Life*. Translated by J. Swain. London: Allen & Unwin.

Geertz, Clifford. 1980. *Negara: The Theatre State in Nineteenth-Century Bali*. Princeton, NJ: Princeton University Press.

Hage, Ghassan. 1998. *White Nation: Fantasies of White Supremacy in a Multicultural Society*. Sydney: Pluto Press.

Halbwachs, Maurice. 1992. *On Collective Memory*. Translated by L. Coser. Chicago: University of Chicago Press.

Hobsbawm, Eric and Terence Ranger. 1983. *The Invention of Tradition*. Cambridge: Cambridge University Press.

Inglis, Ken. 1965. 'The Anzac Tradition.' *Meanjin Quarterly* 24(1): 25–44.

1999. 'Anzac, the Substitute Religion.' In *Observing Australia: 1959–1999*, edited by Craig Wilcox, 61–71. Melbourne: Melbourne University Press.

Ireland, Judith. 2015. Tony Abbott Urges Australians to Turn up on Anzac Day in Wake of Terror Raids. *The Sydney Morning Herald*. 19 April 2015. Accessed 10 January 2016 at www.smh.com.au/federal-politics/political-news/tony-abbott-urges-australians-to-turn-up-on-anzac-day-in-wake-of-terror-raids-20150418-1mnv5d.html.

Kapferer, Bruce. (1988) 2012. *Legends of People, Myths of State: Violence, Intolerance, and Political Culture in Sri Lanka and Australia*. Washington, DC and London: Berghahn Books.

Lake, Marilyn. 1994. 'The Republic Sphere.' *Arena Magazine* 12: 51–52.

Leach, Edmund. 1961. *Rethinking Anthropology*. London: Athlone Press.

McAllister, Patrick. 2012. *National Days and the Politics of Indigenous and Local Identities in Australia and New Zealand*. Durham, NC: Carolina Academic Press.

McKenna, Mark. 2010. 'The Crown.' In *Symbols of Australia: Uncovering the Stories Behind Australia's Best-Loved Symbols*, edited by M. Harper and R. White, 33–37. Sydney: UNSW Press and National Museum of Australia.

McKenna, Mark and Stuart Ward. 2007. '"It Was Really Moving, Mate": The Gallipoli Pilgrimage and Sentimental Nationalism in Australia.' *Australian Historical Studies* 38(129): 141–51.

Meade, Amanda. 2015. 'SBS Sports Reporter Scott McIntyre Sacked over "Despicable" Anzac Tweets.' *The Guardian*. 26 April 2015. Accessed 10 January 2016 at www.theguardian.com/media/2015/apr/26/sbs-sports-reporter-scott-mcintyre-sacked-over-direspectful-anzac-tweets.

Murphy, Damien. 2015. 'Anzac Day Centenary: Record 30,000 Turn Out for Sydney Dawn Service.' *The Sydney Morning Herald.* 25 April. Accessed 1 May 2018 at www.smh.com.au/national/anzac-day-centenary-record-30000-turn-out-for-sydney-dawn-service-20150425-1msxvr.html.

Schwartz, Barry. 2008. 'Collective Memory and Abortive Commemoration: Presidents' Day and the American Holiday Calendar.' *Social Research* 75(1): 75–110.

Seal, Graham. 2004. *Inventing Anzac: The Digger and National Mythology.* St Lucia, Queensland: University of Queensland Press.

Serle, Geoffrey. 1967. 'Godzone: 6) Austerica Unlimited?' *Meanjin Quarterly* 26(3): 237–50.

Thomson, Alistair. 2003. 'Anzac Day.' In *The Oxford Companion to Australian History*, edited by Graeme Davison, John Hirst and Stuart Macintyre. Oxford Reference Online. South Melbourne: Oxford University Press.

Turner, Victor. 1967. *The Forest of Symbols: Aspects of Ndembu Ritual.* Ithaca, NY: Cornell University Press.

Twomey, Anne. 2006. *The Chameleon Crown: The Queen and Her Australian Governors.* Sydney: Federation Press.

Vedelago, Chris and Cameron Houston. 2016. 'Camp Gallipoli: Federal Government Orders Probe into Anzac Charity.' *The Sydney Morning Herald.* 23 April 2016. Accessed 1 May 2018 at www.smh.com.au/national/camp-gallipoli-federal-government-orders-probe-into-anzac-charity-20160423-godhjh.html.

Warhurst, John and Malcolm Mackerras (eds.). 2002. *Constitutional Politics: The Republic Referendum and the Future.* St Lucia, Queensland: University of Queensland Press.

West, Brad. 2008. 'Enchanting Pasts: The Role of International Civil Religious Pilgrimage in Reimagining National Collective Memory.' *Sociological Theory* 26(3): 258–70.

Winterton, George. 1986. *Monarchy to Republic: Australian Republican Government.* Melbourne: Oxford University Press.

7

Localising the Crown

Royals and (Re)Patriation

JAI PATEL AND SALLY RAUDON

George V, by the Grace of God, of Great Britain, Ireland and the British Dominions beyond the Seas King, Defender of the Faith, Emperor of India

Balfour Declaration 1926

The Crown, in fact, symbolises the unity and the co-operation of the freely associated members of the Commonwealth

Michael Joseph Savage, Prime Minister of New Zealand
(Business Publications 1937)

It is appropriate that we should symbolise our status showing that New Zealand is a kingdom in its own right

Attorney-General John Ross Marshall, on changes to
the New Zealand Coat of Arms (replacing the
British Lion with St Edward's Crown), 1956

Elizabeth the Second, by the Grace of God Queen of New Zealand and Her Other Realms and Territories, Head of the Commonwealth, Defender of the Faith

Royal Titles Act 1974 (NZ)

The epigraphs for this chapter illustrate the transformation of the monarchy in New Zealand. Today the Crown has quite different connotations in New Zealand than it did for Michael Joseph Savage in 1937. Then, New Zealand was not a sovereign kingdom but a dominion with equal status to other members of the British Empire and under the reign of the same singular British Monarch. This principle was codified in the 1926 Balfour Declaration, which stated that the dominions 'are autonomous Communities within the British Empire, equal in status, in no way subordinate one to another ... though united by a common allegiance to the Crown, and freely associated as members of the British Commonwealth of Nations' (Balfour Declaration 1926). However, once the dominions chose to adopt the Statute of Westminster (Canada in 1931, Australia 1942 and New Zealand 1947), they became realms with their own legal sovereign persons. The changing royal titles shown above reflect this shift. The 1927 royal title refers to George V as King of Great Britain, Ireland and the British Dominions. By 1953, Queen Elizabeth II was proclaimed as Queen of the United Kingdom of Great Britain and Northern Ireland, as well as her other realms, territories and the Commonwealth. However, in 1974, the Queen became legally known in New Zealand as the Queen *of New Zealand*.

Since the 1930s, the symbols of the British monarchy have gradually been adapted in Canada, Australia and New Zealand as each became legally separate realms with their own Crowns. During the Queen's coronation, military regiments from the various Commonwealth nations marched in the procession, and several of their prime ministers and heads of state sat in the Abbey to witness the Queen being crowned (Cannadine 1983: 153). The Queen's coronation gown featured embroidered faunal symbols of the various realms such as the Canadian maple leaf, the Australian wattle flower and the New Zealand silver fern, each of which have become powerful national symbols. Since 1967, New Zealand governors-general have been selected from among New Zealand citizens where previously they had all been British appointments. Government House, the residence of New Zealand's governor-general, has been redecorated with carved *pou* (pillars) in the official entranceway and colour schemes in the various rooms which represent native flora and fauna. A new flag was designed for the governor-general in 2008, and state rituals now include Māori elements (see Chapter 5).

This chapter focuses on this process of transformation. We ask: in what ways has this process differed between the realms? Is it a natural process of constitutional drift, or do certain actors drive it? If so, what does it achieve? The first section examines the changes made to official symbols of state in Canada, as well as efforts by monarchist organisations to construct the Crown as a distinctly Canadian institution. The second section draws on our collaborative fieldwork at a monarchist conference in New Zealand in 2015, to explore the perspectives of monarchist organisations and their attempts to shore up support for monarchy in the realms.

Once a unifying symbol of empire, the Crown has developed various local meanings and forms. We argue that monarchist organisations have played an important role in domesticating and localising the Crown. If affection for the monarchy remains high within the different realms, monarchist organisations can claim some credit for this. The monarchist conference we attended was held inside New Zealand's Parliament Buildings and organised by Simon O'Connor, an MP from the then governing National Party, which gave the impression that this was an official government event. In Australia, unlike the other realms, constitutional monarchism provided a significant pathway to political power for both John Howard and Tony Abbott (as republican politics has for Malcolm Turnbull). Just as the Crown has developed differently across the various realms, so monarchist movements have taken on different national characteristics and rationales.

'Canada Has Always Been a Monarchy'

The former colonial territories that now make up Canada came under British rule after the end of the Seven Years War (also known in North America as the French and Indian War) against France in 1763. According to the Royal Proclamation of that year, the Crown acquired sovereignty over these territories, which were to be ruled directly as colonial assets. These colonies became federated as the Dominion of Canada a century later under the British North America Act of 1867 (now known as the Constitution Act, 1867); the Dominion then comprised four provinces – Ontario, Québec, Nova Scotia and New Brunswick – but today includes ten provinces and three territories. The 1867 Act established responsible government in Canada, but still allowed the British government to amend or block legislation passed in Canada, or even to pass its own. The passing of the Statute of Westminster in Britain (which Canada adopted in the same year) made Canada a realm with complete legislative independence in all matters except for constitutional amendments. It was only with the Constitution Act of 1982 that Canada could amend its constitution without approval from Britain. This is often referred to as the 'patriation' of the constitution, as opposed to repatriation, as the constitution was not being returned – it had never previously been Canadian.

It was as the Queen of Canada that Elizabeth signed the Act in 1982 on Parliament Hill in Ottawa. The Act retained the Queen's constitutional powers and the position of the Crown as the sovereign, with her powers to be exercised only on the advice of Canadian ministers and not British ones. This had largely been the case since the adoption of the Statute of Westminster, excepting constitutional matters. It is often said that

Canada now has eleven Crowns: a federal one with a governor general[1] to represent the Queen, and a lieutenant-governor representing each of the ten provincial Crowns. The Crown in Canada is in this way distinct from the Crowns in both New Zealand and Britain, who have only one Crown (the Commonwealth of Australia also has multiple Crowns due to its federal constitution).

Transformations of state symbols have accompanied this legal evolution. For instance, in 1988, the Canadian Heraldic Authority was established, which gave the governor general the right to grant armorial bearings, a right previously held by the College of Arms in London (which still holds armorial authority in Australia and New Zealand). According to the Monarchist League of Canada (hereafter MLC), this authority was 'patriated so that they [arms] would more clearly be the gift of the Canadian Crown' (MLC 2012: 24). Numerous arms of state institutions, such as the Canadian Armed Forces, the Territory of Nunavut, and the Royal Canadian Mounted Police, incorporate national symbols – like maple leaves, narwhals and bison – but are topped by the St Edward's Crown, giving the Canadian Crown an omnipresent quality that is enmeshed with local identity. Canada was the first of the realms to have unique flags for members of the Royal Family to recognise their roles as members of the Canadian Royal Family (Government of Canada 2017a).

However, there have recently been strong efforts, both within the Canadian government and by monarchist lobbyists, to assert that the Canadian Crown is unique in other ways. For instance, in recognition of Queen Elizabeth's sixtieth jubilee in 2015, then Prime Minister Stephen Harper stated:

> The Crown is a symbol of our unique Canadian identity, and a fundamental institution not just in our system of government, but in our very way of life. It embodies our rich traditions of parliamentary democracy, freedom and justice – the values under which we thrive; the values that we love.
>
> (MacLeod 2015: v)

This statement comes from a letter in the frontmatter of *A Crown of Maples: Constitutional Monarchy in Canada*, a governmental publication that depicts the Crown as not merely a Canadian institution from a legal or political perspective, but also as one strongly connected to national

[1] In Canada, unlike New Zealand and Australia, the term governor general is spelled without a hyphen.

identity. Significantly, while this was an official publication of state, its lead author is Kevin MacLeod, a monarchist and former Canadian secretary to the Queen (see later). The MLC, a monarchist lobby established in 1970, states that the Queen 'is the representation of all Canada within one person . . . she promotes "all that is best and most admired in the Canadian ideal"' (MLC 2012: 3). Such assertions depart significantly from the constitutional arrangements prescribed by law or the tinkering with official state symbols. How do monarchists come to see the Crown as a Canadian institution, and the Queen as the embodiment of the Canadian ideal?

According to Canadian monarchists, much of the monarchy's appeal and relevance comes from its deep historical roots. They believe that 'Canada has always been a monarchy' (MLC 2012: 4). This notion recognises that Canada in fact has two monarchical lines, as the French monarch ruled over parts of Canada until the Treaty of Paris was signed in 1763 (MLC 2012: 30). Moreover, they claim that the Canadian monarchy echoes indigenous forms of political organisation:

> Many Aboriginal groups were headed by a chieftain who was advised by a council of elders, not unlike the series of French and British monarchs in whose name the original colonies of North America were founded. Although not all Aboriginal communities were governed in this way, the concept of monarchy has never been 'foreign' to the inhabitants of Canada.
>
> (MLC 2012: 4)

Furthermore, many claim that Canadians actively chose constitutional monarchy as their form of government. During the 1864 Québec Conference, attendees (known as the 'Fathers of Confederation') unanimously agreed that Canada should select a constitutional monarchy as the guiding framework for the new state. As *The Crown of Maples* asserts:

> Canada thus did not have monarchy forced upon it. Rather, the Fathers of Confederation understood the key role that the Crown played – and would continue to play – in bringing the colonies together as one country. . . . the Fathers were continuing the long and proud tradition of maintaining an institution that was relevant, valued, and traced its very roots to the beginnings of Canada itself.
>
> (MacLeod 2015: 7)

Monarchists also depict Canada as a historical refuge for Crown subjects. When the American War of Independence in 1783 culminated in a republic south of the border, Canada received tens of thousands of

Loyalist migrants, which 'served to further deepen the attachment between the Crown and people' (MacLeod 2015: 6). The Crown remains an important element for differentiating Canada from its neighbour, the United States – a point frequently mentioned in our Canadian interviews. Canadian monarchists often fear that the cultural and economic strength of the United States threatens to 'overwhelm Canada's national identity' (MLC 2016a). They argue that:

> Every nation needs to understand and foster the existence of distinct images and institutions; thus for Canada, constitutional monarchy is of particular importance . . . Its focus of loyalty and allegiance to a respected monarch, and so to our system of governance, rather than to a politician, an ideology, a symbol or a single document, underlies the notably tolerant, mature society which is a source of pride for all Canadians.
>
> (MLC 2016a)

They also claim that the monarchy sits at the very fount of Canada's most significant and visible symbols of national identity – the Maple Leaf flag. While the maple leaf itself has been a national symbol of increasing importance since the eighteenth century (when it appeared on coats of arms and coins), the national colours, red and white, originate from a Royal Proclamation by King George V in 1921 (Government of Canada 2017b). The new flag design was also confirmed by a Royal Proclamation by the Queen in 1965. For these reasons, monarchists portray the adoption of the Maple Leaf flag as an affirmation of the Canadian Crown.

'Homecomings, Not Visits': The Queen and Royal Tours

Efforts to construct the Crown as something central to Canadian identity are most clearly illustrated in royal tours. First, Canada has been by far the biggest recipient of royal tours since Queen Elizabeth II took the throne. She has visited twenty-two times since 1952, participating in important events like Canada's centenary celebrations in 1967; the opening of the 1976 Montréal Olympics; the proclamation of the Constitution Act on Parliament Hill in 1982; and her own Golden Jubilee in 2002. She has visited other nations in her capacity of Queen of Canada: in 1959 she visited the United States and in 2007 she visited France to rededicate the Canadian National Vimy Memorial (which commemorates the Battle of Vimy Ridge in 1917, regarded as a watershed moment for Canadian national identity) (MLC 2016b). The Department of Canadian Heritage, which organises royal tours, has even sought to focus tours around particular themes that resonate with nationhood: for example, the Queen's 2010 visit centred around the hundredth anniversary of the Royal Canadian Navy, and strongly emphasised service to the national community (MacLeod 2015: 56).

Canadian monarchists have made strenuous efforts to brand royal tours as 'homecomings': they argue that 'our Royal Family does not "visit" . . . as, for instance, the monarch or president of a foreign country might do. Instead, they come home to one of The Queen's realms – and feel very much at home here' (MLC 2016c). The Queen herself has promoted this notion. After her 1951 visit to Canada as Princess Elizabeth, she explained that '[f]rom the moment when I first set foot on Canadian soil, the feeling of strangeness went, for I knew myself to be not only amongst friends, but amongst fellow countrymen' (MacLeod 2015: 3). As she prepared to visit Canada in 1983 following a trip to the United States, she told President Ronald Reagan that 'I am going home to Canada tomorrow' (MacLeod 2015: 46). Even Prince Charles, her heir, stated in 1996 that '[e]very time I come to Canada, and I've been here many times since 1970, a little more of Canada seeps into my bloodstream and, from there, straight into my heart' (The Royal Household 2018).

Finally, monarchists claim that the Crown has come to resonate with First Nations in Canada, adding a completely indigenous dimension to the institution (see Chapter 4). Most notably, the Royal Proclamation of 1763, in which First Nations ceded sovereignty and secured land-use rights and fiduciary obligations, has taken on renewed significance in Crown/indigenous relations and reconciliation efforts over recent decades. Despite the ongoing negotiations between the Crown and First Nations, the Monarchist League of Canada argues that 'the prestige of the Crown stands behind the promise of the treaties. Its relationship with Aboriginal Canadians continues to this day' (2012: 14). This relationship appears valued by many First Nations peoples themselves, as is illustrated by their interactions with members of the Royal Family during their 'homecomings': in 2009, then lieutenant governor of British Columbia, Steven Point (who was also a former chief of the Skowkale First Nation), presented Prince Charles with a talking stick and a Coast Salish First Nation cedar headband; in 2011, Prince William and Catherine participated in a Mi'kmaq smudging ceremony; and in 2005, the Queen presented the First Nations University of Canada with a stone tablet sourced from Buckingham Palace, which she explained was given 'in the hope that it will serve as a reminder of the special relationship between the Sovereign and all First Nations people' (MacLeod 2015: 13). During his time as lieutenant governor Point also bequeaved several gifts for the people of British Columbia: he erected a totem in the Government House garden, wrote a song and made a hand-carved dug-out cedar canoe named Shxwtitostel which now lives on display at the British Columbia legislature (Figure 7.1) According to monarchist and constitutional expert Nathan Tidridge, '[p]erhaps the most "Canadian" aspect of the Crown in these lands is its ability to act as a conduit between communities, as well as a gatherer of community' (Tidridge 2016).

Canadian monarchists' efforts are somewhat unique in their focus on the Crown as an inherently local institution. For instance, monarchists in New Zealand often emphasised their interest in the monarchy as a superior political form, one that promotes and safeguards democratic practice. For Sean Palmer, chair of Monarchy New Zealand, it is not some mystical democratic ethos that maintains the stability of the state, but the constitutional role of the monarch. For him the Crown 'is very much tied into the nature of democracy', and the monarch was 'raised

Figure 7.1 Shxwtitostel, the canoe carved by Steven Point (Stó:lō Nation) while Lieutenant Governor of British Columbia as a gift to the province's people (Cris Shore)

believing that it was their responsibility to uphold the constitution' (Palmer, Interviews, 2015). Simon O'Connor, National Party MP and former chair of Monarchy New Zealand, was quick to distinguish himself as a 'constitutional monarchist' as opposed to a royalist (someone who supports the monarchy for its ceremony and character alone):

> Royalists will say 'Oooh, it's the Queen – give me the biscuit tin and the commemorative mug'. Personally, I couldn't care less. I'm not worried by the personalities. It's the structure which works for a variety of reasons . . . [it provides] . . . good solid functioning democracy. That's why I'm a constitutional monarchist.
>
> (O'Connor, Interviews, 2015)

Canadian monarchists are perhaps able to make the strongest claims on the Queen as local embodiment of the nation and the state. She certainly has visited Canada more than any other realm, and there are strong official statements of affection and kinship between her and the Canadian public. And while monarchists in Australia and New Zealand actively pursue the goal of localising their monarchies, our research found a diversity of monarchist responses to the different meanings that the Crown holds in these realms. In 2016, Neil James, a senior member of Australians for a Constitutional Monarchy (ACM), publicly branded the Australian Monarchist League (AML) as 'royalists' who are far too interested in personalities in comparison with 'reasoned constitutional monarchists' like himself (Iggulden 2016). Moreover, considering the colonial history of Australia, it is striking that neither ACM nor the AML focus on the importance of the Crown for indigenous issues in the manner of monarchists in New Zealand or Canada (see Chapter 4 for discussion of the Crown in Australia).

The Australian Counter-Example

The Australian Crown has not been as successfully localised as the Crowns of Canada and New Zealand. Although Queen Elizabeth has been styled Queen of Australia since 1973, many Australians see the Crown primarily as representing the British monarchy; indeed, republicans often emphasise this in nationalistic appeals for reform. However, that has not stopped two prominent members of Australians for Constitutional Monarchy from making the case that the Crown is Australian. Throughout the constitutional reform debates of the 1990s, future prime minister Tony Abbott consistently called for 'keeping the Crown in the

Australian system of Government without relying on any appeal to "British-ness"' (Abbott 1997: 6). Abbott believed that 'the Australian Crown has become egalitarian and democratic in a way the British Crown never has' (95). The Crown, he asserted, had shed its English elitism, class associations and formality to become as woven into the Australian national character as cricket, rugby and Shakespeare (105). David Flint (1999) argued that the Crown, like the English language and the rule of law, 'is as Australian as our beaches and our forests' (49). In an interview, he elaborated that 'If the Crown is an anachronism, so is Parliament, so is the rule of law, so is the English language, because all of those came with Governor Phillip!' (Interviews, 2015). Australia's other monarchist group, the Australian Monarchist League, also has a discourse of the Crown as Australian but undermines this rhetoric with practices celebrating the explicitly British nature of the Crown in Australia, such as holding events in Anglican churches and furnishing royal-watching crowds with Union Jacks.

Efforts to localise the Crown in Australia began early but often carried an ambivalence that ultimately resolved in favour of the status quo, as demonstrated by two creative efforts to develop a distinctively Australian currency using local symbols. Today, coins and banknotes throughout the Commonwealth still bear the image of a crowned monarch as a sign of sovereign authority. Australia's first official gold coin was a sovereign made at the Sydney Mint between 1855 and 1870. On the reverse side was the word 'Australia' (a remarkable assertion of nationhood given that the continent's independent colonies would not federate as Australia until 1901). The obverse side was engraved with a youthful Queen Victoria crowned, from 1857, with native banksia. This was produced until 1871 when the Mint received instructions from London to remove the banksia crown. Then, between 1919 and 1921 the Melbourne Mint experimented with small square coins of light alloy metals. The obverse side shows an uncrowned King George V, with the reverse engraved with a kookaburra (a large native kingfisher bird known for its 'laughing' call). Much criticised for its irreverence, light weight and unconventional shape, the 'Kookaburra Penny' apparently lacked the gravitas required for currency and was never issued into circulation.

If symbolic attempts to localise the monarchy proved difficult, the monarch's lack of presence in Australia is equally problematic. Republicans often emphasise that an Australian head of state should reside in Australia, which would disqualify the Queen. Prince Charles had spent six months at an Australian high school and consistently claims strong personal ties to Australia, even expressing interest in becoming Australia's governor-general (Atkinson 1993: 89–93). The Royal Family began visiting regularly again during the 1990s, and in efforts to display their cultural competence, Royals are often seen connecting with Australian lands, traditions and national ceremonies. Several monarchists emphasised the good relationships between Royals and Aboriginal Australians (a point not always supported by our indigenous interviewees) and stressed that royal visits always included some time in an indigenous Australian community, often in a remote area. However, these rituals fall short of autochthony: this is not an attempt to indigenise the Crown but rather a marking of sovereign territory according to some 'exemplary and mimetic' (Geertz 1983: 134) symbolic order. If the Queen's habitual sequestration from Australia underscores the Britishness of the Crown, her occasional presence in Australia has strategic political effect. Britishness remains part of the Crown's significance in Australia.

Localising and Patriating the Crown: A Monarchist Conference Observed

Emulating Canada's success in localising the Crown was a central goal for the 2015 conference 'Constitutional Monarchy in the Commonwealth Realms' in New Zealand. The event was organised by Sean Palmer, who worked in the office of MP Simon O'Connor. Palmer was the chair, and O'Connor the former chair, of Monarchy New Zealand, a small lobby group founded in 1995 that aims to 'celebrate and support' the monarchy, 'to promote, and engage in' research around it and to educate New Zealanders as to its importance (Monarchy New Zealand 2015).

Held in the old Legislative Chamber in the Parliament Building, this was an opportunity for politicians, officials, academics and the public to engage in discussions around the functions of constitutional monarchies. Some attendees brought an academic approach to relatively obscure constitutional matters, and some were drawn by what seemed a general non-partisan interest in constitutional affairs. However, it was by no means a non-partisan event. For instance, most attendees and presenters identified as monarchists, often bemoaning the declining support for the monarchy in their countries. No critiques of constitutional monarchies were offered and republicanism was mentioned dismissively and only in passing. There was also a notable networking between monarchists from across the realms. Sean Palmer shared stories about the conference's origins in his meetings with other monarchists overseas. Members of Australians for Constitutional Monarchy were present, after one session we found pamphlets from the Monarchist League of Canada on our table, and we shared the company of several young members of Monarchy New Zealand who had volunteered to help run the proceedings. However, we did notice that the Australian Monarchist League (AML) had not been invited, much to their irritation. One delegate referred to the AML as 'those divisive diamonds-and-pearls people'.

An important guest was Kevin MacLeod, then Canadian secretary to the Queen of Canada, who advised his government on royal ceremony, protocol, tours and vice-regal appointments. MacLeod shared epic accounts of his victories in promoting the monarchy as a Canadian institution – for instance, when he succeeded in having a six-foot portrait of the Queen installed in the Parliament Buildings. He emphasised at length that when Royals come to Canada, they are on royal tours, not visits, because they are Canadians, not foreigners. His efforts have been central to localising the Canadian monarchy. In fact, MacLeod told us, 'that's why Simon [O'Connor] brought me down [to New Zealand]'. In his presentation, he stated that today, 'the Crown is uniquely Canadian' – it is 'an essential building block of Canadian culture'.

O'Connor admitted that the aim of the conference was to 'look at what certain countries are doing, and how we can learn from one another'. In his view, New Zealand needed 'to use the Royal Family more. They are there to serve us and that's their role … [we should get] our Royal Family to engage with things that are Kiwi, you know, have a *hāngi* [food cooked on heated stones] and a beer.' Monarchists often referred to these processes as 'patriation', referring to the patriation of the Canadian constitution. While the monarchy has been a factor of life in the realms since colonisation, it was a rather omnipresent entity that stood over all the realms at once – the Crown being patriated is a local one, not an imperial one.

This purpose of the conference became even clearer during one of the keynote presentations by University of Auckland political scientist Jennifer Lees-Marshment, who spoke on 'marketing the modern monarchy'. As a British expatriate and expert in political marketing, she stressed the importance of 'face-to-face' engagement to improve the 'brand experience' of the monarchy, that is, to encourage national connection with royal bodies. For instance, she suggested that Plunket clinics, the largest provider of healthcare in New Zealand to children under five, could celebrate royal births with new mothers.

Lees-Marshment pressed the need to make royal occasions nationally significant, and asserted that 'what we need to do is find our own Kiwi versions of these rituals.' Later, Lees-Marshment also suggested that one way to keep the connection up would be to have more royal tours or, when the next monarch is crowned, 'have a service as a commemoration here, where you would have a live stream or connection. You need to have the events to market here, street parties, that kind of thing' (Interviews, 2015). Her presentation inspired an inventive conversation during a workshop on patriating the Crown: someone even noted that the role of vice-regal offices developed out of a problem of geographical distance between colony and metropole, but with advances in communication technology some vice-regal duties could, and should, be handed back to the Queen!

One young member of Monarchy New Zealand, who defined himself as politically left-wing, told me during a coffee break that 'I wouldn't be a monarchist if the monarchy wasn't able to evolve'. He pointed to the Royal Succession Act 2013, which removed the male right of primogeniture, and the announcing of the birth of Princess Charlotte over Twitter. For these monarchists, the Crown also adapts to changing cultural forces: note the title of Monarchy New Zealand's journal, *Crown and Koru* (an unfurling fern frond, a symbol prominent in Māori culture and now popularly associated with national identity – not to mention the brand logo for the national airline Air New Zealand).

Conclusion

The twentieth century was an extraordinary era for the British Crown. Through decades of constitutional development and the rise of national independence, what was once indivisible became several separate Crowns, which share the same physical person, Queen Elizabeth, as their embodied representative. These legal steps were taken by the other realms to achieve legislative independence from the United Kingdom. Republicans continue to call on this notion of independence (see Chapter 8). Since the division of the British Crown, symbols of state and monarchy throughout the realms have been transformed to accommodate this pursuit of legislative independence. This is visible in the current titles and flags that each realm has for their own sovereign, in the combination of local symbols with crowns on armorial bearings, and in the honours systems that recognise national service in the name of the Queen.

It would be a mistake to dismiss these alterations as simple attempts to avoid dealing with larger questions around republicanism by making monarchical symbols palatable to postcolonial sensibilities. Rather, monarchists see such action as an exercise of independence, or the act of an independent realm. For instance, Sean Palmer (Canadian by birth) related a story to me about a discussion he had with a journalist where he was asked whether Australia, compared to Canada and New Zealand, had advanced most (towards independence, referring to the 1999 republic referendum). He told the journalist:

> No, I think that's ridiculous, actually. I think the most developed of all the realms is Canada, in terms of what they have achieved in making the Crown a Canadian institution. . . . New Zealand, actually, is the second most successful realm in nationalising it. And then Australia is actually quite distant because . . . the general public treat it as though it is a very British institution.
>
> (Interviews, 2015)

Palmer talked about how both Canada and New Zealand have their own flags for *their own* Queens. For him, independence was not about abandoning the monarchy and becoming a republic; it was about emphasising that it is a local institution.

During the British Raj, there were three ceremonies held (in 1877, 1903 and 1911) known as durbars, which commemorated the coronation of the new monarch. They recreated the Westminster ritual through a Mughal lens to express the nature of sovereignty in India, which otherwise may not have carried over into the Indian context, at least not with the same efficacy. One lesson here is that the monarchy, or sovereign authority, needs to be celebrated in ways that are locally relevant to people from heterogeneous cultural backgrounds. Perhaps because white settler states like Australia, New Zealand and Canada had stronger cultural affinities with Britain, local and more multicultural ways of celebrating and understanding the Crown have only recently become necessary with the recognition of diversity as a fact of modern national identity.

Canadian monarchists are not simply attempting to mould the Crown to fit national identity or legitimise the Crown by attaching to it symbols of nationhood: rather, they see the Crown as an inherently Canadian institution that lies at the heart of national identity – just as the British monarchists we interviewed saw the Crown in Britain as a fundamental element of British history. It would be much harder to argue the same in

Australia or New Zealand. Indeed, some British monarchists reflected that the Australian example had taught them about the risks of complacency. Yet the monarchy in Australia and New Zealand has also acquired its own unique meanings, and monarchists must therefore argue their case according to different rationales.

These symbolic shifts, which reflect the constitutional realities of realms that are now separate entities from Britain, are nonetheless actively contested, particularly by political actors with strong republican beliefs. In all three of the jurisdictions outside of Britain there has been notable oscillation between continuing and discontinuing the trappings of British monarchy. In 2009, the Harper government in Canada made the position of Canadian secretary to the Queen a full-time role (Office of the Prime Minister 2009). While it had existed for more than fifty years, the responsibilities of the position were always tacked onto other portfolios. However, when the new Trudeau Liberal government took power in 2015, the role was left vacant after MacLeod retired (Beeby 2017). In 2017, the new government took down the portrait of the Queen that the previous Harper government had installed in the Department of Global Affairs in 2011 (Beeby 2017). In Australia, Bob Hawke's Labor government removed knighthoods in 1986. These were subsequently reinstated by the monarchist Tony Abbott in 2014, only to be removed again the following year by his republican Liberal Party successor, Malcolm Turnbull. During this brief period one of the three people to be awarded this knighthood was Prince Philip. In New Zealand, the Supreme Court sat for the first time in 2004 – as a symbol of independence, it replaced the right to petition the Judicial Committee based in London, yet was actually opened by Prince William. In the next chapter we explore the other side of this symbolic jostling: we ask, how do republicans contest the monarchy? Which of the realms is most likely to move towards a republican constitution? What are the strengths and weaknesses of republican arguments? And how difficult is it to find alternatives to the symbols of monarchy?

References

Abbott, Tony. 1997. *How to Win the Constitutional War and Give Both Sides What They Want.* Adelaide: Australians for Constitutional Monarchy in association with Wakefield Press.

Atkinson, Alan. 1993. 'The Australian Monarchy: Imperfect but Important.' *Australian Journal of Political Science* 28(4): 67–82.

Beeby, Dean. 2017. 'Liberals Leave Royal Position Vacant in Queen's Sapphire Jubilee Year.' *CBC News.* September 19. Accessed 21 March 2018 at www.cbc.ca/news/politics/queen-canadian-secretary-royal-visits-heritage-1.4295322.

Business Publications. 1937. *New Zealand Official Souvenir Programme of the Coronation of His Majesty King George VI.* Dunedin, New Zealand: Business Publications.

Cannadine, David. 1983. 'The Context, Performance and Meaning of Ritual: The British Monarchy and the "Invention of Tradition", c. 1820–1977.' In *The Invention of Tradition*, edited by Eric Hobsbawm and Terence Ranger, 101–64. Cambridge and New York: Cambridge University Press.

Flint, David. 1999. *The Cane Toad Republic: Why to Vote No.* Kent Town, South Australia: Wakefield Press.

Geertz, Clifford. 1983. *Local Knowledge: Further Essays in Interpretive Anthropology.* New York: Basic Books.

Government of Canada. 2017a. 'Canadian Flags of the Royal Family.' Web page. Accessed 18 March 2018 at www.canada.ca/en/canadian-heritage/services/royal-symbols-titles/canadian-flags-royal-family.html.

2017b. 'Official Symbols of Canada.' Web page. Accessed 18 March 2018 at www.canada.ca/en/canadian-heritage/services/official-symbols-canada.html.

Iggulden, Tom. 2016. 'Monarchists Split in Wake of Latest Republic Push, David Flint Urged to Stand Down.' *ABC.* Accessed 22 March 2018 at www.abc.net.au/news/2016-01-27/monarchists-compete-for-traction-david-flint-republic/7116130.

MacLeod, Kevin. 2015. *A Crown of Maples: Constitutional Monarchy in Canada.* Gatineau, QC: Department of Canadian Heritage.

MLC (Monarchist League of Canada). 2012. *The Canadian Monarchy.* Monarchist League of Canada: Oakville, Ontario.

2016a. 'The Case for the Crown: A Crown for the 21st Century: Arguments in Support of Canada's Constitutional Monarchy.' Web page. Accessed 18 March 2018 at www.monarchist.ca/index.php/our-monarchy/canada-s-monarchy/the-case-for-the-crown.

2016b. 'The Queen & the Duke of Edinburgh.' Web page. Accessed 18 March 2018 at www.monarchist.ca/index.php/our-monarchy/our-royal-family/the-queen-of-canada.

2016c. 'The Queen's Representatives in Canada.' Web page. Accessed 18 March 2018 at www.monarchist.ca/index.php/students-and-teachers/canada-s-monarchy/the-queen-s-representatives-in-canada.

Monarchy New Zealand. 2015. Homepage. Accessed 5 January 2015 at www.monarchy.org.nz.

Office of the Prime Minister. 2009. 'Prime Minister Stephen Harper Announces the Appointment of Kevin MacLeod as Canadian Secretary to the Queen.'

News release, 1 April. Accessed 20 March 2018 at www.canada.ca/en/news/archive/2009/04/prime-minister-stephen-harper-announces-appointment-kevin-macleod-canadian-secretary-queen.html.

The Royal Household. 2018. 'Canada: History and Present Government.' Web page. Accessed 19 March 2018 at www.royal.uk/canada.

Tidridge, Nathan. 2016. 'The Key Role of the Queen and Her Representatives in Reconciliation.' *The Public Policy and Governance Review*. Web page. Accessed 19 March 2018 at ppgreview.ca/2016/03/19/the-key-role-of-the-queen-and-her-representatives-in-reconciliation/.

PART III

The Crown and Constitutional Reform

8

The Republican Move

Cutting Colonial Ties?

JAI PATEL

As part of their 2014 tour of New Zealand, Prince William and Kate, the Duke and Duchess of Cambridge, visited Auckland, also known as the 'City of Sails'. Auckland played host to the America's Cup sailing regatta in both 1999 and 2003 and is scheduled to host it again in 2021. Thousands of yacht masts dot the cityscape, moored at marinas or cruising around the harbour. Larger yachts belonging to the national sailing team, Team New Zealand, who enjoy wide support from the public, are often seen practicing as you pass over the Auckland Harbour Bridge. William and Kate were to visit Team New Zealand as part of their tour, and a media frenzy ensued as the royal couple tacked up and down the harbour in a head-to-head race.

The visit was part of a well-orchestrated attempt to showcase the Royal Family's engagement with local institutions and passions, infusing the imagery of the monarchy with nationalist sentiment. Recent royal visits have occurred at an unprecedented rate (there have been four since 2012); Prime Minister John Key explained that 'future visits should occur more regularly than in the past, to build on the close and special links between New Zealand and Their Royal Highnesses' (Beehive 2015). This particular stunt reinforced that message: here were two royals, one a future monarch, supporting and participating in a sport that many New Zealanders love – that is, they were being Kiwis (a colloquial term for New Zealanders). It is this domestication of the royals that monarchists in New Zealand see as vital for the future of the current constitutional arrangements (see also Chapter 7).

However, as the Duke and Duchess sailed, a small plane flew above the harbour dragging a banner proclaiming: 'Time for a Kiwi Head of State' (Figure 8.1). The statement was made by New Zealand Republic, an organisation established in 1994 that campaigns to have a republic in

Figure 8.1 A small aircraft, sponsored by New Zealand Republic, tows a sign reading 'Time for a Kiwi head of state' above Prince William and Catherine, Duchess of Cambridge as they sail with Team New Zealand in Waitemata Harbour in Auckland; 11 April 2014
(Michael Bradley/AFP/Getty Images)

place of the constitutional monarchy. They believe that the head of state should be an elected New Zealand citizen rather than a British monarch, as only a citizen is capable of truly representing the nation. In a sense, they were using the same sentiment to contest the monarchy as was being used officially to legitimise or naturalise it as a local institution. Where monarchists would point out that the royal couple were performing Kiwi identity, the image that New Zealand Republic's banner evoked was of the monarchy as something foreign, irrelevant and outdated.

Whenever royals visit New Zealand, details of where and when to catch them and photos of the visitors shaking hands with delighted crowds are front-page features in the news media. However, no tour passes without reference to republicanism and a recycling of soundbites about the royals being 'a bit of an anachronism' (RNZ 2015) or 'a colonial hangover' (*New Zealand Herald* 2014a). As bold as these statements are, they appear to have little resounding effect on public support for republicanism. It remains a marginal political discourse in New Zealand, especially in comparison with Australia, which has a well-established republican lobby. New Zealand Republic remains the most prominent permanent organisation but receives little public attention outside of the profile provided by royal tours.

Despite this, politicians across the political divide often describe New Zealand becoming a republic as a certainty. In the 1980s, Labour prime minister David Lange proclaimed that 'New Zealand will become a republic just as Britain will be blurred into Europe' (Stuff 2016b). This was echoed in the 1990s by Prime Minister Jim Bolger, who stated that 'the tide of history is moving in one direction' (New Zealand Parliamentary Debates 1994). Prime Minister Helen Clark, in her valedictory speech some 20 years later, declared: 'It is inevitable that our constitutional status as a monarchy will also change. It's a question of not if, but when' (*New Zealand Herald* 2010a). More recently, former prime minister and self-confessed monarchist John Key said, 'I think in my heart of hearts it probably is inevitable it will happen' but conceded that it probably would not happen during his lifetime (Newshub 2014). These prime ministerial prophesies raise interesting questions: why is it assumed that republicanism is inevitable when so little progress has been made in the decades since Lange? Are the realms of New Zealand, Canada and Australia all bound to become republics and, if so, when and how, and who might be first?

In this chapter, I examine the rationales of organised republicanism in New Zealand. First, I discuss New Zealand Republic's project to change the head of state to fit their idea of national identity. I contrast this with efforts by Sir Geoffrey Palmer, constitutional lawyer and former prime minister and attorney-general, along with Andrew Butler, legal scholar and former Crown counsel, to reform constitutional arrangements in favour of a more rational, accountable and republican system of government. I also consider some of the obstacles to republican reform in New Zealand, Canada and Australia. I then ask: how easy it is to create new symbols, to replace the Crown with another symbol, like the state? How easily can political symbols be made to serve nationalist ends?

I make three main arguments. First, despite the claimed inevitability of republicanism in the realms, republican reform in Canada and Australia is extraordinarily difficult to achieve due to these countries' stringent requirements for constitutional change and complex federal systems. While constitutional reform in New Zealand is by no means common or straightforward, it is certainly easier from a legal point of view, and for that reason, New Zealand may be the first to become a republic. Second, I complicate this prediction by highlighting the challenges raised by the unique place of the Crown in New Zealand and its association with the Treaty of Waitangi (the Treaty). Third, I suggest that as inevitable and rational as republicanism claims to be, the symbolic transformation it requires is far more complicated, and this element is something that republican reformers typically underestimate.

'Not the New Zealand Way'

Republicanism, for New Zealand Republic, is primarily about bringing constitutional arrangements into line with their perception of nationhood. This is not so much a matter of improving political or constitutional processes as finding an appropriate way to represent the nation at the highest level. In a news article after the Duke and Duchess of Cambridge had left the country in 2014, the chair of New Zealand Republic, (Mr.) Savage (who legally has only one name), wrote:

> Traditions are a good thing, but some traditions are exclusionary and no longer serve our needs. New Zealand is more diverse than ever before and our head of state needs to reflect contemporary values and embrace future trends. . . . Only a New Zealander, who lives in New Zealand, can properly serve us as our head of state . . . It is not the New Zealand way that someone should be born into public office.
>
> (*New Zealand Herald* 2014b)

Here, Savage invokes an imagined national character – the 'New Zealand way' – which the head of state ought to embody. Though numerous values may be attributed to the 'New Zealand way', in this case he is referring specifically to the notion that New Zealanders value egalitarianism, which is incompatible with succession to office by birthright, especially by someone born in another country. Dean Knight, legal scholar and the constitutional advisor for New Zealand Republic, told me that 'the sovereign, the monarch we have got is not a symbol of "New Zealandness". . . . In a formal sense they might be the head of the Realm of New Zealand, Queen of New Zealand. . . . But they are not Kiwis!' (Knight, Interviews, 2015).

One of the key markers of national allegiance in New Zealand is which sport and team you support. For instance, rugby is often described as a national religion, a marker of egalitarianism and of Kiwi masculinity (Phillips 1984). Knight used this notion to point out how he thinks the monarchy is an inadequate embodiment of New Zealand identity. He described to me how at the Rugby World Cup in 2015:

> Prince William, you know, the doyen of all the monarchists in New Zealand, is going to be wearing the red rose of England. . . . it is who they are, it's where they come from of course, it's where their heart is, but it tells you what a part-time foreigner they are in that role [as New Zealand head of state].
>
> (Knight, Interviews, 2015)

For Knight, the royals' inability to reflect 'New Zealandness' arises from their being 'part-time foreigners', neither born nor raised in New Zealand, and never having spent enough time there to truly understand what it means to be a New Zealander. He draws an image of the second in line to the throne at the Rugby World Cup (an event close to the heart of millions of New Zealanders) wearing his true identity on his literal sleeve, to show the incomprehensibility of indigenising a royal family that is equally loyal to sixteen different realms simultaneously. It is exactly this symbolic dissonance – between the monarchy of New Zealand in the formal sense and the lived realities of the British Royal Family – that events like royal tours and organisations like Monarchy New Zealand seek to resolve.

On the face of it, New Zealand Republic are not campaigning for radical political reform. They advocate for a referendum process that would ask New Zealanders whether they want an independent head of state, with the same powers and duties, in place of the current monarch. Essentially this would involve promoting the governor-general. Knight reiterated that their aim is simply to 'cut ties with the British sovereign', which speaks to a coming-of-age narrative that has its roots in the colonial experience and culminates in a republic which signals 'New Zealand's independence and maturity to the world' (New Zealand Republic 2015). This sort of teleological argument is central to the republican cause and is often articulated through the imagery of medieval anachronism. For instance, Savage told me that 'New Zealand has been around long enough now for us to have our own traditions, and for us to understand our democracy without having to refer back to some past pre–New Zealand tyranny' (Savage, Interviews, 2015). The notion that the monarchy's time has run out, or that the wheels of history have moved on, is articulated in the banner that New Zealand Republic flew above the sailing royals, and in Savage's claim that 'our head of state needs to reflect contemporary values and embrace future trends'. This sort of construction conceptualises the nation as modern but somehow held back by its archaic symbols of government, holding up republicanism as the final stage for the realisation of independent nationhood. Part of the aim in this chapter is to disrupt this assumed teleology (which, as seen earlier in this chapter, has also been championed by major political figures under the notion of inevitability) by drawing attention to the practical and symbolic obstacles to republicanism.

The first question to be asked is: how would one appoint a republican head of state? One of the central tenets of monarchy is that the successor to the throne is identified long before the current monarch dies; a republican model, however, demands a new mechanism for selecting a new head of state when the current head of state's term comes to an end. Both Knight and Savage indicated that they have made recent efforts to simplify their model of republicanism (they also recently changed their name from the Republican Movement of New Zealand to New Zealand Republic to place emphasis on the nation rather than a political ideology). They believe that election via a supermajority of 75 per cent in Parliament would be the best way to appoint a new head of state. This position is in part inspired by the difficulties republicanism has faced in Australia. The Australian republican movement, while much larger than in New Zealand, was stunted by the failure of the 1999 republic referendum. Many have claimed that the primary cause of its defeat was that monarchists, including the then prime minister, were able to split the republican vote between those who favoured a direct popular vote of the head of state versus those who favoured a parliamentary appointment. Parliamentary appointment may be the simplest and most effective way of appointing a head of state but risks political partisanship on the part of those appointed. On the other hand, there is a risk that the public might perceive a directly elected head of state to have a democratic mandate to disrupt the normal workings of parliamentary government.

Despite New Zealand Republic's efforts to simplify the debate, New Zealanders appear to be split on how best to appoint a republican head of state. A 2016 poll showed that while 59 per cent of respondents favoured having a New Zealand head of state instead of the Queen's successor (compared to 34 per cent in favour of retaining the monarchy), of those, 44 per cent preferred the head of state to be directly elected by popular vote and the remaining 15 per cent preferred parliamentary appointment (Stuff 2016a). It is also worth noting that David Farrar, the principal researcher for Curia, the firm that conducted the poll, has previously held a position on the New Zealand Republic board.

The model proposed by New Zealand Republic is not the only one put forward by organised republicans. In 2016 Geoffrey Palmer and Andrew Butler staked their own claim in the republican arena with the release of their draft constitution for New Zealand. For them, the adoption of a new constitution goes hand in hand with a move to a republic; however, their republican rationale differs substantially from that of New Zealand Republic. We met with Palmer in Old Government House, once

Auckland's vice-regal residence, to discuss the future of New Zealand's constitutional arrangements. As we sipped coffee and talked, I decided to play devil's advocate and asked about New Zealand Republic's position on models of republicanism that avoid confronting the wider issues of constitutional reform. Palmer told us, 'I totally disagree with that, because if you are actually going to settle this thing, you have got to realise that every part of the constitution works together. You cannot fiddle with power in one place and not consider the effects in the other places' (Palmer, Interviews, 2016). Palmer's primary concern is with constructing constitutional arrangements that are more accountable and suited to what he would call 'bridled power' (see Chapter 2). Palmer and Butler see a new written constitution as the best means to achieve this, and creating a new constitution should be accompanied by the move towards a republic.

When asked if he thought elevating the governor-general's role could have ramifications for the practice of government, he replied firmly, 'I do, because where do the Queen's powers go? Who gets them? You have got to answer that from a legal point of view'. Some might argue that these powers could simply be transferred to the new head of state via statute, but Palmer contended that the powers of the sovereign are problematic because they are currently unclear. He contends that things like royal prerogative are not adequately codified, and that notions of the sovereign acting on the advice of ministers can be used as a smokescreen by the executive to bypass the democratic process (see Chapter 10). As he put it:

> If you are going to have accountability of politicians, the mystery is not appropriate, because they will hide behind it. The biggest difficulty we have is ministerial responsibility, accountability for those people who make decisions. Mystery is hardly appropriate.
>
> (Palmer, Interviews, 2016)

For Palmer and Butler, a republican constitution would demystify how power is exercised. In other words, Palmer and Butler are less concerned with pursuing republicanism to achieve nationalist ends than with establishing a more transparent, durable and principled political system. This is not to suggest that they are unconcerned about the issues that New Zealand Republic raises. Indeed, they argue that 'we are not British, and it is absurd to have a head of state living 12,000 miles from our shores' (Palmer and Butler 2016a). However, Palmer and Butler do not believe that this constitutional reform should be made as a symbolic gesture but rather that it should follow more systematic changes to, or clarifications of, the practice of government. During our conversation, Palmer stressed the pragmatism of their approach, stating that:

> One of the motivations for this project is that we had a referendum on the flag, and the flag seems to me to be a symbol of the government. If you do not know what your identity is in constitutional terms, or what you stand for in terms of values, how can you decide what the appropriate symbol is? It would be better to concentrate on the substance rather than the symbol, to start with.

This statement highlights a point of difference between the republicanisms of Palmer and Butler and of New Zealand Republic. While both support a move towards a republic with a simple promotion of the governor-general to head of state, and preferably by election of super-majority in Parliament, they are motivated by very different ends. It remains to be seen which of those motivations for republicanism will, if at all, mobilise the public into pushing for constitutional reform.

Obstacles to Reform

Republicanism is far more relevant to both politicians and the public in Australia than it is in New Zealand. For instance, on 26 January 2016, Australia Day, a declaration of support for a republic was signed by all but one state premiers and all chief ministers. The statement was organised by the Australian Republican Movement, and its chair, Peter FitzSimons, described it as no less than a 'declaration of desired independence' (*New Zealand Herald* 2016). It of course followed almost 20 years after the unsuccessful republican referendum of 1999, which was preceded by years of constitutional deliberation amongst experts and debate in the public domain. In October 2017, Labor, the opposition party at the time, went so far as to appoint Matt Thistlethwaite to be the new shadow minister for an Australian head of state: describing his role, Thistlethwaite told the press that 'I'm going to work with other political parties but most importantly I am going to work with the Australian people to build the consensus for this important change [republicanism] to our Constitution' (News Corp 2017).

From these strong gestures of republican sentiment and this widespread support among political leaders, it might seem safe to suggest that Australia might become a republic before Canada and New Zealand – Canadian and New Zealand politicians rarely show such interest in the republican cause. Indeed, when it comes to political and legal reforms,

New Zealanders often look to Australia for precedent and are willing to let them do the hard work in drafting legislation. For instance, former governor-general Sir Anand Satyanand told us:

> My own sense is that New Zealanders are conservative in the sense that they go along with the status quo. . . . So New Zealand will not be putting its hand up first to become a republic. The republican idea is, I think, a little more alive in Australia. And were Australia to become a republic I think that the debate would suddenly quicken in New Zealand and that we would in all probability do something similar. I do not think that New Zealand would diverge from Australia on something like that.

This was a common feeling amongst our New Zealand participants, who were relatively ambivalent about the claims made by republicans. But how accurate is this notion – that reform is more advanced in Australia? What impediments does republicanism face, and does this differ between the realms?

Much of the work that republican organisations engage in consists in dispelling the fears and concerns that arise whenever discussion turns to the question of republican reform. For instance, in New Zealand, discussions around republicanism inevitably raise questions around codified constitutional documents (usually called written constitutions), in the manner of Palmer and Butler. Opponents to written constitutions argue that the current arrangement allows for a level of flexibility in deciding how government is practised, seeing as new constitutional rules are introduced simply by passing legislation. Furthermore, some would argue, having a written constitution might empower the judiciary to deem certain executive acts as unconstitutional, raising fears that a republic might result in a drift towards an American-style arrangement. Another issue that is often raised is whether a move to a republic would result in a country leaving the Commonwealth. While this is factually incorrect – almost all the members of the Commonwealth are republics – this theme features prominently in public discourses of republicanism. Opponents also argue that a republican move would be costly, that monarchy provides a head of state at a bargain rate, that constitutional reform is low on the public agenda and that staying with the status quo is preferable to the risks of adopting an untested system.

However, there are more specific obstacles to republican reform that arise in each realm. In Australia, the constitution stipulates that reform requires a double majority: not only must the majority of voters across the country vote for a proposed reform, it must also have the support of the majority of voters in at least four out of six states. It is for this reason that constitutional reform rarely occurs in Australia – of the forty-four proposals made since the constitution was signed in 1901, only eight have passed (Australian Electoral Commission 2012). To complicate matters further, the republican debate in Australia always draws reference to the failed 1999 referendum. For a new referendum to succeed, it would not only need to overcome the stringent constitutional requirements but also require a huge amount of political will from a party willing to revive a once-lost cause, in the face of more pressing public interest – a poll in 2018 showed that a slim majority of 52 per cent support republican reform (News Corp 2018).

Republicanism in Canada faces similar practical issues. Section 41 of the Constitution Act of 1982 states that any changes to the Office of the Queen would require a successful resolution in the Senate, the House of Commons and each provincial legislature. The difficulty of passing such major constitutional amendments is evident in the failure of the Meech Lake Accord in 1990 and the Charlottetown Accord in 1992. Moreover, given that the Canadian republican movement is relatively weak compared with those in New Zealand and Australia, there is little momentum behind organising a referendum in the first instance. As Chapter 7 illustrates, there has also been relatively strong progress towards localising the monarchy in Canada, which perhaps blunts the republican rhetoric.

By contrast, constitutional reform in New Zealand is remarkably simple from a legal point of view. New Zealand is neither a federal polity comprising multiple states or provinces nor does it have a Legislative Council or upper house of Parliament (abolished in 1950). A constitutional amendment therefore requires only a majority in the House of Representatives (the lower house). However, this does not mean that constitutional reform is common in New Zealand – for instance, the Constitutional Arrangements Committee (CAC) which reviewed the constitution in 2005 used the phrase 'pragmatic evolution' to describe New Zealand's history of irregular and crisis-driven reform (CAC 2005). Moreover, reform related to the monarchy has proven difficult in recent years. In 2000, the Labour government replaced damehoods and knighthoods, as a system of honouring extraordinary citizens, with the New Zealand Order of Merit. According to Helen Clark, the prime minister at that time, the change was made to strengthen 'our own cultural and national identity' by providing a means 'for New Zealanders to be honoured in a distinctive New Zealand way' (Beehive 2000). However, the subsequent National-led government reinstated the former titles in 2009. That year also saw the National-led government reverse the previous Labour-led government's decision to replace the title of Queen's Counsel (given to lawyers of exceptional ability and record) with the title Senior Counsel in 2006 (Beehive 2009).

In 2005, the Oaths Modernisation Bill attempted to make oaths available in te reo (the Māori language) and added a statement of loyalty to the nation (without replacing the statement of loyalty to the Queen). Debate in Parliament raged during its second reading, despite the relative conservativeness of the proposal. National Member of Parliament Wayne Mapp argued that 'the current [Labour] Government is moving towards republicanism secretly and covertly' (New Zealand Parliamentary Debates 2005: 20716), while Maurice Williamson, also from the National Party, suggested that it was not the right time to debate the suitability of oaths to the Queen (New Zealand Parliamentary Debates 2005: 20726). The Bill failed to pass after the majority of members voted against it. The difficulty facing reforms that aim at the wider symbolic assemblage of the monarchy shows that while constitutional reform in New Zealand is legally far simpler than in either Australia or Canada, appetite for change is by no means assured. Political will, rather than constitutional drift, is the only way that New Zealand will become a republic ahead of the other former British dominions that remain as constitutional monarchies.

Colonial Ties or Sacred Links?

While the failed referendum of 1999 may still be a topic of conversation best avoided at some Australian dinner tables and barbecues, few New Zealanders remember their country's own failed attempt at republican reform. In 2009, the Head of State Referenda Bill, drafted by Green Party MP Keith Locke, went before Parliament. It proposed two referenda to decide whether to promote the governor-general to the position of head of state. Supporters suggested that a change to a republic would properly reflect national identity, describing the Queen's role as an anachronism. Members opposing the bill raised issues of cost and priority: National Party MP (and later party leader) Simon Bridges explained that

> [o]ver time, New Zealand may look more seriously at becoming a republic, but many New Zealanders will share my view that now is not the time. Today our nation has so many pressing and, frankly, real issues to grapple with that a head of State debate may well be a divisive distraction.
>
> (New Zealand Parliamentary Debates 2010: 10375)

Others argued that there was no strong public call to abolish the monarchy, and that moving to a republic would raise questions around a wide range of complex constitutional issues. Locke's attempt to make it possible for a New Zealander to become head of state did not even make it past this first reading and was rejected by sixty-eight votes to fifty-three.

What was particularly noteworthy in this instance of attempted reform was the reference to the Crown as an invaluable constitutional symbol. Māori Party MP Rāhui Katene told the House 'the bill has the potential to make the Māori-Crown relationship obsolete, which would be a major concern for all *iwi* [tribes]' (New Zealand Parliamentary Debates 2010: 10379). The provocation refers to the unresolved issues surrounding sovereignty in New Zealand: whether Māori signed away their sovereignty to the Crown under the Treaty in 1840; what obligations the Crown has to Māori; what shape the relationship between Māori and non-Māori should take and what the nature of shared sovereignty might be. Locke's response was, 'Yes, the Crown is important, but the Crown is in this room. The Parliament and the Government are the Crown, and that determines the relationship between Māori and the Crown', not the nature of the head of state (New Zealand Parliamentary Debates 2010: 10384). In this case, Katene views the Crown as inseparable from the British monarch, Queen Elizabeth II, whose ancestors entered into agreement with Katene's ancestors under the Treaty in 1840. To remove the monarchy and the Crown would jeopardise that relationship. For Locke, however, the New Zealand state, and in this case, the legislature, had long since taken on the moniker of the Crown, and along with it, the Treaty relationship. Nonetheless, Locke told me that 'one of the big barriers I had in advocating for republicanism was it should be associated with a broader constitutional debate and changes and the role of Māori and the Treaty' (Locke, Interviews, 2015).

So, while New Zealand is likely to have the simplest legal framework for constitutional reform, it also faces unique challenges in the role of the Crown as a Treaty partner with Māori (while the Crown entered into treaties with the indigenous peoples of Canada, it is not raised as frequently as a barrier to republicanism as it is in New Zealand). For many of our New Zealand participants, the Treaty relationship was almost an automatic reply when we asked them about republican reform. For instance, Peter Andrews, who has worked as Crown Counsel with the Waitangi Tribunal, told us that while he favoured republicanism, 'I always hope that that should not affect the Treaty relationship. Quite what the legal mechanism is for securing the rights and obligations under the Treaty in a republican state, I am not entirely clear about'. Former Labour MP and Speaker of the House, Margaret Wilson, told us that

> The Crown is a major obstacle to constitutional reform because it appears Māori see the notion of the Crown as being fundamental to a current government fulfilling obligations under the Treaty of Waitangi. It is for Māori to decide if it is necessary to continue with the notion of the Crown as a Treaty partner . . . I suspect most New Zealanders are also comfortable for nothing to happen.
>
> (Wilson, email correspondence, 2011)

Michael Cullen, another Labour politician and former attorney-general who has been non-committal on the issue of a republic, has said that 'the biggest problem of becoming a republic was how to deal with the Treaty of Waitangi . . . The way that issue can be resolved could result in immense political difficulties' (*New Zealand Herald* 2010b).

The relationship between the Crown and Māori certainly does not foreclose a republican future in New Zealand. Discussions around possible future roles for the Treaty have taken place with more regularity, and recent efforts, particularly by the constitutional working group Matike Mai, have explored the potential for new arrangements that might reflect notions of *tino rangatiratanga* (Māori self-determination). The recently elected Labour government of 2017 even established a new ministerial role of Crown–Māori relations, which seems to be focussed on a post-Treaty settlements relationship between the state and Māori. During the lead up to the 2017 election, Labour Party leader Jacinda Ardern announced that she thought it time to talk about becoming a republic. She commented that 'there are a lot of issues that need to be resolved on that path', including the Crown–Māori relationship (*New Zealand Herald* 2017).

The view that a republic might threaten the status of the Treaty is by no means universally held by Māori. For instance, Labour MP Louisa Wall supported Ardern's republican stance, while acknowledging that Māori needed to be at the forefront of such discussions. Morrie Love, former director of the Waitangi Tribunal, told us that 'before you look at that step and before you fully deal with the constitutional questions, it is probably better to get historical claims dealt with, just to make life a little easier I suspect' (Interviews, 2011). Shane Solomon, legal adviser to the Tainui confederation of *iwi* (tribes), agreed, telling us that, 'if we were to become a republic, we'd be a unique republic' (Interviews, 2011). Tom Roa, a member of the executive board of the Waikato-Tainui *iwi*, saw a republic as an opportunity for his *iwi* to establish their own state (Interviews, 2011). Academic and activist Margaret Mutu told us, 'It is up to *Pākehā* [Europeans/non-indigenous people] whether they want to keep the Crown', which speaks to her view that the Treaty established the rights of Pākehā and Māori alike to decide how they want to be governed (Interviews, 2015). On the other side of the spectrum, Morgan Godfery, a Māori unionist, political commentator and member of New Zealand Republic, told us that while a republic would mean no practical changes to the Treaty relationship, 'Treaty settlements, Treaty negotiations, none of that changes. But at that conceptual level, the *whakapapa* [shared ancestry] level it, changes. And you will see speeches on the *marae* [meeting houses] – people will be bemoaning the severance' (Interviews, 2016). Whether or not Māori opponents to republicanism are right in being concerned about the Treaty relationship, or whether a republican state would inherit the Crown's obligations to Māori, is beside the point. What is more important is that in the New Zealand republican debate, the Crown is much more than just the Queen, and proposals to simply switch people or transfer legal rights ignore the symbolism that surrounds states and their heads.

Building the Republican Nation

Palmer, like members of NZ Republic, played down the implications of republican reform for the Treaty relationship, which they suggest would continue unimpeded. However, republicans had different views about how to actually replace the Crown. For Palmer and Butler (2016b), the Crown is 'too complicated, ambiguous and mystical' for practical political use (214). As Palmer put it to us, the Crown sits 'like a brooding omnipresence over every part of the government' and this is 'a very big problem in trying to understand how we are actually governed' (Palmer, Interviews, 2016). In *A Constitution for Aotearoa New* Zealand, Palmer and Butler argue that '[m]atters would be much more straightforward legally and politically if we used the term "state" . . . With this change from the Crown to the State we would secure clarity' (2016b: 216–17). Palmer told us that 'there is no difficulty with transferring the rights and obligations of the Crown in Right of New Zealand to the state, there are no difficulties in that at all, and it is only a question of appearance . . . it is not complicated legally'. For Palmer, the symbolic dimensions of the Crown are simply window dressing for its technical and legal substance.

Strangely, however, New Zealand Republic – who see republicanism as a battle for the soul of the nation – had no policy on the alternative symbols that might accompany a republic. They seemed happier to leave these issues to be resolved after a reform has been made. Knight argued that 'the symbol of the Crown would have to go . . . It is a package'. He talked about replacing the Crown with something like 'the state' or 'the people of New Zealand'. Knight emphasised that 'the head of state is the key thing; the rest is just dotting i's and crossing t's' (Interviews, 2015). For him, what would replace the Crown is incidental and a simple technical issue: the *New Zealand Herald* has quoted him as saying '[w]e can deal with symbols, flags later on. They are distractions. That is the puffery around the edges' (*New Zealand Herald* 2010a). Savage had a relatively conservative, though novel, approach: he said 'it is actually possible for us to keep the name "Crown", to keep the picture of the Crown . . . people would come to understand that whereas the Crown once meant the authority of one person or one family, now it represents the authority of all of us, that we all are holders of the Crown' (Interviews, 2015).

However, political symbolism poses a serious challenge for republicans. On one hand, there is an apparent relegation of symbols and the symbolic to epiphenomena and therefore of secondary or marginal importance. But on the other hand, their calls for a republic make strong symbolic and emotive claims – and a quick browse of their websites reveal the importance of nationalist symbols like native flora and fauna. It is hardly a winning formula to paint the monarchy as the antithesis of national identity without providing an alternative symbol around which interested citizens can mobilise and unite. To suggest that replacing the Crown is simply a technical task akin to 'dotting the i's and crossing the t's' is to ignore the Crown's fundamental symbolic importance, particularly for many Māori. This reflects the rationalist way that republicans tend to approach constitutional reform. Republicans claim that public support for a republic hinges on citizens being correctly informed. Republicans we interviewed all shared their frustrations over misunderstandings of the monarchy and its role. Savage told me that 'people think you can write to the Queen' and appeal for her intercession in New Zealand politics. Knight explained, however, that 'my sense is once they get information about the nature of the role, the possibility for change and all that sort of thing, that they move to the republican side of the debate'. Here, republicanism appears to be the rational choice of informed actors – the idea being that once people know how the current constitutional arrangements work, they will identify how this stands at odds with their sense of nationhood.

According to Ernest Gellner, 'nationalism is not the awakening of nations to self-consciousness: it invents nations where they do not exist'

(Gellner 1964: 168). In other words, nationalism is not something primordial that arises during national celebrations or tragedies: rather, nations are imagined – and organised republicanism is a form of nation building. If a move to a republic is about 'cutting the colonial ties' and growing up as a nation, this begs the question: whose colonial ties are being cut, and what kind of identity should this grown-up nation create? Who is a Kiwi anyway? How seriously does the republican model take the Crown–Māori relationship? To contemplate shifting the locus of sovereignty from the monarch to a local head of state without resolving wider issues pertaining to sovereignty itself fails to truly escape the colonialism that republicans relegate to the past.

Conclusion

One of the key aims of this chapter has been to disrupt the notion that republicanism is an inevitable outcome of a constitutional drift towards a pre-determined endpoint of socio-political development. Clearly republicanism takes different forms and faces different obstacles throughout the realms. Republicans have different reasons for pursuing reform that range from nationalism to rationalism and legal pragmatism. The republican movement in Australia has by far the strongest lobby and public presence and seems to have the greatest momentum behind it in political circles. By contrast, republicanism in New Zealand and Canada (and the UK) is a far less salient public issue, and in New Zealand the debate is at times a touchstone for much more fundamental discussions around sovereignty and the Treaty. On the other hand, New Zealand appears to have the best legal environment for republican reform, given that it has a far simpler political structure and less stringent requirements for constitutional amendment. Some might argue that it is unlikely that Australia or Canada will ever become republics.

A further complication raised with republicanism is what appears to be a lack of engagement with the symbolic dimensions of reform. The Crown is much more than the Queen or the Royal Family; it is a symbol that is deeply embedded in political practice and history. Without suggesting that republicanism is impossible or undesirable, I do challenge the notion that republicanism is inevitable – a transition to republic is not a teleological certainty, the final realisation of nationhood that will emerge naturally though an informative campaign and rational deliberation. Rather, it involves a serious discussion around what the nation is in the first place. There is no consensus around national identity in New Zealand; indeed, on Waitangi Day, which commemorates the signing of the Treaty and is often described as the national day, the contested nature of national identity always comes to the fore. Nationhood is always contested, but in New Zealand, any attempt to replace the Crown and move to a republic entails explicitly engaging with such unresolved issues.

Moreover, creating new symbols that break from the anachronisms of the past, yet reflect the collective national sentiment, is extremely difficult – as the 2016 campaign to replace New Zealand's national flag demonstrated (see Chapter 9). The Flag Consideration Panel, created to consult with the public on the selection of a new flag, was greeted with widespread scepticism and a lack of engagement – the public session that I attended had more panel members present than attendees. The process was unable to generate a consensus over which alternative best symbolised New Zealand. If choosing a new flag is problematic, how much more problematic would be selecting or electing a new head of state? In the chapter that follows we address some of these themes. More specifically, we examine the reasons why constitutional reform projects that aim to engage the public according to the principles of 'deliberative democracy' so often result in the sort of apathy that typified the flag design and referendum process in New Zealand, and which would likely plague future attempts to move to a republic.

References

Australian Electoral Commission. 2012. 'Referendum Dates and Results.' Accessed 26 November 2017 at www.aec.gov.au/Elections/referendums/Referendum_Dates_and_Results.htm.

Beehive. 2000. 'Titles Discontinued.' Media release, 10 April. Accessed 3 January 2016 at www.beehive.govt.nz/release/titles-discontinued.

2009. 'Government to Restore Queen's Counsel.' Media release. 18 June. Accessed 3 January 2016 at www.beehive.govt.nz/release/government-restore-queen%e2%80%99s-counsel.

2015. 'The Prince of Wales and Duchess of Cornwall to Visit New Zealand in November.' Media release, 3 July. Accessed 24 June 2017 at www.beehive.govt.nz/release/prince-wales-and-duchess-cornwall-visit-new-zealand-november.

CAC (Constitutional Arrangements Committee). 2005. 'Inquiry to Review New Zealand's Existing Constitutional Arrangements: Report of the Constitutional Arrangements Committee.' Report presented to the New Zealand House of Representatives. Accessed 22 May 2016 at www.victoria.ac.nz/law/pdf/cg2-constitutional-review-2005.pdf.

Gellner, Ernest. 1964. *Thought and Change*. University of Chicago Press: Chicago.

New Zealand Parliamentary Debates. 1994. 'Address-in-Reply Debate.' 8 March. p. 139. Accessed 15 July 2017 at www.parliament.nz/en/pb/hansard-debates/historical-hansard/#1990.

2005. 'Oaths Modernisation Bill – First Reading.' 18 May. Accessed 03 January 2016 at www.parliament.nz/en/pb/hansard-debates/rhr/document/47HansD_20050518_00001235/oaths-modernisation-bill-first-reading.

2010. 'Head of State Referenda Bill – First Reading.' 21 April. Accessed 4 January 2016 at www.parliament.nz/en/pb/hansard-debates/rhr/document/49HansD_20100421_00001343/head-of-state-referenda-bill-first-reading.

News Corp. 2017. 'Major Step in Push for Australian Republic: Labor Appoints a "Shadow Assistant Minister for an Australian Head of State".' 24 October. Accessed 12 January 2018 at www.news.com.au/national/major-step-in-push-for-australian-republic-labor-appoints-a-shadow-assistant-minister-for-an-australian-head-of-state/news-story/d561ffcd9aeb895db55acf70afcfc679.

2018. 'Majority of Australians in Favour of Becoming a republic, Poll Shows.' 21 February. Accessed 16 March 2018 at www.news.com.au/entertainment/celebrity-life/royals/majority-of-australians-in-favour-of-becoming-a-republic-poll-shows/news-story/9a068f60a6512d3babd782fa466d9778.

Newshub. 2014. 'Key: NZ Becoming a Republic "Inevitable".' 7 April. Accessed 15 July 2017 at www.newshub.co.nz/politics/key-nz-becoming-a-republic-inevitable-2014040717.

New Zealand Herald. 2010a. 'Putting Monarchy on a Short Reign.' 29 August. Accessed 15 July 2017 at www.nzherald.co.nz/nz/news/article.cfm?c_id=1&objectid=10669697.

2010b. 'NZ as a Republic "Inevitable" – Cullen.' 2 September. Accessed 23 September 2017 at www.nzherald.co.nz/nz/news/article.cfm?c_id=1&objectid=10670608.

2014a. 'Morgan Godfery: The Monarchy Has Lost Meaning.' 13 April. Accessed 12 July 2017 at www.nzherald.co.nz/opinion/news/article.cfm?c_id=466&objectid=11237269.

2014b. 'Savage: Now Is the Hour to Make Head of State Our Own.' 15 April. Accessed 2 January 2016 at www.nzherald.co.nz/opinion/news/article.cfm?c_id=466&objectid=11238122.

2016. 'Republic Debate: Australian Leaders Call for Head of State.' 25 January. Accessed 13 June 2017 at www.nzherald.co.nz/world/news/article.cfm?c_id=2&objectid=11579366.

2017. 'Jacinda Ardern in the PM Job Interview: "It's Time to Talk about a Republic".' 22 August. Accessed 22 August 2017 at www.nzherald.co.nz/nz/news/article.cfm?c_id=1&objectid=11908796.

Palmer, Geoffrey and Andrew Butler. 2016a. 'Monarchy or Republic?' *Constitution Aotearoa NZ: Archive*. Web site. Accessed 5 September 2017 at archive.constitutionaotearoa.org.nz/the-conversation/topics/monarchy-or-republic/.

2016b. *A Constitution for Aotearoa New Zealand.* Wellington: Victoria University Press.
Phillips, Jock. 1984. 'Rugby, War and the Mythology of the New Zealand Male.' *New Zealand Journal of History* 18(2): 83–103.
RNZ (Radio New Zealand). 2015. 'Greens Question Timing of Visit.' Accessed 2 January 2016 at www.radionz.co.nz/news/political/288575/greens-question-timing-of-royal-visit.
Stuff. 2016a. 'Nearly 60 Per Cent of Kiwis Want the British Monarchy Out – Poll.' 4 September. Accessed 2 April 2017 at www.stuff.co.nz/national/politics/83864989/nearly-60-per-cent-of-kiwis-want-the-british-monarchy-out–poll.
2016b. 'Opinion: A New Zealand Republic Is Less Than Inevitable.' 12 September. Accessed 15 July 2017 at www.stuff.co.nz/world/84165372/opinion-a-new-zealand-republic-is-less-than-inevitable.

9

Constitutional Reform and the Politics of Public Engagement

CRIS SHORE AND DAVID V. WILLIAMS

Advocates of republicanism and constitutional reform often argue that a key obstacle to political change is ignorance, or 'lack of public understanding' about what the constitution *is* and what its provisions actually mean in terms of the allocation of legitimate power and authority.[1] If only people were better informed so the argument goes, they would naturally draw the right conclusions and accept the logic of the republican arguments that constitutional monarchy is an archaic, opaque, neo-colonial and outdated form of government. In the course of our interviews and conversations with republican activists and supporters in Australia and New Zealand, many told us that what was needed is more civics education or public educational programmes, targeted particularly at young people and taught systematically in schools. Paradoxically, these arguments were often echoed by monarchists, who also claimed that civics education and a better understanding of how constitutional monarchy works would inevitably lead people to recognise that their current system is by far the most stable and superior form of government compared to many countries with republican constitutions. These competing claims about constitutional reform and public engagement/apathy recall political and legal debates over the constitutional arrangements that best guarantee more deliberative forms of democracy.

New Zealand has had three major constitutional deliberations since 2005. Framed by successive governments as 'national conversations' on 'the future of New Zealand', these included an initiative aimed at engaging the public's views on constitutional reform and a consultation

[1] This chapter developed out of a series of seminars on deliberative constitutionalism held in London and Canberra in 2016. An earlier version of it was published in *The Cambridge Handbook of Deliberative Constitutionalism*, edited by Ron Levy, Hoi Kong, Graeme Orr, and Jeff King (Cambridge: Cambridge University Press, 2018).

followed by two binding referenda over proposals to change the national flag. Yet what was striking about these constitutional reform initiatives was not their capacity to mobilise the measured consideration and interest of citizens but rather the lack of enthusiastic public engagement and, more pertinently, the lack of serious government commitment to the principles of deliberative democracy except on minor matters of its own choosing. These 'non-events' – or what might be termed 'pseudo-deliberations' – highlight one of the key challenges for advocates of deliberative constitutionalism and participatory democracy: how to prevent the 'performative' and theatrical aspects of the democratic process from overshadowing substantive and meaningful participation in political debate and constitutional decision-making.

Our use of the term 'performativity' here draws on the idea of 'speech acts' developed by anthropologists and philosophers of language (Austin 1962; Habermas 1984; Turner 1988; Butler 1997) who argue that the capacity of speech and communication is not simply to communicate but rather to consummate action. Part of the work of constitutional deliberation – like other kinds of speech act – is to perform an identity and bring particular kinds of social reality into being. As these authors have all noted, public events and rituals – from the highly ritualised routines in courtrooms to the political oratory government ministers use to advance legislative reforms – are invariably governed by particular codes of performance, signal systems that are designed to communicate one's place within a social group (see also Goffman 1969).

In this chapter we explore these themes in the context of New Zealand, but the debates also have implications for understanding and assessing the impact of referenda in other contexts, including Australia's vote on a republican constitution (1999), Ontario's 'Citizen's Assembly' (2007), Scotland's vote on independence (2014) and the UK's 'Brexit' referendum on continued membership of the European Union (2016). The New Zealand case, as we illustrate in this chapter, highlights a further problem for deliberative constitutionalism in countries whose political systems are based on the Westminster model of constitutional monarchy, namely, the difficulties of creating meaningful public consultation when key terms of reference – such as 'Crown', 'monarchy' and 'constitution' – are so notoriously ambiguous, amorphous and opaque. To echo Stephen Sedley (2011: 269), 'an uninstructed observer today might well find difficulty in discerning either the constitution or – except in its ceremonial form – the monarchy'. Politicians acting in the name of the Crown go through the motions of public engagement. Yet the constitutional and political deliberations they initiate, if they are to have democratic legitimacy, have to be communicated and performed, and herein lie the politics and poetics of performativity. The concept of performativity, we suggest, helps us to recognise that there are other issues and agendas going on in most democratic events; that is, these are communicative acts that are wrapped up in issues of national identity and political interest.

Our argument is set out in four steps. First, we reflect on the rationalistic assumptions and normative frameworks that dominate most legal writing about, and advocacy for, deliberative democracy and deliberative constitutionalism. Second, we illustrate why greater attention should be paid to the symbolic and performative dimensions of political deliberation and the implications for understanding how democracy works in practice. Third, we exemplify our arguments drawing on two case studies of deliberative democracy from New Zealand and one from Australia. Finally, we consider the utility and implications of this analysis of deliberative constitutionalism for understanding proposals for constitutional reform in New Zealand, Australia, Canada and the United Kingdom.

Deliberative Constitutionalism as a Normative Order

Debates about the role of deliberations in a democracy go back to Aristotle and the problem posed by the ancient Greeks as to whether ordinary people who do not know much should control constitutional change (Werhan 2012). As Keith Werhan sums it up:

> At its most pungent, the popular constitutionalism project is nothing less than an appeal that the People, or their elected representatives, replace the Court (at least to a substantial degree) as the day-to-day decision maker regarding the meaning and application of the Constitution.
>
> (Werhan 2012: 68)

The epithet 'deliberative constitutionalism' has a complex genealogy (Kong and Levy 2017), but seems to draw together at least two strands of literature. The first is the ongoing debate among political theorists, philosophers and scientists on the conditions that promote or hinder democracy. These questions, which also featured prominently in the writings of political philosophers from Edmund Burke and J. S. Mill to John Dewey and Hannah Arendt, have attracted renewed interest since the publication of John Dryzek's influential book *Deliberative Democracy and Beyond: Liberals, Critics, Contestations* (Dryzek 2000). The second is the more recent debate, particularly among European Union (EU) scholars, on constitutionalism in the EU and how to redress Europe's legitimacy problem arising from its 'democratic deficit'. The common perception of a 'democratic deficit' in Europe stems from the fact that the EU, unlike its member-states, has no obvious or self-identifying 'European public', except at the level of political and economic elites. As critics note, 'demos' without democracy leaves only 'cratos', or power. That exercise of power by European policy elites can lay claim to little more than a second-order or derived legitimacy. This form of power often appears tantamount to mere assertions based on raison d'état (Leicester 1996; Shore 2000). Many scholars have sought a solution in Habermas's theories of communicative action and constitutional patriotism (Habermas 1992), and the idea that political legitimacy can be garnered through a more rational (and less emotional) type of loyalty to the institutions and ideals of a post-national constitutional order. Habermas's normative framework and his arguments about the dangers of emotion and the affective dimensions of political life highlight many of the same assumptions that underlie deliberative constitutionalism (Chappell 2012). To echo Patchen Markell (2000), these are all about replacing passion, '*polis* and *patria* for the calm certitudes of reason' with the aim of 'making affect safe for democracy' (Markell 2000: 38–39). The desire for post-national patriotism or loyalty to some abstract constitutional principle may have made sense for some in the aftermath of the Second World War, but recent events suggest that prospects for the emergence of a Habermasian-style constitutional patriotism – and a public sphere serenely detached from the loyalties that feed it – are waning, not waxing.

As in the case of the EU, much of the debate over deliberative constitutionalism hinges on the idea that a clear distinction can be drawn between the rational and deliberative effects of constitutionalism and less savoury emotional forms of political persuasion based on ideology, propaganda and the appeal to baser instincts. Deliberative democracy is thus framed as something that encourages critical reflection and rational debate, thereby somehow promoting a freer, more open, 'authentic', 'reasoned' and participatory form of public engagement (Bohman 1998: 401–2). According to Dryzek, the end of the twentieth century was marked by a strong 'deliberative turn' in theories of democracy as democratic legitimacy has increasingly come to be recognised as a corollary of people's ability to participate meaningfully and effectively in decision-making. As he wrote:

> The essence of democracy itself is now widely taken to be deliberation, as opposed to voting, interest aggregation, constitutional rights, or even self-government. The deliberative turn represents a renewed concern with the authenticity of democracy: the degree to which democratic control is substantive rather than symbolic, and engaged by competent citizens.
>
> (Dryzek 2000: 1)

This 'renewed concern' was doubtless a response to growing voter apathy and disenchantment with Western liberal democracies. As Colin Crouch (2004) summed it up in his provocative book *Post-Democracy*:

> While elections certainly exist and can change governments, public electoral debate is a tightly controlled spectacle, managed by rival teams of professionals expert in the techniques of persuasion, and considering a small range of issues selected by those teams. The mass of citizens plays a passive, quiescent, even apathetic part, responding only to the signals given them. Behind the spectacle of the electoral game, politics is really shaped in private by interaction between elected governments and elites that overwhelmingly represent business interests. … Under the conditions of a post-democracy that increasingly cedes power to business lobbies, there is little hope for an agenda of strong egalitarian policies for the redistribution of power and wealth, or for the restraint of powerful interests.
>
> (Crouch 2004: 4)

The key condition for 'authentic deliberation', Dryzek (2000) wrote, is 'the requirement that communication induce reflection upon preferences in non-coercive fashion' (1–2). The aim of this definition is to distinguish deliberation from forms of 'domination via the exercise of power, manipulation, indoctrination, propaganda, deception, expressions of mere self-interest, threats … and attempts to impose ideological conformity' (2). Dryzek's goal, like that of other writers on deliberative democracy, was to define the conditions that would produce a purer and more authentic form of democracy freed from the distorting influences of emotion, ideology and political interests. As Bohman put it:

> The attraction of deliberative democracy for many was precisely its promise to go beyond the limits of liberalism and to recapture the stronger democratic ideal that government should embody the 'will of the people' formed through the public reasoning of citizens. Deliberative democracy, broadly defined, is thus any one of a family of views according to which the public deliberation of free and equal citizens is the core of legitimate political decision-making and self-government.
>
> (Bohman 1998: 401)

The problem, however, is how to create such conditions when the two 'basic expectations of public governance' – democratic participation by citizens and deliberative decision-making – 'appear to lie in sharp tension' (Levy 2013: 355).

Democracy, Performativity and the Work of Symbols

This neat differentiation between 'reflection' and 'manipulation' and the Enlightenment ideals of free and equal citizens engaging meaningfully in rational self-government is problematic and far removed from the way that democratic debate occurs in practice. While critics have argued that theories of deliberative democracy are often naïvely utopian and freighted with normative assumptions (Gutmann and Thomson 2004), Dryzek's (2007, 2012) later work has responded to these criticisms by defending deliberative democracy's normative dimension and arguing that the theory is not a naïve quest for consensus but simply offers a 'set of standards' against which democratic practices can be 'analysed, criticized and further improved' (Ercan and Dryzek 2015: 243).

Deliberative theory thus 'offers a lens upon which "real-world" practices can be contextualized, interpreted, and evaluated, rather than "tested" in order to be verified or falsified' (Ercan and Dryzek 2015: 244). However, perhaps a more useful and reflexive approach would be to reverse this analytical framing and use those 'real-world' practices as a lens to contextualise, interpret and re-evaluate some of these misplaced and de-contextualised theoretical assumptions.

While Dryzek and other deliberative democrats acknowledge that deliberation is a 'social process', the implications of that insight are overlooked. To argue that the essential condition for 'authentic democracy' is that 'democratic control is substantive rather than symbolic, and engaged by competent citizens' (Dryzek 2000: 1) is to reduce symbols to filigree or window dressing, mere epiphenomena of the supposedly more substantive, institutional aspects of democracy. From an anthropological perspective, this argument completely misses the point about the power of symbols or the work they perform. Symbols do not simply reflect political reality; they actively constitute it (Turner 1967; Abélès 1988; Kertzer 1988). For example, most of the concepts that frame democracy – nation, state, sovereignty, freedom, justice, etc. – can only be meaningfully grasped or understood through their symbolic forms. In short, it is only through such symbols that citizens can ever come to know or engage with the social, political and legal worlds that they inhabit.

The ephemeral and symbolic nature of state has become a central theme in contemporary theories of the modern state (Mitchell 1999; Trouillot 2001; see also Chapter 3), but they also highlight the point that symbols are more than simply representational; they are performative and have considerable agency. As we illustrate in this chapter, New Zealand's recent constitutional debates can usefully be seen as performances that serve various political purposes. These include defining the nation and focusing public attention on issues of importance to the government and political elites rather than the public (a category which, perversely, these speech acts work recursively to create and sustain). In developing this argument our aim is to question some of the assumptions underlying democratic theory and to expand the theoretical repertoire surrounding debates over deliberative constitutionalism. To do this, it is necessary to deconstruct the term 'deliberation' and explore what constitutional debate and engagement mean in practice, particularly in those contexts where few citizens understand their constitution or how it works.

The invisibility of the state and its implications for democracy are particularly salient issues for Britain's former dominions that still share its system of constitutional monarchy. In New Zealand and Canada, for example, the term 'Crown' typically serves as a substitute or 'conceptual placeholder' for the state in civil law jurisdictions (Cox 2008). This adds further layers of complexity to what is an already complex and opaque entity, particularly as the concepts of 'Crown' and 'state', while often used interchangeably, have different meanings and do not map the same semantic terrain (see Chapter 3). Taking New Zealand's history of recent constitutional reforms as our focus, two key questions arise:

1. What insights can recent experiences of referenda offer to debates about democracy and deliberative constitutionalism?
2. How can citizens engage with the substantive issues of constitutional reform when the key aspects of their constitution are so opaque and obscure?

Indeed, considering the many obstacles to meaningful constitutional deliberation, we might also ask, 'to what extent can the ideals of deliberative democracy and deliberative constitutionalism ever be achieved?'

We turn to two case studies on deliberative processes. It is worth noting first, though, that New Zealand has effected several major constitutional changes without much or any democratic deliberation. Examples include the move to appointing New Zealanders (rather than British notables) as governors-general; the creation of New Zealand orders and honours to replace British Empire honours; the creation of a Supreme Court of New Zealand as the final appellate court to replace appeals to the Judicial Committee of the Privy Council; and the abolition of knighthoods and damehoods in 2000, followed by their restoration in 2009.

Case Study One: New Zealand's Constitutional Review (2010–2013)

The 2010–2013 constitutional review arose from a confidence-and-supply agreement between the National Party and the Māori Party (2008) to allow the former to form a government with majority support in the House of Representatives. It arose initially out of controversy about the future status of dedicated Māori constituency seats in the House that have existed since 1867. Their continuation or abolition was an issue during the 2008 election campaign. The New Zealand Business Roundtable had published a working paper that proposed the 'abolition of separate Māori representation in parliament' (Joseph 2008). The National Party subsequently published its policies about Treaty of Waitangi negotiations, Māori affairs and electoral law, announcing that it would pursue 'one voting franchise' following the settlement of historic Treaty claims between the Crown and Māori (Taonui 2012).

The Māori Party won a number of the Māori constituency seats in the 2008 election, and it was very determined that the seats should not be abolished. Thus, in the confidence-and-supply agreement between the governing parties, the following compromise was reached:

> [B]oth parties agree to the establishment (including its composition and terms of reference) by no later than early 2010 of a group to consider constitutional issues including Māori representation. . . . The National Party agrees it will not seek to remove the Māori seats without the consent of the Māori people. Accordingly, the Māori Party and the National Party will not be pursuing the entrenchment of the Māori seats in the current parliamentary term.
>
> (National Party and Māori Party 2008)

As a result, in December 2010 Deputy Prime Minister Bill English (National Party) and Minister for Māori Affairs Dr Pita Sharples (Māori Party) announced a 'wide ranging cross-party government review of New Zealand's constitution' over the next three years (English and Sharples 2010), establishing eight key areas of focus under three headings, as follows:

1. 'Electoral matters': size of Parliament, length of the term of Parliament and whether or not the term should be fixed, size and number of electorates, and electoral integrity legislation;
2. 'Crown–Māori relationship matters': Māori representation (including the Māori Electoral Option), Māori electoral participation, Māori seats in Parliament and local government, and the role of the Treaty of Waitangi in New Zealand's constitutional arrangements; and
3. 'Other constitutional matters': Bill of Rights issues (e.g., property rights and entrenchment of some elements of the constitution by requirements for a special majority in Parliament to effect reforms), and the question of a more comprehensive written constitution.

(English and Sharples 2010: 15)

The review provided for additional matters to be discussed during the public engagement phase if the ministers advised cabinet that an issue 'appears to be of widespread interest and merits consideration' (English and Sharples 2010: 15).

Conspicuously absent from the review's terms of reference was the possibility of replacing the monarchy with a republic, arguably the most important constitutional reform issue of all. Faced with repeated questions from journalists about this omission, English claimed that it would 'inevitably be part of the discussion' but was not included as the government did not want it 'overshadowing a range of other issues, some of which are more immediate'. Sharples added that a republic was 'not an issue for Māori', but conceded that the question of a republic did have implications for Māori–Crown relations and the Treaty. Perhaps the most important, yet unspoken, implication was that becoming a republic would effectively render obsolete the idea of the Crown and the institutional architecture that sustains it. Despite this, the review was portrayed as the start of a major national conversation on the future of New Zealand's constitution. At the press conference launch, English noted that the review was intended to canvass the opinions of 'all New Zealanders' as constitutions 'belong to the people, not politicians' (Scoop News 2010). While this may appear to be the language of deliberative constitutionalism, as we shall see, the participation sought did not amount to a serious exercise in deliberative democracy.

English and Sharples established a cross-party reference group of MPs to support the project and, by August 2011, had appointed a Constitutional Advisory Panel (CAP), an independent group whose role was to 'listen, facilitate, and record New Zealanders' views on constitutional issues' (CAP, n.d.), aided by a secretariat based in the Ministry of Justice. The twelve CAP members (half of whom were Māori) were selected to represent a cross-section of New Zealand society. The review took place over a three-year period. It included phases of clarifying issues and preparation, an election hiatus (to 'avoid compromising the 2011 General Election and [Mixed Member Proportionality] Referendum' [English and Sharples 2010]), and then a series of public engagement exercises. That engagement included meetings with specific community groups and cohorts such as ethnic groups, 'disability communities' and youth; a series of radio debates to raise awareness and generate interest; national TV advertisements; and an online media campaign to solicit submissions from the general public (CAP 2013: 91). The Panel produced an interim report and then a final report in December 2013.

Despite being promoted as a 'national conversation', the constitutional review attracted only modest popular interest, and curiously little media attention. By January 2013, for example, it had still not launched its promised 'engagement website' and it had appointed only one permanent administrative staffer. In the end, although it did receive 5,259 individual and group submissions from the public, the review process attracted limited or no input from the major political parties. One party – New Zealand First – refused to participate, describing the process as a democratic 'sham' and (it alleged) part of a government coalition deal to promote formally enshrining the Treaty of Waitangi as part of the constitution. Only the two smallest political parties in Parliament (ACT and United Future) made submissions to the panel.

Surprisingly, neither the National Party nor the Māori Party who initiated the process provided any sustained commentary or policy announcements on the review other than at its launch. The Māori Party's website placed constitutional change as number eight on a list of its fifteen policy agreements signed with the National Party. A round-up of the political events of 2012 in the prime minister's Christmas message in December made no mention of the review at all (Key 2012), and his opening statement to the new Parliament in 2013 referred to it only in passing ('the Government will continue to progress the review of constitutional arrangements') towards the end of a twenty-four-page document (Key 2013). The rationale behind the Crown's constitutional review initiative was not so much to engage the public in serious constitutional deliberation. Rather, it seems, it was political expediency for coalition-building politics in a parliamentary democracy where members are elected by a proportional representation system and no one party wins a majority of the seats. This would seem to fit a pattern, all too familiar in Westminster-style democracies: deal with awkward or inconvenient issues by 'kicking them into the long grass' through the use of Royal Commissions or protracted official inquiries. Of course, sometimes such commissions can produce surprisingly critical reports with significant consequences, as with the 1981 Mahon Erebus inquiry in New Zealand and the 2016 Chilcot Iraq inquiry initiated by Prime Minister Gordon Brown in the United Kingdom. There were no surprises, however, in the CAP report.

The main recommendations of the CAP final report were that government 'invites and supports the people of Aotearoa New Zealand to continue the conversation about our constitutional arrangements [and] develop a national strategy for civics and citizenship education in schools and in the community' (CAP 2013: 3), including affirming the unique role of the Treaty of Waitangi 'as a foundational document' (17). It found a lack of broad support for any constitutional changes such as enacting a written constitution that would be supreme law and enhancing the legal status of the Treaty of Waitangi. However, it did find some support for entrenching elements of the constitution such as the New Zealand Bill of Rights Act 1990 and Constitution Act 1986 and noted a minority perspective in favour of 'a constitution which better reflects the Māori–Crown relationship or which establishes New Zealand as a republic' (CAP 2013: 24).

Unsurprisingly, given its anodyne recommendations, the report received little media attention. More tellingly, the same governing parties when re-elected in the 2011 and 2014 general elections did not take constitutional reform issues any further – except for the proposal to adopt a new national flag, to which we now turn.

Case Study Two: Changing the New Zealand Flag

Our second example of a Crown political process that might resemble performative constitutionalism concerns the 2015–2016 referendum campaigns to change New Zealand's national flag. This was something of a pet project – and legacy-building initiative – of the then prime minister John Key, who did much to spearhead the campaign. Although the flag could have been changed by ordinary legislation, Mr Key insisted that this was a 'constitutional issue' that required wide public consultation. The current flag – a blue ensign with the Union Jack in the top left-hand corner and with the four stars of the Southern Cross in red and white – was first designed for use on colonial naval ships in 1869, to implement an imperial statute (the Colonial Naval Defence Act 1865 [UK]). This blue ensign was then adopted as New Zealand's national flag in 1902. On occasion since the 1970s there have been calls for New Zealand to discard the Union Jack and create a new national identity by changing the flag, but none have gained traction. In 2010 Mr Key publicly announced his support for replacing the flag with the image of a silver fern (also used on the jerseys of the national rugby team, the All Blacks, and other sports teams). In a speech at Victoria University in 2014 he set out his case, arguing that the existing flag 'symbolises a colonial and postcolonial era whose time has passed', whereas efforts by New Zealand athletes had given 'the silver fern on a black background a distinctive and uniquely New Zealand identity' (BBC News 2014). Changing the flag, he added, represented 'one more step in the evolution of modern New Zealand by acknowledging our independence'. Confusion over the similarity between Australia's and New Zealand's flags was cited as another compelling reason for the change. Yet the flag issue was not tied to any deeper postcolonial questions such as New Zealand becoming a republic, or even to relaxing ties with the United Kingdom, both of which Mr Key (a self-professed monarchist) opposed.

Unlike the CAP review, this exercise in constitutional deliberation was extremely well resourced. The Crown spent over NZ$27 million promoting its 'nationwide engagement programme'. This included a ten-month consultation process with national roadshows, publicity events and social media campaigns. The public were also invited to submit their own draft designs, some 10,300 of which were received, which were then reduced to a shortlist of five. Among the more ironic designs was James Gray's 'Fire the Lazer' (Laser Kiwi), which has enjoyed a life after the competition at sports matches (Figure 9.1).

Official government leaflets presented this as 'your chance to be part of history'. Yet opinion polls consistently showed most of the public had little desire to follow Mr Key's lead, and a TV3 Poll conducted in September 2015 found that some 70 per cent of the public were opposed to changing the flag.

The process involved two binding referenda. The first, in November 2015, invited the public to select their preferred alternative from a list of five designs. The second, in March 2016, then asked the electorate which of two options – the current flag or the most favoured alternative (a silver fern with the stars of the Southern Cross (Figure 9.2)) – they preferred.

In the event, by a narrower than expected but still substantial majority, the public voted by 56.6 per cent to 43.2 per cent (and 0.2 per cent informal votes) to retain the status quo (with 67.8 per cent of eligible voters participating). This was a relatively high voter turnout. General

Figure 9.1 James Gray's 'Fire the Lazer' (Laser Kiwi) entry to the Flag Consideration Panel, 2015
(James Gray, 2015)

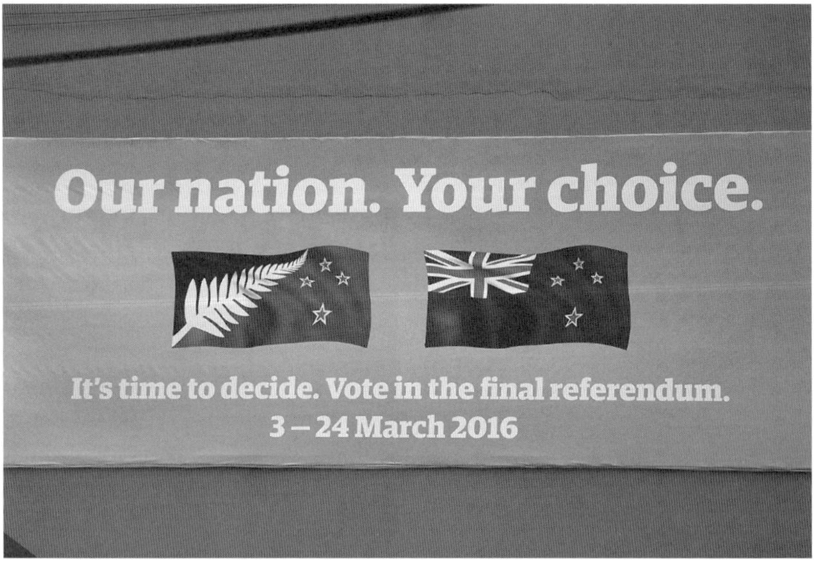

Figure 9.2 A billboard advertising New Zealand's 2016 flag referendum, comparing the current flag (right) with the alternative design
(Marty Melville/AFP/Getty Images)

elections in New Zealand in recent decades have achieved between 77 per cent (in 2014) and 93 per cent (in 1984) voter turnouts. The problem for this Crown initiative, though, was that those who wished for more thoroughgoing constitutional reform combined with conservative voters to defeat the prime minister's pet project. As one veteran reporter, Duncan Garner, summed it up:

> I consider myself a proud and patriotic Kiwi who cares deeply for this country. I love this place – what we stand for, how we live and how much we achieve internationally. But I couldn't give a toss about changing our current flag. I just can't get excited about the debate, it's a totally meaningless and expensive exercise. I'd much prefer a genuine debate about whether we cut ties with Mother England because I support us becoming a republic, with our own constitution. ... This flag debate is completely superficial – we're having a nationwide drawing competition to pick a winning flag to flog off in a referendum up against the current flag. Exactly who is demanding a change? I can't find anyone.
>
> (Garner 2015)

One answer to Garner's question was provided in an interview with economic geographer Nick Lewis. The flag debate, he notes, was 'led by a group of celebrity New Zealanders and brand developers' deeply invested in the Brand New Zealand Campaigns of the last 20 years (Hargreaves 2015). These somewhat blatant links with corporate and national branding probably helped to sink Key's campaign. However, it is worth noting that the silver fern had, for many decades prior, been a symbol of amateur sporting teams and has been the insignia used on Commonwealth war graves for New Zealanders since the First World War.

More importantly, many voters rightly saw the flag referendum as a diversion from more important constitutional issues. It took place as government ministers and Crown officials were negotiating a highly controversial and secretive Trans-Pacific Partnership Agreement (TPPA) – the largest international free-trade agreement in New Zealand's history – without any reference either to Parliament or to the electorate. The public was not invited to offer its views on this far more substantive constitutional matter. The flag debate also provided a useful distraction from mounting concerns about increasing economic inequalities and government attempts to further open up New Zealand's economy and assets to overseas investors (including oil and gas prospecting, farmland, urban real estate, education and even the right to citizenship). As critics of the TPPA argued, the powers it would grant to foreign corporations would threaten New Zealand's sovereignty, undermine environmental protections and copyright laws, weaken labour rights and business regulation, and place constraints on the ways the Crown can honour its Treaty of Waitangi obligations (Kelsey 2015). Paradoxically, the government was happy to rely on the Crown's unreviewable prerogative powers for treaty-making to negotiate the extensive commitments in the TPPA – signed with eleven participating nations in 2018 and renamed the Comprehensive and Progressive Agreement for Trans-Pacific Partnership (CPTTP) – whilst requiring two binding referenda to decide on a symbolic changing of the national flag. The prime minister's hope, it seems, was that these concerns would be eclipsed by the flag spectacle. In the event, the government's discourse around constitutional change failed to create a nationalistic narrative about a young and little nation at the end of the earth, defying the odds and punching above its weight whilst waving a silver fern flag.

Conclusion: The Limits of Constitutional Deliberation

We began this chapter by asking what insights can be gleaned from New Zealand's recent experience in apparent attempts to foster deliberative democracy leading to constitutional reform. We conclude with two points.

First, our case studies highlighted some of the tensions that exist between the ideals of deliberative constitutionalism (and deliberative democracy as a set of abstract and elusive principles) and the practices of performativity and political expediency that typically shape how constitutional debate and engagement are enacted empirically. In terms of performance theory, these are what we might term the 'perlocutionary' effects of these speech acts. As we have argued, constitutional deliberations should be viewed as *performances* that serve a variety of social purposes, including defining and mobilising the nation, focusing public attention on issues of importance to the government, and distracting attention from other potentially sensitive issues.

Introducing the idea of 'performance' to theories of democracy and constitutionalism may help to provide a more critical and reflexive lens through which to analyse the concept of 'deliberation'. It also helps us to understand how instruments ostensibly designed to enhance public engagement may have the opposite effect. Indeed, as Lawrence LeDuc observes, '[t]he theoretical concepts of *deliberative democracy* and the institutions and processes associated with *direct democracy* often pull in different directions, despite their surface similarity' (LeDuc 2015: 139). LeDuc suggests that this is because deliberative democracy is less interested in resolving issues than in discussing them. It is also because popular referenda often tend to inhibit a deeper commitment to genuine deliberation, as New Zealand's flag debate demonstrates. We need to take symbols and the performative dimensions of politics more seriously when analysing processes of democracy and deliberation. This is not simply an acknowledgement of the emotional bases of political engagement or the 'bread and circuses' nature of much of what passes for participation in the political process, but rather a recognition that there is more to politics than rational actors and institutions operating in accordance with defined roles, interests and path dependencies. Symbols are performative and have a powerful influence over the way democracy is enacted; they do not merely describe or represent our political realities but actively constitute them.

Second, our chapter raised the question of whether meaningful and rational constitutional deliberation is possible when the constitution in question is so ambiguous and opaque that most members of the public find it incomprehensible. New Zealand's system of government – an unwritten constitution based around the elusive central conceit of a constitutional monarchy featuring the role of 'the Crown' in all three branches of government – leaves even constitutional experts struggling to grasp what this might mean for the process of reform. Significantly, the term 'Crown' features 79 times in the Constitutional Advisory Panel's 134-page report, yet nowhere is it defined, discussed or even questioned. It appears as an immutable fact, an entity so axiomatic and unquestionable that it lies beyond any constitutional conversation. Much like its presence in the commemoration of Anzac Day in Australia (Chapter 6), it is 'hidden in plain sight'. In short, for most people in New Zealand, the Crown and its constitutional role are obtuse and invisible. One lesson from this, it would seem, is that government proposals need to provide a good deal more clarity about the existing constitutional arrangements before seeking to engage ordinary citizens in a meaningful conversation about constitutional alternatives. Theories of deliberative democracy risk ignoring structural constraints (like class, cultural histories and unequal access to information) that inhibit meaningful participation in the democratic process. In this respect, liberal democracies may indeed have helped to foster an apathetic citizenry (De Greiff 2000) and a political environment that places emotion and personal belief above objective facts in what is coming to be termed our 'post-truth' era.

Perhaps the most relevant point that these New Zealand examples highlight is to note the importance of controlling the terms of reference in any constitutional debate, and who decides those terms. The term 'deliberate', as our examples demonstrate, may mean careful, cautious and reflective, but it can also mean intentional, calculated and manipulated. The main difference between these tropes lies not so much at the level of abstraction as in the way that constitutional deliberation is performed in practice by those in power. Serious constitutional deliberation is certainly possible in constitutional monarchies such as New Zealand, but that requires much greater public understanding of the work that political symbols do and the shifting meanings of concepts like 'the Crown', and an acknowledgement of what is at stake in the key terms of reference that frame these nationwide deliberations.

References

Abélès, Marc. 1988. 'Modern Political Ritual: Ethnography of an Inauguration and a Pilgrimage by President Mitterrand.' *Current Anthropology* 29(3): 391–404.

Austin, J. L. 1962. *How to Do Things with Words: The William James Lectures Delivered in Harvard University in 1955*. Edited by J. O. Urmson. Oxford: Clarendon Press.

BBC News. 2014. 'New Zealand to Hold Referendum on National Flag.' 11 March. Accessed 16 May 2016 at www.bbc.co.uk/news/world-asia-26524132.

Bohman, James. 1998. 'Survey Article: The Coming of Age of Deliberative Democracy.' *Journal of Political Philosophy* 6(4): 400–25.

Butler, Judith. 1997. *Excitable Speech: A Politics of the Performative*. New York and London: Routledge.

CAP (Constitutional Advisory Panel). 2013. *New Zealand's Constitution: A Report on a Conversation*. Wellington: New Zealand Government.

N.d. 'Our Role – Tō mātau kaupapa.' Website. Accessed 11 May 2018 at ndhadeliver.natlib.govt.nz/ArcAggregator/arcView/frameView/IE28514444/http://www.ourconstitution.org.nz/.

Chappell, Zsuzsanna. 2012. *The Palgrave Macmillan Deliberative Democracy: A Critical Introduction*. London: Palgrave Macmillan.

Cox, Noel. 2008. *A Constitutional History of the New Zealand Monarchy: The Evolution of the New Zealand Monarchy and the Recognition of an Autochthonous Polity*. Saarbrücken, Germany: VDM Verlag Dr. Müller.

Crouch, Colin. 2004. *Post-Democracy*. Cambridge: Polity.

Dryzek, John S. 2000. *Deliberative Democracy and Beyond: Liberals, Critics, Contestations*. Oxford: Oxford University Press.

2007. 'Theory, Evidence, and the Tasks of Deliberation.' In *Deliberation, Participation and Democracy: Can the People Govern?*, edited by Shawn W. Rosenberg, 237–50. Basingstoke and New York: Palgrave Macmillan.

2012. *Foundations and Frontiers of Deliberative Governance*. Oxford: Oxford University Press.

English, Bill and Pita Sharples. 2010. 'Consideration of Constitutional Issues.' Office of the Deputy Prime Minister and Office of the Minister of Māori Affairs. Wellington. Accessed 16 January 2017 at www.beehive.govt.nz/sites/default/files/CR_Cab_paper_8.12.10.pdf.

Ercan, Selen A. and John S. Dryzek. 2015. 'The Reach of Deliberative Democracy.' *Policy Studies* 36(3): 241–48.

Garner, Duncan. 2015. 'Opinion: Flag This Irrelevant Debate and Spend $26m on Hungry Kids.' *The Dominion Post*. 9 May. Accessed 10 May 2018 at www.stuff.co.nz/dominion-post/comment/columnists/68392405/duncan-garner-flag-this-irrelevant-debate-and-spend-26m-on-hungry-kids.

Goffman, Erving. 1969. *The Presentation of the Self in Everyday Life*. London: Allen Lane.

De Greiff, P. 2000. 'Deliberative Democracy and Group Representation.' *Social Theory and Practice* 26(3): 397–415.

Gutmann, Amy and Dennis Thompson. 2004. *Why Deliberative Democracy?* Princeton, NJ: Princeton University Press.

Habermas, Jürgen. 1984. *The Theory of Communicative Action, Vol. 1: Reason and the Rationalization of Society*. Translated by Thomas McCarthy. Boston: Beacon Press.

1992. 'Citizenship and National Identity: Some Reflections on the Future of Europe.' *Praxis International* 12(1): 1–19.

Hargreaves, Lynley. 2015. 'Is Our Flag a Brand?' *Science Media Centre Sciblogs*. Blog post, 29 June. Accessed 16 May 2016 at sciblogs.co.nz/infrequently-asked-questions/2015/06/29/is-our-flag-a-brand/.

Joseph, Philip A. 2008. 'The Māori Seats in Parliament. Te Oranga o te Iwi Māori: A Study of Māori Economic and Social Progress.' Working Paper 2. Wellington: New Zealand Business Roundtable. Available at www.nzcpr.com/wp-content/uploads/2014/08/TheMaoriSeatsInParliament.pdf.

Kelsey, Jane. 2015. 'The TPPA: Treaty Making, Parliamentary Democracy, Regulatory Sovereignty and the Rule of Law.' Trans-Pacific Partnership Agreement: New Zealand Expert Paper Series, No. 1. Accessed 19 May 2018 at tpplegal.files.wordpress.com/2015/12/tpp-treaty-process.pdf.

Kertzer, David I. 1988. *Ritual, Politics & Power*. New Haven, CT: Yale University Press.

Key, John. 2012. 'Merry Christmas!' YouTube video. Published 20 December 2002 by user 'NZNats'. Accessed 25 January 2012 at www.youtube.com/watch?v=x48TNjVbSHk.

2013. 'Prime Minister's Statement to Parliament.' January 29. Accessed 23 February 2013 at www.parliament.nz/en/pb/papers-presented/current-papers/document/50DBHOH_PAP24173_1/statement-to-parliament-rt-hon-john-key-prime-minister.

Kong, Hoi and Ron Levy. 2017. 'Deliberative Constitutionalism.' In *Oxford Handbook of Deliberative Democracy*, edited by André Bächtiger, John Dryzek, Jane Mansbridge and Mark Warren, 625–39, Oxford: Oxford University Press.

LeDuc, Lawrence. 2015. 'Referendums and Deliberative Democracy.' *Electoral Studies* 38 (2015): 139–48.

Leicester, Graham. 1996. 'A Pragmatic Approach to the Construction of Europe.' In *Europe: A Time for Pragmatism*, edited by Miguel Herrero de Miñón and Graham Leicester, 6–19. London: European Policy Forum.

Levy, Ron. 2013. 'The Law of Deliberative Democracy: Seeding the Field.' *Election Law Journal* 12(4): 355–71.

Markell, Patchen. 2000. 'Making Affect Safe for Democracy? On "Constitutional Patriotism".' *Political Theory* 28(1): 38–63.

Mitchell, Timothy. 1999. 'Society, Economy, and the State Effect.' In *State/Culture: State-Formation after the Cultural Turn*, edited by George Steinmetz, 76–97. Ithaca, NY: Cornell University Press.

National Party and Māori Party. 2008. 'Relationship and Confidence and Supply Agreement between the National Party and the Māori Party.' Accessed 19 May 2018 at img.scoop.co.nz/media/pdfs/0811/NationalMaori_Party_agreement.pdf.

Scoop News. 2010. 'Sharples and English Announce Constitutional Review.' *Scoop News Audio*. 8 December. Accessed 19 May 2018 at www.scoop.co.nz/stories/HL1012/S00066/audio-sharples-and-english-announce-constitutional-review.htm.

Sedley, Stephen. 2011. *Ashes and Sparks: Essays on Law and Justice*. Cambridge: Cambridge University Press.

Shore, Cris. 2000. *Building Europe: The Cultural Politics of European Integration*. London: Routledge.

Taonui, Rawiri. 2012. 'Ngā māngai – Māori representation: Controversy over Māori Seats.' *Te Ara: The Encyclopedia of New Zealand*. Published 20 June 2012; reviewed and revised 15 July 2016. Wellington: Manatū Taonga Ministry for Culture and Heritage. Accessed 19 May 2018 at www.TeAra.govt.nz/en/interactive/33915/john-key-on-the-maori-seats-2008.

Trouillot, Michel-Rolph. 2001. 'The Anthropology of the State in the Age of Globalization: Close Encounters of the Deceptive Kind.' *Current Anthropology* 42(1): 125–38.

Turner, Victor. 1967. *The Forest of Symbols: Aspects of Ndembu Ritual*. Ithaca, NY: Cornell University Press.

1988. *The Anthropology of Performance*. New York: PAJ Publications.

Werhan, Keith. 2012. 'Popular Constitutionalism, Ancient and Modern.' *UC Davis Law Review* 46(1): 65–131.

10

Crown Prerogative

Reining in the Powers

DAVID V. WILLIAMS

Every New Zealander goes to bed tonight knowing that Her Majesty reigns over us and the government rules.

I think you can go to bed tonight knowing that Her Britannic Majesty the Queen of New Zealand reigns over New Zealand and that John Key is validly the prime minister.

Christopher Finlayson, Attorney-General of New Zealand, 2014a/b

In assessing the propriety of the Governor General's decision to prorogue Parliament, it is necessary to answer two questions: (1) Did the Governor General have a discretion to refuse the Prime Minister's advice to prorogue Parliament and (2) if so, did she make a wise decision in accepting the advice?

Peter W. Hogg, legal adviser to the Governor General of Canada, 2009

The government eventually acted more wisely than was at first proposed.

Sir Paul Hasluck, former Governor-General of Australia, 1979

Seven of the ten judges who were on the Chagos Islanders' case agreed that using the prerogative power to exile the Chagos Islanders was an abuse of the royal prerogative and should be struck down. ... The House of Lords overturned the decision, but even they agreed that there were legal limits to the use of the royal prerogative – they simply disagreed on whether those limits had been breached in that particular case. So the Chagos Islanders' case has established, very importantly, that the royal prerogative was subject to the rule of law.

Sir Stephen Sedley, retired Lord Justice of Appeal, UK, 2016

Reigning or Ruling

Westminster constitutions are now based on the supremacy of Parliament, and most governmental powers are exercised in accordance with rules prescribed by Acts of Parliament as interpreted and applied by courts. Nevertheless, there remain a number of important governmental powers that derive purely from royal prerogatives (Bartlett and Everett 2017). The exercise of Crown prerogatives can be potent political weapons for those who control the executive government. They may manipulate the paradoxical arrangement of powers sourced in monarchical sovereignty to legitimise actions taken with little or no democratic accountability in nations that purport to now be based on the will of the people as expressed in democratic politics. This was an issue close to the heart of the late British Labour politician Tony Benn, who said:

> We are told that power has moved over time from the throne to the Lords, from the Lords to the commons and from the commons to the people. But in practice power has now moved to the prime minister who then, exercising the powers of the crown without explicit consent from parliament, dominates the whole system. The House of Commons is the only elected part of Parliament and democratic principles should require that all prerogative powers be controlled by that house.
>
> (McKie 2000)

Benn's expectations have yet to be met.

Questions also arise as to the role of the courts in relation to prerogative powers. Richard Gordon observes that between 1688, the beginnings of constitutional monarchy, and 1985 prerogative power could not be challenged, any more of course than an act of Parliament could be challenged (Gordon, Interviews, 2016; Blick and Gordon 2016: 18). In the 1985 *GCHQ* case, a UK government prerogative decision to ban employees of the Government Communications Headquarters from joining a trade union was challenged. The restrictions on trade unions was eventually justified on national security grounds, but the House of Lords established new law in holding that exercises of prerogative power were amenable to judicial review if illegality, irrationality or procedural impropriety could be shown (*Council of Civil Service Unions* v. *Minister for the Civil Service* [1985]).

That precedent was highlighted by many of those whom we interviewed in the UK on controversies involving contemporary uses of prerogative powers. Also important to this chapter is the notion, based on an aphorism in Thomas Macauley's *History of England* (1855), that a constitutional monarchy 'can be defined as a state which is headed by a sovereign who reigns but does not rule' (Bogdanor 1997: 1). So what is it to 'reign', and who actually 'rules'?

Reserve Powers

A few of the Crown prerogative powers, known as the reserve powers, have to be exercised by the monarch (or representative) in person. Canadian academic (and expatriate New Zealander) Peter Hogg describes the rare situations when the governor-general 'possesses a personal prerogative, which provides her with the discretion as to whether or not to accept any advice that is tendered' (Hogg 2009: 196–97). This was a matter of great significance in Canada in 2008 in a dispute over whether Parliament should be prorogued on the advice of a prime minister who may well have been about to lose the confidence of the House of Commons. Less controversial are the personal decisions the Queen, governors-general and lieutenant governors must make subsequent to each general election. As Sir Anand Satyanand, former governor-general of New Zealand, put it to us, 'the vital thing that the governor general has to do' was 'passing the parcel of power.' It is his personal responsibility to accept the resignation of an outgoing prime minister and 'pass the parcel' of political power to the person who now has a majority in the House (Interviews, 2015).

Over time prerogative powers have been circumscribed by constitutional conventions (Hazell and Morris 2017), and in some realms Cabinet Manuals clarify what the conventions now require of those who act in the name of the sovereign. They do not appear in any constitution or statute and they are not enforceable in courts. They are described as being part of the 'unwritten' constitution in Westminster systems based on parliamentary supremacy (Wade 1955; Willis 2015; Eleftheriadis 2017). The 'unwritten' nature of these conventions constraining prerogative powers was described to us by Martin Loughlin: 'Our whole tradition is one in which we don't write things down. Back to the common law. The common law is – in the classical expression – *lex non scripta*, unwritten law.' Further to that, he added, 'keeping things opaque but maintaining indivisible authority at the centre was always part of that governing tradition' (Interviews, 2016).

The Exercise of Reserve Powers

Given their origin in powers created by authoritarian English monarchs in the distant past, constitutional monarchs and their vice-regal representatives tend to be discreet in the exercise of reserve powers that might be perceived to undermine choices made by democratically elected heads of government. The reserve powers remain, however, and there are instances when they are invoked. Convention has it that it is not appropriate to do so just because a government's policy is not liked by a governor-general, but they may be relied upon if there is a perceived danger that a government may be acting in breach of norms of legal and procedural propriety. Little is publicly known about specific instances, but Anne Twomey relies on her own personal knowledge and involvement in New South Wales to write that government ministers do indeed modify or rescind decisions in the light of vice-regal communications behind closed doors:

> [It has been] argued that if a monarch today were to reject prime ministerial advice … the Prime Minister would be likely to resign in protest. While that might be the academic and theoretical position, it is most unlikely to occur in practice. Few governments are prepared to give up the right to govern and resign because of disagreement with the head of state. … It is simply not worth the political capital to engage in the fight.
>
> (Twomey 2018: 113)

Even with freedom of information laws in place, those communications and their impact on acts or omissions of elected governments will not become a matter of public record until well after all relevant actors are dead. Perhaps even then they may not see the light of day. Some scholars have an intense interest in the role of Buckingham Palace (if any) in the dismissal of Gough Whitlam as prime minister of Australia by the governor-general, Sir John Kerr, in 1975. Evidence of the Queen's involvement has been alleged but archival material will not be made public any time soon. In 2018 the Federal Court ruled that the Palace letters between Kerr and the Queen relating to Kerr's dismissal of the Whitlam government are 'personal' and not Commonwealth records, thus continuing the embargo on their release at least until 2027 (*Hocking* v. *Director-General, National Archives of Australia* [2018]).

What we do know is that Westminster constitutions continue to bestow reserve powers on the sovereign. They include the appointment and dismissal of prime ministers and ministers and summoning, proroguing and dissolving parliaments. Clearly, these are matters of the highest constitutional significance. One of the crucial issues facing those who argue for a more formal written constitution to replace the flexibility of the Westminster system is how reserve powers and political conventions might be defined in a new constitution – especially if constitutional reform includes the move from constitutional monarchy to a republican head of state.

More in the public gaze are exercises of royal prerogative powers by members of the executive government on matters such as entering, ratifying and withdrawing from treaties, declaring war and dispatching armed forces personnel to theatres of war, and dealings with British subjects in directly ruled Crown overseas territories. There is no requirement for a parliamentary mandate or public scrutiny when prerogative powers are exercised even though what the powers actually are, and when they can be appropriately used, remains ambiguous and debatable. While some argue that one of constitutional monarchy's chief merits is that there are checks on executive power, others maintain that the Crown's chameleon nature can provide a mask for the exercise of executive power without democratic mandate.

Genuflecting to Bagehot's *The English Constitution*

It was Walter Bagehot who drew attention to the importance of the monarchy's symbolic power. Though purporting to be merely describing the monarchy, Bagehot promoted the myth that Britain's constitution was or certainly ought to be understood as a 'disguised republic'. That notion was current in nineteenth-century English debates on the monarchy (Craig 2003), and it is a myth that resonates still in some quarters – including the emphasis, discussed in Chapter 6, that Australians for Constitutional Monarchy put on the 'crowned republic' to describe the status quo. Hence, they argue, there are no good reasons for republicans to advocate for constitutional change.

In debates on such issues in realms with a Westminster-based parliamentary system, Bagehot's name is invariably *the* primary authority on the role of the sovereign in a constitutional monarchy. For Craig (2003), '[t]he spectre of Bagehot haunts the historiography of the monarchy' (168). Twomey (2018) notes a constant genuflection to Bagehot's 'extremely influential' ideas that have moulded 'the view of the public and academics . . . even though they did not accurately reflect the reality' (94). Bogdanor (1997) observes that 'the writings of Bagehot were to attain canonical status' (40–41). He mentions that George V, George VI,

Elizabeth II and the Prince of Wales have all studied *The English Constitution* (32–33), as has Prince William, it seems (Smith 2013: 89).

In one respect Bagehot's prominence in constitutional discourse is surprising. Bagehot studied law only briefly. His career was as a journalist. He co-founded the *National Review* and was editor-in-chief of *The Economist*. A series of articles in the *Fortnightly Review* were collated and published as *The English Constitution* in 1867. Yet his writings contain quotable passages about aspects of constitutional monarchy that reverberate strongly to this day. Amongst the best known are these:

- No one can approach to an understanding of the English institutions . . . unless he divide them into two classes. . . . first, those which excite and preserve the reverence of the population – the *dignified* parts, if I may so call them; and next, the *efficient* parts – those by which it, in fact, works and rules (Bagehot 1867: 4–5).
- A cabinet is a combining committee, – a *hyphen* which joins, a *buckle* which fastens, the legislative part of the state to the executive part of the state. In its origin it belongs to the one, in its functions it belongs to the other (15).
- The sovereign has, under a constitutional monarchy such as ours, three rights – the right to be consulted, the right to encourage, the right to warn. (103).

The third excerpt is our focus in this chapter. Among Bagehot's arguments for the success of the English constitution is that it was unnecessary to explain to 'the mass of uneducated men' who 'really believe that the Queen governs . . . the recondite difference between "reigning" and "governing"' (40). This 'recondite difference' has morphed into the now trite aphorism attributed to Bagehot that 'the Queen reigns, but she does not rule' (British Monarchist League website). That precise wording can be found earlier than 1867 in Macauley's writings (Bogdanor 1997: 1), but Bagehot advocated the same dichotomy. The principle appears in Sir Kenneth Keith's introduction to New Zealand's *Cabinet Manual* as 'the Queen reigns, but the government rules' (Keith 2017: 3). The United Kingdom *Cabinet Manual*, which drew heavily on the New Zealand precedent (Hazell and Morris, Interviews, 2016), strongly reflects the influence of Bagehot's writings:

> The Sovereign is the Head of State of the UK, providing stability, continuity and a national focus. By convention, the Sovereign does not become publicly involved in the party politics of government, although he or she is

> entitled to be informed and consulted, and to advise, encourage and warn ministers. For this reason, there is a convention of confidentiality surrounding the Sovereign's communications with his or her ministers. The Sovereign retains prerogative powers but, by constitutional convention, the majority of these powers are exercised by, or on the advice of, his or her responsible ministers, save in a few exceptional instances (the 'reserve powers').
>
> (Cabinet Office 2011: 3)

Challenge and Response in New Zealand, 2014

The enduring significance of Bagehot's assertions and Macauley's aphorism in constitutional discourse can be seen in government responses to a finding of New Zealand's Waitangi Tribunal in 2014. After a detailed inquiry into the significance and meaning of the Declaration of Independence 1835 and the Treaty of Waitangi 1840, the Tribunal found that those who signed the Treaty 'did not cede their sovereignty in February 1840: that is, they did not cede their authority to make and enforce law over their people and within their territories. Rather they agreed to share power and authority with the Governor' (Waitangi Tribunal 2014: 526–27). In light of this finding of historical fact, what might be the status of Crown assertions as to the sovereignty of New Zealand now? How was British sovereignty acquired if not by that Treaty? Was it a colonialist imposition, followed by conquest in some areas, and eventually general acquiescence that the Queen's writ ran throughout the land in the decades that followed? The attorney-general, Christopher Finlayson, did not engage with such issues. Instead, he invoked the language of Bagehot and Macauley. There was no question the Crown had sovereignty in New Zealand, and the report did not change that. As quoted in the preface to this chapter, his response to media inquiries included:

> I think you can go to bed tonight knowing that Her Britannic Majesty the Queen of New Zealand reigns over New Zealand and that John Key is validly the Prime Minister.
>
> (Finlayson 2014b)

This distinction between 'reigning' and 'ruling', as anthropologist Declan Quigley observes, quoting Lucien Scubla, is that 'to reign does not mean to govern or to give orders, but to guarantee the order of the world and of the society by observing ritual prescriptions' (Quigley 2005: 1).

Monarchs and Governors Do Not Always Follow Bagehot

The Bagehot tripartite mantra was that the monarch's job when responding to advice from ministers was restricted to the right to be consulted, to encourage and to warn. A modified version set out in the UK *Cabinet Manual* holds that the monarch has the right 'to be informed and consulted, and to advise, encourage and warn ministers' (Cabinet Office 2011: 8). Was that actually the case in 1867, and is it the case now? Harold Laski, writing in the late 1930s, argued that Queen Victoria was no 'passive instrument in the hands of her ministers' but rather an 'active and insistent agent in the conduct of government' – blocking army reforms, securing the appointment of some ministers and preventing the appointment of others, etc. (Laski 1938: 397). Later kings were also 'more interventionist in their relations with the government than Bagehot's constitutional idyll would have allowed' (Twomey 2018: 94, citing Laski 1938: 398–401). This suggests that Bagehot's work, far from being a description, is another instance from Victorian Britain of the 'invention of tradition' (Cannadine 1983). Bagehot sought to transform the monarchical constitution to that of a 'disguised republic', and he used his journalistic abilities with language to try to constitute such a reality. Over 150 years later his myths have become much closer to actual constitutional practice. Yet, there are known instances of divergence from the Bagehot picture and perhaps many more examples that will never be known publicly.

A striking example of non-compliance was King George V's fateful intervention after the revolution in Russia that overthrew the monarchy in February 1917 (but before the Bolshevik revolution of October 1917) to reverse government decisions to grant asylum to the Romanov royal family and to send a Royal Navy vessel to rescue them. Mindful that it would be taken amiss for a constitutional monarch to extend a hand of friendship to an autocrat, George V urged the foreign secretary, Arthur Balfour, and Prime Minister David Lloyd George to rescind the government's rescue offer. When Balfour responded that the offer had already been made and could not be taken back, the King through Lord Stamfordham (his private secretary) kept up the pressure anyway. If Bagehot's version of the constitution was correct, George V had no power to insist that the naval warship already on its way should be recalled, but the government bowed to the King's pressure and the mission was aborted. In hindsight, Lord Stamfordham and George V claimed that the King had wanted to rescue his cousin all along, and it was his wicked leftist prime minister who would not allow him to do it (Aronson 2015). Lloyd George never publicly disputed his King's highly inaccurate version of the facts. Only when the official government records were declassified in the 1980s was the maligned prime minister posthumously vindicated (Rose 1983: 210).

Much more public was the decision in 1926 of the governor-general of Canada, Lord Byng, to refuse the advice of the prime minister of a minority government, W. L. Mackenzie King, to dissolve Parliament and call another general election. Instead the governor-general invited the leader of the somewhat larger party (in a multi-party House) to become prime minister, but he could not retain the confidence of the House either and a subsequent election was won by King (Forsey 2013). This use (or abuse) of royal prerogative powers was a primary catalyst for the strong stance taken by Canadian delegations to imperial conferences in the 1920s that led to the enactment of the Statute of Westminster 1931 – thus entrenching the legal status of Dominions as independent nations within the British Empire.

Memories of the Byng–King crisis returned to centre stage in Canada in 2008. Several commentators suggested that the governor-general, Michaëlle Jean, would have been acting within her reserve powers if she had refused advice offered by Stephen Harper, the incumbent prime minister leading a minority government, in the light of a publicly notified agreement between three opposition parties (commanding an overall majority in the lower house) to pass a vote of no confidence in the government when Parliament was scheduled to reconvene four days later (Russell and Sossin 2009). After some deliberation, Jean eventually chose to act on Harper's advice. Unlike King in 1926, Harper's advice was not to dissolve Parliament shortly after an inconclusive general election but rather to have it prorogued for two months whilst the government prepared a budget to put before the re-assembled House of Commons. Though not at liberty to disclose his own confidential advice to Jean, Hogg is on public record as to his views of the constitutional issues in the answers to the questions he posed at the beginning of this chapter. In his estimation, the governor-general's personal prerogative, freed from the usual obligation to accept the advice of a prime minister, is in play if that prime minister has lost the confidence of the House and that this extends to a situation when the government is about to lose the confidence of the House. Jean did have the power and discretion to refuse Harper's advice, but in the actual political circumstances at the time (justified by later events), she chose wisely to exercise her discretion in favour of granting the prorogation that the prime minister sought.

Less dramatic, but highly pertinent to this narrative, are two New Zealand examples. Governor Gordon in 1881 commuted a death sentence to penal servitude for life 'according to my own deliberate judgment' (1881: 1). In 1941 Governor-General Newall stood his ground in the face of explicit advice in favour of clemency for prisoners (Twomey 2018: 110–11). Doubtless it is difficult to draw a line between the sovereign's representative exercising the Bagehot-approved right to warn and encourage – as Newall thought (Quentin-Baxter and McLean 2017: 209) – and his or her objections being seen as a blatant refusal to act on the advice proffered by ministers, as Acting Prime Minister Nash perceived it (Sinclair 1976: 204).

The English Constitution: From Desirable Myth to Agreed Convention?

In Chapter 2 I argued that Sir Edward Coke's efforts to limit Charles I's royal autocratic powers by the enactment of the Petition of Right 1627 were based on ahistorical myths about an ancient constitution and a romanticised Magna Carta. Yet those myths were transformed into constitutional fact half a century later following a Dutch invasion (the 'Glorious Revolution') and the supremacy of Parliament asserted in the Bill of Rights 1688. The strict confidentiality of communications between those acting for the sovereign and their ministers makes it difficult to know whether a similar argument can be advanced about Bagehot's writings on constitutional monarchy being in the nature of ahistorical myth. While these were not an accurate representation of how Queen Victoria acted during her long reign, has 'constant genuflection' to Bagehot nonetheless produced some firm conventions limiting the powers of the sovereign? Can the Queen or her vice-regal representatives in the realms, states and provinces on occasion intervene to divert a government from a course of action it had decided on? Should ministerial advice always be implemented straightaway?

Westminster constitutions do evolve. Bagehot's wording now appears in Cabinet Manuals in some realms. Yet, behind the scenes, can a long-serving monarch or an astute and respected vice-regal officer still deflect ministers from their initial decisions without breaching political conventions? It is unlikely to be true that the Queen's personal prerogatives have been so diluted during the course of her reign, as Hazell and Morris (2017) suggest, that the sovereign has no effective reserve powers left (6). Some of our interviewees, who preferred not to be cited, suggested that

Elizabeth II, whilst firmly avoiding party political issues, has exercised a good deal more influence than the phrase 'to encourage and to warn' would suggest (anonymous, Interviews, 2015 and 2016). A possible instance, late in her reign, is the suggestion that 'the Queen put her foot down' over the ill-conceived attempt of the Blair government in 2003 to abolish the office of Lord Chancellor without enacting legislation (Hardman 2012: 184–85).

Outside the UK, we do have published reflections of a person who fulfilled a vice-regal role. Sir Paul Hasluck was governor-general of Australia 1969–74. He is quoted in the third of the set of statements prefacing this chapter. Archival material shows that Hasluck managed to steer the Australian prime minister away from implementing a decision (without clear cabinet support) to dispatch defence forces to maintain order in Papua New Guinea (Twomey 2018: 100–2). Without breaching confidentiality in the details recounted, on Hasluck's own published account of his vice-regal tenure, there were four or five occasions on which major issues arose and 'the government eventually acted more wisely than was at first proposed' (Hasluck 1979: 40–41).

The Crown's Prerogative Executive Powers and War

If we cannot be certain about the full extent of the monarch's reserve powers, we are in a better position to assess public actions of the executive based on Crown or royal prerogative powers. The executive branch of government frequently finds it useful and necessary – indeed 'efficient' in Bagehot's terms – to invoke prerogative powers. Though parliamentary supremacy is a pillar of the Westminster constitution, that does not mean that the executive branch of government must always seek legislative authority for its actions nor indeed seek any democratic scrutiny of decisions made. Ministers often act in important matters without much or indeed any reference to Parliament – though, ultimately, they are accountable to that institution whose confidence they must retain to remain in power unless and until voted out of office. This chapter now turns to canvas briefly a few controversial examples of the use of prerogative powers that cropped up in the interviews for our project.

One of the most controversial instances was the United Kingdom government decision to rely on the war prerogative when invading Iraq in 2003. British armed forces were ordered into combat by their government as an ally of the United States of America and other members of a coalition of states willing to take part in invading a foreign nation (other than in self-defence) without explicit authorisation from the Security Council of the United Nations. This triggered anti-war demonstrations in over 600 cities worldwide, including London, where an estimated 2 million people attended a rally in Hyde Park, making this perhaps the largest protest march in UK history (Jeffrey 2003). As it transpired, the prerogative power was utilised without full and frank disclosure of relevant facts to members of the British Parliament. The report of a Committee of Privy Counsellors (chaired by Sir John Chilcot) into Britain's role in the Iraq war was published in 2016 when a number of our interviews were in progress. That report found some severe failings in the manner the prerogative to enter into military hostilities was exercised by the then government. It concluded that the government of President Saddam Hussein did not pose an urgent threat to British interests, that intelligence regarding weapons of mass destruction was presented with unwarranted certainty, that peaceful alternatives to war had not been exhausted, that the United Kingdom and United States had undermined the authority of the United Nations Security Council, that the process of identifying the legal basis for the entire enterprise was far from satisfactory and indeed that war in 2003 was quite unnecessary (Committee of Privy Counsellors 2016). Sedley's comment on that report was that 'the power to make war is the ultimate prerogative power. And it was misused systematically by ministers' in 2003 (Interviews, 2016). Sir Edmund (Ted) Thomas, a retired New Zealand appellate judge, went so far as to frame a twelve-point indictment of Tony Blair listing offences and misjudgments he had committed in ordering the Iraq invasion: 'Tony Blair, in foreign policy, exerted unbridled and unchecked power to pursue his personal vision. When that vision was threatened he was able to manipulate the political process to his own ends' (Thomas 2007: 48). Sir Stephen Laws, on the other hand, was more circumspect. A senior public servant who rose to be First Parliamentary Counsel and thus responsible for the drafting of all government legislation submitted to Parliament, he suggested to us that you have to distinguish between getting authorisation from Parliament for doing something and being accountable for doing it:

> I don't think there's any doubt at all that governments are accountable to Parliament for the way they carry on military conflict. In the last resort Parliament has control over the money. So, go back to the Middle Ages: you can't wage a war without money. And one of the proposals when Gordon Brown was thinking about giving more formality to the approval of military action was to do it via the voting of money.

As Laws noted, though 'various proposals were brought forward, nothing was ever enacted, certainly on war powers' (Interviews, 2016).

The various proposals included a Select Committee report in 2004, *Taming the Prerogative: Strengthening Ministerial Accountability to Parliament*; a green paper, *Governance of Britain*, issued in 2007 by Gordon Brown when he became prime minister; a white paper, *The Governance of Britain – Constitutional Renewal*, along with a draft Constitutional Renewal Bill 2008; and a 'Review of the Executive Royal Prerogative' in 2009 (Bartlett and Everett 2017: 16–18). Then, in 2014 the succeeding coalition government published a House of Commons Committee report, *Roles and Powers of the Prime Minister*, which also argued for 'more powers to be placed on a statutory footing, with parliamentary approval' (Bartlett and Everett 2017: 18–19). With respect to ratification of treaties and regulation of the civil service, prerogative powers were supplanted by the Constitutional Reform and Governance Act 2010. As for the rest of the ancient, ambiguous and significant executive powers of the Crown wielded by prime ministers and ministers, these remain intact in the UK.

Thus, the war prerogative power remains vested in the Crown, exercised by the executive, and there is no procedural legal requirement to seek parliamentary approval for executive actions. Yet whilst the Chilcot inquiry did not make findings concerning the criminal or civil liability of anyone responsible for the manner in which the war prerogative was used in 2003, the report did influence the political landscape and, for a while at least, the level of accountability to Parliament became more pronounced. For example, the House of Commons voted down a government motion to approve direct military action in Syria in 2013. When the vote was lost the prime minister, David Cameron, accepted that, in the light of the Commons decision, he should not seek alternative methods of authorisation for the desired military intervention. In 2015 the government returned to the Commons seeking support for the government's more limited proposal to order British air strikes against ISIS targets in Syria. On this occasion majority support was forthcoming. The coalition government in 2011 suggested that 'a convention had emerged by which Parliament would be consulted before the deployment of troops' (Bartlett and Everett 2017: 19) – although that wording may not cover other war actions such as missile attacks. In an interview Martin Loughlin suggested 'the government will not engage in [troop deployments] without tabling a debate in Parliament and presumably will not precede with the military action unless Parliament has acquiesced by a majority vote. So that's another way in which those powers get regularised, institutionalised, rendered more accountable' (Interviews, 2016). The Chilcot Report doubtless contributed to rendering the executive more transparent and accountable when invoking a prerogative power than used to be the case. On the other hand, also in 2016, the minister of defence was firm that the government 'would not be bringing forward legislation to codify the convention into law, in order to "avoid such decisions becoming subject to legal action"' (Bartlett and Everett 2017: 20).

The Crown's Treaties Prerogative

What then might be the role of Parliament and/or the courts in relation to government decisions under prerogative powers to enter into treaties, to ratify them or to withdraw from them? In Commonwealth jurisdictions there is a strong trend towards seeking some form of parliamentary approval for treaties negotiated using prerogative powers, or at least offering Parliament the opportunity to veto ratification of a treaty that has been signed by the executive. In the UK, the Ponsonby Rule convention to that effect has been applied since 1924 and was codified into statute by the Constitutional Reform and Governance Act 2010 (Bartlett and Everett 2017: 14). It was the withdrawal element of the treaties prerogative, however, that became a white-hot political and legal issue in the UK in 2016 and 2017. The word 'Brexit' was coined to describe Britain's decision to withdraw from the European Union (EU) following a narrow majority for such an exit in a national referendum conducted on 23 June 2016. The government of the since-resigned prime minister, David Cameron, had stipulated no process as to how to deal with a vote in favour of exiting the EU. As Andrew Blick told us:

> It wasn't actually made clear in advance whether this would be a binding or non-binding referendum. There wasn't really much thought given to what would happen if one or more parts of the UK voted to remain if the UK as a whole voted to leave. So we've got that problem that Northern Ireland and Scotland both voted to remain, but the UK as a whole voted to leave. What do you do about that? That wasn't really thought through.
>
> (Interviews, 2016)

Paul McHugh suggested to us that Cameron's lack of forethought about such matters was utterly irresponsible: 'Why do you have representatives if they don't represent you?' (Interviews, 2017).

Nevertheless, the post-referendum government immediately deemed it a non-negotiable political reality that triggering Article 50 of the Treaty of Lisbon 2007 (which would enable exit negotiations to commence) must be implemented sooner rather than later. The incoming prime minister, Theresa May, indicated that this was a matter to be dealt with by the executive under prerogative powers. Other people had different ideas, and one of them was a British-Guyanese business owner, Gina Miller. She thought that if the statutory rights of British citizens under EC laws directly applicable in Britain were to be taken away, then only a parliamentary enactment could lawfully trigger Brexit negotiations. The litigation she launched, supported by counsel acting largely pro bono, provided ample food for thought and debate in academic circles (Robinson 2017; Young 2017) and very different responses indeed in other circles. The tabloid press in Britain, led by the *Daily Mail*, launched vitriolic personal attacks on members of the judiciary who found in favour of Miller's application and branded them 'enemies of the people' (Slack 2016). The government's strong preference for relying solely on prerogative powers was such that an appeal was taken to the Supreme Court. An eleven-member full bench of the Supreme Court decided by an 8–3 majority to uphold the decision of the judges pilloried by the *Daily Mail*. The impact of triggering Article 50 on statutory rights under EU laws was so significant, the court found, that explicit parliamentary consent was a condition precedent to triggering that article (*R (Miller) v. Secretary of State for Exiting the European Union* [2017]). As a consequence, the government was compelled to draft a statute for parliamentary scrutiny. It chose to draft and push through the Houses a minimalist measure enacted as the European Union (Notification of Withdrawal) Act 2017. The *Miller* litigation highlighted the contestation for legitimacy that reliance on ancient royal prerogative powers may provoke in a modern democracy, and especially so in the context of the antagonism between the principles of direct democracy and representative democracy that the Brexit referendum has provoked.

Prerogative Rule in British Overseas Territories

Of the vast territory and large populations of people that were once part of the Empire over which the sun never set, just a few specks of land with tiny numbers of inhabitants still remain under the direct rule of the United Kingdom government, though they are not part of the UK. There are fourteen entities that are not part of the UK as such. Known as

British Overseas Territories (BOTs), all of them are insignificant in terms of their area (except for territorial claims suspended under the Antarctic Treaty 1959). These BOTs along with the somewhat different, but still tiny, category of Crown dependencies (such as Jersey and Guernsey in the Channel Islands) attract a good deal more attention in world news than their size should warrant. This is because legal and financial advice firms based in British territories such as Bermuda, the Cayman Islands and the British Virgin Islands devise complex tax avoidance and tax minimisation regimes that enable wealthy individuals from other nations to hide their wealth and to avoid scrutiny as to how it was accrued. Customers availing themselves of their expertise hope and expect anonymity. Their expectations have been dashed by two immense troves of confidential information being put into the public domain. The Panama Papers in 2015 comprised some 11.5 million documents that 'show the myriad ways in which the rich can exploit secretive offshore tax regimes' (Harding 2016). The Paradise Papers added a further 13.4 million leaked documents on those 'who have sheltered their wealth in secretive tax havens' in Britain's offshore empire (Garside 2017). The scandal about the Panama and Paradise papers is that the millions of transactions they disclose are in fact in many instances entirely lawful. That is precisely the problem. How is it that territories ruled in the name of the British Crown can allow so much lawful latitude to the wealthiest people of the world so that they can contribute so little in tax revenues for the benefit of tax-paying citizens in the countries where their wealth was generated?

Protecting the interests of the super rich in Crown territories contrasts starkly with the history of the egregiously oppressive treatment of British subjects in the British Indian Ocean Territory (BIOT). Though BOTs are British, they are ruled by constitutional arrangements that puts the executive branch of the UK government in a position of power that is not all that different to the absolutist royal powers that Charles I sought to retain for himself in seventeenth-century England. There are few or no constitutional checks and balances, and there is no parliamentary body to which the executive is formally accountable. The majority of House of Lords judges in the decision on the Chagos Islands (*R* v. *Secretary of State for Foreign and Commonwealth Affairs, ex p Bancoult (No 2)* [2008]) held that British subjects whose ancestors had lived on the islands for centuries never had a legal right of abode on their own islands, and could be denied any chance to return (even temporarily) to their homeland – now the site of a United States military facility.

The quotation from our interview with Sedley – the last of the quotations that precede the text of this chapter – is the small solace that remained to him after the House of Lords reversed the Court of Appeal decision in which he had delivered the leading judgment (*R* v. *Secretary of State for Foreign and Commonwealth Affairs, ex p Bancoult (No 2)* [2007]). In principle the royal prerogative power used to dispossess the Chagos Islanders of their homeland was subject to the rule of law. Sedley and other lower court judges had applied the *GCHQ* precedent mentioned earlier. They held that actions by British governments over a number of years in the BIOT were a flagrant abuse of the royal prerogative to issue Orders in Council and should be struck down. In the final outcome, though, the government's actions were found to be lawful. Even citation of the rights of subjects under the Magna Carta did not suffice to win the day in court.

That outcome has been subject to a great deal of adverse criticism from legal academics (Poole 2015), anthropologists (Vine 2011) and many others. Vine was particularly harsh in his comments on the final decision:

> Indeed, when one strips away the ideological and linguistic window dressing of the 'royal prerogative', the 'Crown', and 'Her Majesty's Government', the Chagossians' case is fundamentally about the power of one group of predominantly 'white' people to control the lives of another group of relatively powerless 'black' people. As the Chagossians' US lawyer Michael Tigar said of the British government one night after the court, 'Why do they get to make the choices? You're a subject people. That's why.'
>
> (Vine 2008: 27)

One author so despaired of the triumph of pragmatism over legal principle in *Bancoult (No 2)* that he compared it with the pragmatism of Chief Justice Mansfield in a case concerning the slave-trading ship the *Zong* (Arvind 2012). In 1772 Lord Mansfield famously held that a slave could not be owned in England and so 'the black must be discharged' (*Somerset* v. *Stewart* [1772]). Much less well known is that the same judge held as a matter of law – even if not conclusive for the outcome of the particular case – that an insurance claim concerning African slaves thrown into the sea to drown was rightly categorised as a claim for a loss of private property (*Gregson* v. *Gilbert* [1783]). The African slave trade was considered vital to the British economy in the eighteenth century; providing military facilities for an ally was considered vital for Britain's national interests in the twenty-first century.

Concluding Comments

Undoubtedly, the prerogative powers of the Crown have been used for good and important purposes of government, as well as for pragmatic and illiberal reasons of state. But should there be any such powers in a modern liberal democracy? Should British Overseas Territories continue to be governed by uncodified prerogative powers to permit financial sector activities to operate in ways that would not be countenanced in the metropolis? Sunkin and Payne were right to complain that Crown prerogative powers 'remain shrouded in uncertainty and continue to generate controversy' (Sunkin and Payne 1999: 1). Gordon Brown's efforts to modernise and define prerogative powers mostly came to nothing. The vestiges of absolute powers once vested in medieval English monarchs continue to permit a lack of effective constraints on executive government powers.

Some scholars, such as expatriate New Zealander Richard Ekins, are highly critical of the *Miller* decision. Ekins perceives no particular dangers in royal prerogative powers being exercised by the executive without supervision by the courts or parliaments (Ekins 2017). On the other hand, Geoffrey Palmer and Andrew Butler (2018) have drafted a proposed constitution for New Zealand in which '[a]ll powers formerly exercisable by Ministers under the authority of the royal prerogative are abolished' (314). It remains to be seen whether that proposal will be any more successful than Brown's efforts were in the UK. For myself, I would favour constitutionalism and rule of law principles that enable courts to review and constrain potential excesses of executive power not otherwise subject to scrutiny. As E. P. Thompson put it, when reflecting on the importance of the rule of law in the very different context of Whig oligarchy rule in the eighteenth century, 'the inhibitions upon power imposed by law seem to me a legacy as substantial as any' (Thompson 1977: 265). It is a moot point whether twenty-first-century governments in the Commonwealth show sufficient respect for that legacy. The lyrics of a familiar anthem include 'Long to *reign* over us.' Whether or not some realms become republics in which the hereditary monarch ceases to reign – the subject of our next chapter – her prerogative powers most certainly do need to be codified to prevent abuses of power by those who *rule* over us.

References

Aronson, Theo. 2015. *Crowns in Conflict: The Triumph and the Tragedy of European Monarchy 1910–1918*. London: Thistle Publishing.

Arvind, T. T. 2012. '"Though It Shocks One Very Much": Formalism and Pragmatism in the *Zong* and *Bancoult*.' *Oxford Journal of Legal Studies* 32(1): 113–51.

Bagehot, Walter. 1867. *The English Constitution*. London: Chapman and Hall.

Bartlett, Gail and Michael Everett. 2017. *The Royal Prerogative*. Briefing Paper No. 03861, August 17. London: House of Commons Library.

Blick, Andrew and Richard Gordon. 2016. *Using the Prerogative for Major Constitutional Change: The United Kingdom Constitution and Article 50 of the Treaty on European Union*. London: The Constitution Society.

Bogdanor, Vernon. 1997. *The Monarchy and the Constitution*. Oxford: Clarendon Press.

British Monarchist League. Website. Accessed 14 April 2018 at www.monarchist.org.uk/the-constitution.html.

Cabinet Office. 2011. *The Cabinet Manual*. London: Cabinet Office.

Cannadine, David. 1983. 'The Context, Performance and Meaning of Ritual: The British Monarchy and the "Invention of Tradition" c. 1820–1977.' In *The Invention of Tradition*, edited by Eric Hobsbawm and Terence Ranger, 101–64. Cambridge and New York: Cambridge University Press.

Committee of Privy Counsellors. 2016. *The Report of the Iraq Inquiry*. London: Cabinet Office.

Craig, David M. 2003. 'The Crowned Republic? Monarchy and Anti-Monarchy in Britain, 1760–1901.' *The Historical Journal* 46(1): 167–85.

Ekins, Richard. 2017. 'Constitutional Practice and Principle in the Article 50 Litigation.' *Law Quarterly Review* 133: 347–53.

Eleftheriadis, Pavlos. 2017. 'Two Doctrines of the Unwritten Constitution.' *European Constitutional Law Review* 13(3): 525–50.

Finlayson, Christopher. 2014a. 'Christopher Finlayson on Waitangi Finding.' Radio interview, 14 November. *Checkpoint* programme, Radio New Zealand. Accessed 10 April 2018 at www.radionz.co.nz/national/programmes/checkpoint/audio/20157322/christopher-finlayson-on-waitangi-finding.

2014b. 'Waitangi Tribunal Report.' Radio interview, 14 November. Newstalk ZB. Accessed 10 April 2018 at www.newstalkzb.co.nz/on-air/larry-williams-drive/audio/chris-finlayson-waitangi-tribunal-report/.

Forsey, Eugene. 2013. 'King-Byng Affair.' *The Canadian Encyclopedia*. Accessed 16 April 2018 at www.thecanadianencyclopedia.ca/en/article/king-byng-affair/.

Garside, Juliette. 2017. 'Paradise Papers Leak Reveals Secrets of the World Elite's Hidden Wealth.' *The Guardian*, 5 November. Accessed 14 May 2018 at www.theguardian.com/news/2017/nov/05/paradise-papers-leak-reveals-secrets-of-world-elites-hidden-wealth.

Gordon, Arthur. 1881. 'Commutation of Sentence of Death Passed upon Wiremu Wharepa.' *Appendices to the Journal of the House of Representatives, A.–1A*. Wellington: Government Printer.

Harding, Luke. 2016. 'What Are the Panama Papers? A Guide to History's Biggest Data Leak.' *The Guardian*, 5 April. Accessed 14 May 2018 at www.theguardian.com/news/2016/apr/03/what-you-need-to-know-about-the-panama-papers.

Hardman, Robert. 2012. *Our Queen*. London: Arrow.

Hasluck, Paul. 1979. *The Office of Governor-General*. Melbourne: Melbourne University Press.

Hazell, Robert and Bob Morris. 2017. 'If the Queen Has No Reserve Powers Left, What Is the Modern Monarchy For?' *Review of Constitutional Studies* 22(1): 5–32.

Hogg, Peter. 2009. 'Prorogation and the Power of the Governor General.' *National Journal of Constitutional Law* 27: 193–203.

Jeffrey, Simon. 2003. 'UK's "Biggest Peace Rally".' *The Guardian*, 15 February. Accessed 14 May 2018 at www.theguardian.com/uk/2003/feb/15/politics.politicalnews.

Keith, Kenneth. 2017. 'On the Constitution of New Zealand: An Introduction to the Foundations of the Current Form of Government.' In *Cabinet Manual 2017*, 1–6. Wellington: Cabinet Office, Department of the Prime Minister and Cabinet.

Laski, Harold. 1938. *Parliamentary Government in England*. London: Allen & Unwin.

Macauley, Thomas. 1855. *The History of England from the Accession of James the Second, Vol. IV*. Leipzig: Bernhard Tauchnitz.

McKie, David. 2000. 'How Ministers Exercise Arbitrary Power.' *The Guardian*, 6 December. Accessed 14 May 2018 at www.theguardian.com/uk/2000/dec/06/monarchy.comment4.

Palmer, Geoffrey and Andrew Butler. 2018. *Towards Democratic Renewal: Ideas for Constitutional Change in New Zealand*. Wellington: Victoria University Press.

Poole, Thomas. 2015. *Reason of State: Law, Prerogative and Empire*. Cambridge: Cambridge University Press.

Quentin-Baxter, Alison and Janet McLean. 2017. *This Realm of New Zealand: The Sovereign, the Governor-General, the Crown*. Auckland: Auckland University Press.

Quigley, Declan. 2005. 'Introduction: The Character of Kingship.' In *The Character of Kingship*, edited by Declan Quigley, 1–23. Oxford: Berg.

Robinson, Tim. 2017. *Brexit Reading List: Legal and Constitutional Issues*. Briefing Paper 7702, 20 December. London: House of Commons Library.

Rose, Kenneth. 1983. *King George V*. London: Weidenfeld and Nicolson.

Russell, Peter and Lorne Sossin (eds.). 2009. *Parliamentary Democracy in Crisis*. Toronto: University of Toronto Press.

Sinclair, Keith. 1976. *Walter Nash*. Auckland: Auckland University Press.

Slack, James. 2016. 'Enemies of the People.' *Daily Mail*, 4 November. Accessed 14 May 2018 at www.dailymail.co.uk/news/article-3903436/Enemies-people-Fury-touch-judges-defied-17-4m-Brexit-voters-trigger-constitutional-crisis.html.

Smith, David E. 2013. 'The Crown in Canada Today: How Dignified? How Efficient?' In *Canada and the Crown: Essays on Constitutional Monarchy*, edited by D. Michael Jackson and Philippe Lagassé, 89–100. Kingston/Montreal: McGill-Queen's University Press.

Sunkin, Maurice and Sebastian Payne (eds.). 1999. *The Nature of the Crown: A Legal and Political Analysis*. Oxford: Clarendon Press.

Thomas, Edmund W. 2007. 'An Indictment of Tony Blair, and the Failure of the Political Process.' *The Spokesman* 95: 12–48.

Thompson, Edward. 1977. *Whigs and Hunters: The Origin of the Black Act*. Harmondsworth: Penguin Books.

Twomey, Anne. 2018. *The Veiled Sceptre: Reserve Powers of Heads of State in Westminster Systems*. Cambridge: Cambridge University Press.

Vine, David. 2008. 'Decolonising Britain in the 21st Century? Chagos Islanders Challenge the Crown, House of Lords, 30 June–3 July 2008.' *Anthropology Today* 24(4): 26–28.

2011. *Island of Shame: The Secret History of the U.S. Military Base on Diego Garcia*. Princeton, NJ: Princeton University Press.

Wade, William. 1955. 'The Basis of Legal Sovereignty.' *Cambridge Law Journal* 13(2): 172–97.

Waitangi Tribunal. 2014. *The Report on Stage 1 of the Te Paparahi o Te Raki Inquiry, He Whakaputanga me te Tiriti – The Declaration and the Treaty*. WAI 1040. Wellington: Waitangi Tribunal.

Willis, Edward. 2015. 'Unwritten Constitutionalism: A Study of the Principles and Structures That Inform New Zealand's Distinctively Unwritten Constitution.' PhD thesis. University of Auckland, Auckland, New Zealand.

Young, Alison L. 2017. *Democratic Dialogue and the Constitution*. Oxford: Oxford University Press.

11

The Queen Is Dead! Long Live the King?

SALLY RAUDON

> One of the jobs that I'm doing is preparing for the transition to a new sovereign. We call it 'the demise of the Crown'. And just recently we've gone out to all public sector chief executives and asked them, 'What are the implications for your agency when the Queen dies?' And they're all looking through the legislation ... pointing out that there's references to Queen Elizabeth the Second, Queen of New Zealand, references to 'the sovereign', references to 'the Crown' – and some of them are going to have to do a bit of work in figuring out what is actually meant by each of those. So there's a lot of different phrases that may be equivalent, but may not, depending on the context.
>
> Senior public servant, Wellington (Interviews, 2015)

On some future day, some very young children will need to be told that their great-grandmother, who held them on her kilted lap, let the girls hold her handbag and was rarely seen without her little dogs, has died. Everyone in this large family will sorrowfully prepare for great-grandmother's funeral. For she was terribly old – two birthdays every year! – and had done the same things for so long that it might seem that she could never really die. And something else will be going on too: their parents will gather to kneel and kiss the hand of their grandfather and great-uncle, the new head of the family.

This will be more than just a family affair. The British prime minister will be told immediately. The British Parliament will be recalled (and if an election campaign should be underway, this will be suspended). The British Foreign Office will communicate the death to the prime ministers and governors-general of her fifteen other realms. Simultaneously, Buckingham Palace's website will be stripped of other content to display the news of the Queen's death, a footman will pin a notice to the Palace gates, and the news will be relayed to the BBC and wire services, via secure radio networks, to newsreaders who have kept black mourning clothes at their studios, primed for the day (Knight 2017). Broadcast programming will be interrupted and, in the UK, suspended. *The Times* apparently has some eleven days of coverage prepared. Airline pilots will announce it to passengers and crew mid-flight. Flags across the realms will be lowered to half-mast. We will all remember where we were when we heard the news.

Queen Elizabeth is the longest reigning and oldest monarch in British history. Her longevity and public service have endowed her with immense popularity, even reverence.[1] She is recognised as standing at the 'still centre' of the monarchy (*The Economist* 2012). Inevitably, her time will end and a new reign will begin: the sempiternal Crown comes with concepts of mortality embedded, because it exists to overcome this problem by symbolising sovereignty's perpetual nature. As Bryan Turner notes, perpetuity is monarchy's *illusio* (2012: 86). For the head of state to die is exceptional in a republic; in a monarchy it is inevitable. Even reform advocates recognise that the respect and affection for Queen Elizabeth makes the outcome they seek harder to contemplate during her lifetime. Yet there are other problems of succession that are unevenly distributed throughout the realms.

Further, the issue of the Queen's death raises deeper questions than those of succession, as the institution of monarchy itself may be on the cusp of profound constitutional change. Most lobbyists, lawyers and civil servants we interviewed recognised a sovereign's death as a time of uncertainty and instability for the established constitutional order. While this is true in principle, in Queen Elizabeth's case her enduring popularity increases the potential for great upheaval when her reign ends. Opinions varied about whether and how the Queen's death might precipitate initiatives for new constitutional arrangements in various Commonwealth countries. Most fundamentally, some questioned the purpose and role of the monarchy in a postcolonial world; this was asked not only by committed republicans but by constitutional experts and citizens in each country.

This chapter examines the speculation, anxiety and ambivalence about the significance of the Queen's death and its implications for debates about constitutional reform. The argument is set out in four sections. The

[1] Longevity alone is insufficient: Queen Victoria likewise reigned for decades, but she was deeply unpopular for the 20 years during which she withdrew from public life, prompting a resurgence of republican sentiment.

first examines the mechanics of succession, including the technical issues this entails. The second surveys arguments for and barriers to reform in Australia, New Zealand and Canada, illustrating these by discussing how the Queen's death is imagined in Australia as the potential end of constitutional monarchy. The third examines an Australian attempt to resolve ambivalence about reform by finding a name for the country's brand of *de facto* republicanism. The fourth returns to what will actually happen when the Queen dies, and analyses the fusion of ideology and affect that will be rolled out in the legal, ecclesiastical and political acts that are required to make a monarch. Is the Queen's death the right time for reform?

The Mechanics of Succession

A primary conceptual problem for succession is the Crown's divisibility: each of the sixteen Commonwealth realms has a separate sovereign as head of state, but that office is occupied by one individual, Queen Elizabeth. When the Succession to the Crown Act 2013 (UK) eliminated male primogeniture from succession, the other realms had to decide if and how to maintain uniform succession rules throughout the Commonwealth. Each handled the problem differently. As Anne Twomey (2017) noted, Canada's federal parliament passed a law simply stating that whatever happens in the UK also applies to Canada, which has the political advantage of avoiding the need to promote an amendment to the Canadian constitution (eliding the need to seek agreement from all provinces including Québec). Twomey described this as 'a stark case of short-term political pragmatism taking priority over fundamental constitutional principle' (2017: 41; cf. Lagassé, 2018). The Australian federal and state governments, on the other hand, conducted a two-year programme of legislation to bring Australia's succession laws into accord with the UK law. Unitary New Zealand, with its unwritten constitution, had no difficulty in passing an act to ensure uniform royal succession. With those issues now settled, the law makes no provision for anything else to happen on the present Queen's death apart from her heir's immediate accession. Each realm has a slightly different way of proclaiming the succession of the heir, but it will be achieved promptly and simultaneously. Pegging reform to the Queen's death overlooks the legal and bureaucratic machinery that has long been in place to secure a rapid, smooth and peaceful succession.

Impediments to Reform

Barriers to constitutional reform fall under three broad categories: constitutional, procedural and social. Like Canada, Australia is a constitutional hybrid, melding state federalism with an inherited Westminster system. In many ways Australia already functions as a republic, as even some monarchists argue, albeit one which retains a monarch as ceremonial head of state. The phrase 'Commonwealth of Australia' gave the constitution a republican nuance (Cochrane 1996: 66), but the personified and personalised aspects of the Crown were also made explicit because Queen Victoria and her heirs were named (as was usual in colonial documents of the time) rather than referenced as abstractions of government.

Republican sentiments have never been far from the surface in Australian politics. Since the 1990s, political elites have been especially preoccupied with whether to replace constitutional monarchy with a republic (McKenna 1996, 2004, 2016). However, amending the Australian constitution requires both a majority of all voters nationally and in at least four of the six states. This double majority requirement has ensured a glacial pace of change. Since Federation in 1901, only eight of forty-four proposed amendments to the constitution have been carried. As Quick and Garran's (1901) *Annotated Constitution* explains, this was 'to prevent change being made in haste or by stealth, to encourage public discussion and to delay change until there is strong evidence that it is desirable, irresistible, and inevitable' (988). The constitution ought not be adapted piecemeal, by interpretation or by haphazard drift. Some commentators described Australian's constitutional inertia more bluntly: 'You couldn't introduce free beer by referendum' (Walsh 1965: 4). Geoffrey Sawer noted, 'Constitutionally speaking, Australia is the frozen continent' (1967: 208). Compulsory voting also enhances constitutional conservatism as undecided voters tend to support the status quo.

In 1999 Australia held a referendum on whether to elect for themselves an Australian as head of state. One popular monarchist slogan ran, 'If you don't know, vote no.' The result fell far short of what was required to change the constitution: some 55 per cent of voters preferred to stay with constitutional monarchy. Almost twenty years later republicans still spoke with great emotion about watching the republican vote split and fail: for many, this had become the great political struggle of their lives. For Diana Warnock, a former Western Australia state parliamentarian, broadcaster and women's rights activist, the referendum failure was still painful for her and her activist colleagues:

> It was a symbolic tragedy for the country . . . it probably doesn't mean as much to other people, but I feel immensely sad about it . . . Oh, it's a total grief! I mean I feel total grief about it.
>
> (Interviews, 2015)

Securing voter support for constitutional reform is only one of the many problems facing reformers. Procedural impediments are equally challenging. Anne Twomey estimated that amending state and federal statutes to reflect a republican constitution would require three to five years of legal work, which would need to be completed beforehand to realise the transition promptly when the Queen dies – and making reform at the time of death impractical unless the preparations were well advanced. Nowhere in the countries we studied had such official reform preparations begun. Twomey believed that careless interpretations might create significant problems lasting decades into the future:

> . . . it became apparent . . . that the word 'Crown', or other references to royal, majesty, king, queen, cloaked a range of different meanings, and it was a convenient word to do that, so that people didn't have to think what it meant.
>
> (Interviews, 2015)

The issues raised here by the conceptual slipperiness of the Crown echo that of the New Zealand public servant quoted at this chapter's epigraph, who is charged with clarifying how statutes will require amendment when the Queen dies.

Political scientists often suggest that substantial constitutional reform requires compelling motivation akin to a revolutionary purpose. Peter FitzSimons, head of the Australian Republic Movement and a writer and commentator, thought a crisis could motivate Australians to attempt constitutional reform again. As he put it:

> For the French to become a republic, they had to storm the Bastille, they had to risk their lives, and they *lost* lives. For the Americans to become a republic, they had to beat the English in the War of Independence. Here in Australia, we have to overcome the cult of celebrity.
>
> (Interviews, 2015)

In the absence of such a crisis, financial considerations represent a strong counter-motivation, specifically the costs of expunging the Crown and the monarchy from the statutes and public life and replacing it with new nationalist symbols. Doing this federally and in each state and territory would be enormously expensive. Some Australian republicans believe this cost should be acknowledged as early as possible and accepted as worth paying. However, their opponents will inevitably cite costs as a further deterrent to change.

In New Zealand, where the constitutional barriers to reform are relatively lower, social factors weigh more heavily. There is currently no compelling motivation for change, and politicians perceive that voters regard other issues as more important. Further, following the Australian example, republican politicians recognise that a reform campaign demands substantial political leadership and consumes significant political capital, and anything other than success does not bear contemplation. As one senior public servant stated:

> If there is no particular crisis at hand, what's the compelling problem? We don't seem as a country to be enormously passionate about the monarchy, nor do we seem enormously opposed, you know? It works for us.
>
> (Interviews, 2015)

Other participants noted that their own interest in constitutional matters was unusual, because 'Most New Zealanders don't spend much time worrying about it'. This was generally true in each of the countries we studied. Some speculated that reform would not occur until or unless there was a serious constitutional deadlock:

> It may require something to go really wrong – you'll need some sort of crisis, for a new king to do something outrageous or for some part of the system to fail. And then people say, well, actually, it's not working, can we do better?
>
> (Anonymous, Interviews, 2015)

In New Zealand, a further barrier to reform is the concern that becoming a republic would marginalise Māori by diminishing their status as partners of the Crown in the Treaty of Waitangi (see Chapter 4). An alternative reading is that with most Treaty claims now agreed, Māori and New Zealand governments might have less use for the Crown as a concept. Some Māori leaders are already longstanding republicans (Mahuta, Interviews, 2014; Godfery, Interviews, 2016). Others have followed the assertion from the Waitangi Tribunal (2011) that in the twenty-first century, the Crown now stands for Māori as much as it does for Pākehā (Stephens 2017; Godfery, 2018). There is certainly debate within Māoridom about how to develop a new constitution based on the Treaty and *tikanga Māori* (Māori custom) in which the Crown in Parliament would be only one of several relationally entwined actors (Matike Mai 2016). Further, as one of her first acts as prime minister,

Jacinda Ardern, a committed republican, replaced the ministerial portfolio of Treaty Negotiations with that of Crown–Māori Relations, signalling the government's interest in renewing the relationship now that so many negotiations are settled. Ardern has predicted that republican reform will happen during her lifetime, but the 'very special arrangement [through the Treaty of Waitangi] between Māori and the crown [means that] before any conversation like that occurs, that is something that will needed to be resolved within New Zealand' (Roy 2018).

Imagining the Death of the Queen

Australian reform advocates hope that the Queen's death will prompt meaningful reflection about constitutional monarchy's limitations and argue that any advantages of current constitutional arrangements can be retained. Prince Charles himself stated during the lead-up to the 1999 referendum:

> This is something which only you – the Australian people – can decide. Personally, I happen to think that it is the sign of a mature and self-confident nation to debate those issues and to use the democratic process to re-examine the way in which you want to face the future. Whatever course you ultimately decide upon, I can only say that I will always have an enormous affection for this country.
>
> (The Prince of Wales 1994)

Although the Australian Liberal Party remains committed to constitutional monarchy there is widespread support for reform amongst its senior members. Though Malcolm Turnbull had led the republican campaign through the 1990s, he tempered his reform ambitions once he became liberal prime minister, recognising that reverence for Queen Elizabeth's great age and her personal popularity pose formidable obstacles to reform. Speaking at the twenty-fifth anniversary of the Australian Republic Movement, which he founded, Turnbull declared:

> The vast majority of Australians have known no other Head of State than the Queen. She is so admired and respected that few of us can say – whether monarchists or republicans – that we are not Elizabethans. I do not believe Australians would welcome let alone support another republic referendum during her reign. And as you know I have held this view for some time . . . the cold, unyielding practical reality [is that] it is hard to see how this issue will return to the forefront of debate in this country during the Queen's reign.
>
> (Turnbull 2016)

With its strong Irish Catholic roots, the Australian Labor Party has historically supported republicanism (Warhurst 1993). Although lacking details, both the Labor and Green parties have held republican policies based on nationalist arguments since the 1999 referendum, generally agreeing that the Queen's death would trigger reform. Previous Labor prime ministers Gillard and Rudd both championed reform in principle when the Queen dies. So when Labor voted to pursue republican reform at its 2015 conference it was not fresh policy (BBC 2015); what was new was the insistence that reform need not wait for Queen Elizabeth's death – a point reinforced by its 2017 appointment of Matt Thistlethwaite as shadow assistant minister for an Australian head of state. As constitutional lawyer George Williams argued, using the Queen's death as a marker is 'a bogus delaying tactic . . . a convenient excuse to put things off' because 'if you want to become a republic then you do it independently of the state of the monarchy, [otherwise] it sort of emphasises our connection to Britain . . . you'd have to be ready to do it beforehand' (Interviews, 2015). The Australian Labor Party now agreed.

While Australian and New Zealand political elites often expressed the view that constitutional reform could be conducted only after the Queen dies, the Australian republican debate frequently framed it as a choice between retaining this Queen personally or dispensing with her. Could the death of the Queen mark the death of constitutional monarchy? Some, like Williams, saw this as a flawed argument predicated on an external locus of control: by what logic can republicans argue that the death of 'a foreigner' should trigger local constitutional reform? Others, including Turnbull, took a pragmatic approach. In interviews, republicans discussed the need to make respectful preparations while also hoping Australians would be prompted to review whether monarchy was right for their country.

Republicans might frame the living Queen as an artificial obstacle to reform, but they also see her death as possibly heralding the end of monarchy in their nation. Australians recognised waiting for the Queen's death as a way of promising reform without committing to action, yet some regarded it as a courteous placeholder. It reassures the electorate that republicanism remains official policy while appeasing those with conflicted loyalties towards the Queen. Delaying any decisions until after her death recognises this fundamental ambivalence, because many Australians both feel ideologically and emotionally attracted by republicanism *and also* experience the pull of affective bonds towards Queen Elizabeth as a familiar and quasi-familial presence. This makes possible a republican discourse that contemplates allowing the old regime to die with Elizabeth: 'The Queen is dead. Leave it so'.

The Elizabethan Age

Why is it taboo to consider constitutional reform while the Queen remains alive? After all, the motion was already vigorously debated and voted on once during her life. As Twomey notes, the Crown's visibility 'rises and falls depending upon circumstances, depending upon the monarch of the day. And things may well be considerably different when Prince Charles is around, if he becomes king' (Interviews, 2015). Suspicion about Prince Charles's suitability for the role often underlies equivocation about whether the Queen's death will trigger constitutional reform, but postponing the issue until after the Queen's death will mean addressing it during the life of the new king.

All parties acknowledged affection for the Queen as another strong impediment to reform. Republican arguments were often overlaid with respect for the monarch herself and the ties people feel to her. Veteran journalist Kerry-Anne Walsh was convinced that although change was not politically palatable now, it may become so once these quasi-kinship bonds end.

> She has reigned for a long time so people cannot imagine being without her as a wallpaper to life. I think that the affection for her is such that we don't want to offend Granny, and also because the offending Granny thing would carry over into any vote. So you are not going to do it. Once she is gone, then . . . even John Howard eventually recognised that!
>
> (Interviews, 2015)

Many monarchists emphasised that Queen Elizabeth's character, including her record of public service, made her personally suitable to be the sovereign. The Queen's virtues formed part of a broader argument about her ethical appeal. People who had only very briefly met her used the encounter as evidence of the Queen's impressive human qualities, often elaborating knowledge of the Queen of which they had no direct experience (see Nairn 1988). Critics found it difficult to take these affective bonds seriously, dismissing them as anachronistic, motivated by the pleasures of celebrity and lacking seriousness. However, such sentiment is commonplace and was socially acceptable within living memory (Connors 1993); certainly, many Australian participants had strong memories of the excitement of the 1954 tour, when some three-quarters of the population saw the Queen.

Most monarchists relied on the ritually constructed sense of renewal that follows the death of one monarch and the installation of another, predicting that once Charles became monarch, he would be affectionately embraced. Both monarchists and republicans predicted a great spectacle of grief. Some monarchists anticipate mass mourning followed by soaring public support for the monarchy – and gleefully anticipated the resulting republican dismay. Monarchist Philip Benwell believed Australians will experience the Queen's death as akin to a family bereavement: 'There will be an intense period of grief, like losing one's favourite grandmother. By the time people stop grieving, Charles will be there, and then the coronation will be coming' (Interviews, 2015). Members of the Australian Monarchist League fervently hoped that King Charles's investiture might include similar ceremonies in several Commonwealth realms, including Australia. Retired judge, academic and monarchist Michael Kirby, who was old enough to remember the previous change of monarch, noted the effect of concatenated rituals:

> The death of the present Queen will not alter Australia's constitutional arrangements in the slightest. Because of her long reign, most Australians have not witnessed a change in the monarch. I did, as a schoolboy in 1952, when King George VI died. There was genuine mourning, great pageantry, and the sense of renewal on a new reign. I would expect that the same things would follow.
>
> (pers. comm. 2015)

For many Australians the Queen has been Queen their entire life. However, as Twomey argued:

> People may have a personal attachment to Queen Elizabeth but not to Charles, and so that's obviously an issue – are they attached to the notion of hereditary monarchy, or are they attached to a particular person?
>
> (Interviews, 2015)

The question is whether the institution and the person who holds its office can be separated.

What matters in the speculation about the constitutional implications of the Queen's death is the energy and consideration devoted to something legally and politically impossible. Asked to speculate about what might happen when the Queen dies, many interviewees responded, 'Nothing. Charles will become king.' There is currently no alternative to Prince Charles legally becoming King in Right of Australia, and no practical preparations have been made to make an alternative possible. So why does vacillation about the Queen's death recur in issues of constitutional reform? Paradoxically, it leaves the Queen as politically potent in death as she was in life (cf. Verdery 1999).

Can a Republican Monarchy Bridge the Gap?

... if our slowly-grown
And crowned Republic's crowning common-sense,
That saved her many times, not fail ...

'To the Queen', *Idylls of the King* (Tennyson)

In the 1990s, political elites began describing Australia's constitutional status as a 'crowned republic' (Kirby 1992; Republic Advisory Committee 1993: 39; Hirst 1994; Keating 1995; Brett 1996; McKenna 1996: 4–5; Flint 1999). This phrase has a best-of-both-worlds quality, and both republicans *and* monarchists use it without irony. For instance, the Republican Advisory Committee (1993) described Australia as 'a state in which sovereignty resides in its people, and in which all public offices, except that at the very apex of its system, are filled by persons deriving authority directly or indirectly from the people ... a crowned republic' (39). For some members of Australians for Constitutional Monarchy (ACM), it signified their belief that Australia was already a *de facto* republic, fully independent from Britain, making constitutional reform a mere formality of no urgency or consequence. For them, it signalled that Australia's constitutional monarchy had already successfully incorporated the most salient and useful aspects of a republic to create a new and distinctively Australian form.

While the term gained currency during the 1990s Australian constitutional reform debate, it has an older history. Bagehot ([1867] 2001) famously described the English constitution as a 'disguised republic' (185) which has 'insinuated itself beneath the folds of a monarchy' (44), a gloss required for those who habitually misinterpreted theatrical pomp for actual power. Tennyson ([1873] 1897) first used the term in the closing stanza of *Idylls of the King*, his great Arthurian epic narrative. When the first Australian cardinal, Cardinal Moran (1830–1911), described Australia as a 'crown republic', it was this sense of British Empire that he evoked (Cochrane 1996: 66). H. G. Wells uses the term eleven times in his *A Short History of the World* ([1922] 1958) to describe the Empire as a crowned republic of 'United British Kingdoms'. Yet, contemporary Australian usage suggests a new localised expression.

Today, the term is used almost exclusively by the ACM. Their educational website, *The Crowned Republic*, championed the idea that because 'Australia now enjoys all the desirable features of a republican government and a constitutional monarchy without any disadvantages of either system', republican concerns can be dismissed because 'agitation for change is unnecessary, irrelevant, divisive and distracting' (Australians for Constitutional Monarchy 2016). This vocabulary particularly appeals to that subset of monarchists who maintain that the governor-general is the head of state (Smith 2005) because it undermines the republican argument that Australia should be led by a local rather than a foreigner. Indeed, governors-general are recognised as heads of state unless Queen Elizabeth is in the country and are often treated as heads of state during diplomatic and trade travel. If Australia is already a *de facto* republic and the head of state is already an Australian citizen, what ground remains for the republicans? Yet they remain concerned that the Queen's death should be marked in ways which support the monarchy, and they are not isolated in this.

Orchestrating Kingship Rituals

In each realm, public servants we spoke with have comprehensively detailed plans, regularly reviewed and rehearsed, for what must happen when Queen Elizabeth dies. The goal is to ensure that no unforeseen circumstance occurs. Officials refer to this plan as the Demise of the Crown, after the 1901 Demise of the Crown Act UK (legislated in New Zealand as Section 5 of the Constitution Act; see Chapter 2), which describes how sovereignty passes from one monarch to another without pause. Code-named 'Operation London Bridge', after the key words which will be used to communicate it on secure lines, the plans cover every imagined contingency, from the circumstances and location of death and plans to return the Queen's body to Buckingham Palace's throne room in London to getting their own prime minister and delegation to the 2,000-strong funeral and (in New Zealand) the minutiae of distributing official books of condolence in provincial towns across the nation. Prince Charles becomes king at the moment of his mother's death: the succession is immediate and automatic under the Act of Settlement 1700 (UK).

The day after the monarch's death, the Accession Council meets at St James's Palace. This marks the beginning of the precise choreography which will assent Charles's kingship. This Council body comprises privy counsellors, members of the House of Lords, the Archbishop of Canterbury, Commonwealth high commissioners, the Lord Mayor of London and others. The Accession Council's role is to confirm and proclaim the name of the new monarch. As king, he may choose to be known as Charles or one of his other names (Philip, Arthur or George). Charles's wife Camilla, Duchess of Cornwall, was appointed to the Privy Council in 2016 and so will attend and be presented to the Council as Queen Consort (Knight 2017). Various witnesses sign the proclamation and order that it be read at locations around London, accompanied by gunfire salutes, and around the United Kingdom. Beginning the proclamation with the phrase 'The Queen is dead, long live the King!' is convention rather than part of the official text. King Charles will respond to the Council with his personal declaration and oath – the first assertion of the expressly ecclesiastical nature of the British monarchy. The new sovereign becomes the head of state for the sixteen realms and supreme governor of the state Church of England, and also swears to maintain the Church of Scotland. This formalises the links between the monarchy and its two Protestant churches (Bonney 2013).

Later that day, British parliamentarians will swear oaths of loyalty to the new king. Royal mints around the Commonwealth will begin production using the image, name and emblem of the new king to replace Queen Elizabeth's. These will be gradually phased in on stamps, coins and currency, medals, and everywhere else that royal authority is claimed. In vice-regal residences, parliaments, high commissions and embassies around the world, the portrait of Queen Elizabeth will be carefully stored away and her son's mounted on the wall.

Queen Elizabeth's coffin will lie at Westminster Hall where people may visit it. Managing the public and media interest will place extreme logistical demands on government departments and police. The full state funeral will take place ten days after the Queen's death, which allows time for the sixteen realms and many other nations to send delegations. The funeral procession will take the coffin through London's streets to Westminster Abbey, where people will line the streets to watch and witness. After an appropriate period, King Charles will begin touring the UK and then visiting his realms, and some time over the next year his coronation will occur.

Performing Oaths

Various oaths are sworn by many people in the first hours of a new reign. During this transitional (or 'liminal') period, both the new monarch and those who proclaim and serve him take oaths declaring the monarch's status and role, and prominent members of society promise their loyalty to the new king. Taking oaths is both common in public life and rather taken for granted. Given their centrality in the rituals of king-making it is worth analysing what symbolic work they perform.

The new monarch's personal oath to preserve the Church of Scotland can be made in front of the Privy Council or, as Elizabeth did (because she became queen when in Kenya), at the next state opening of Parliament, where the monarch also takes the oath to maintain the Protestant succession – called the Accession Declaration. The monarch takes the oaths 'by the Grace of God' (not to God or with God's help, which is the commoner contemporary form) and, like the Accession Council, these oaths display the ecclesiastical foundations for the legitimacy of British monarchy.

Taking an oath is an attempt to manifest an aspiration. Oaths are performative utterances (Butler 1997; see also Chapter 9 for a discussion of 'performative constitutionalism'). Taking an oath is a solemn act that should not be made casually. Once issued, like the gun salutes which promptly follow the monarch's oath, they cannot be recalled. Oaths mark an attempt to transform the future, while evoking a sense of timelessness and transcendence (Herzfeld 1990). In cultures that valorise the potency of speech, oaths are also dramatic and dangerous. The oath-taker strikes a deal with the divine order, akin to prayer (Kerrigan 2011: 69), which carries the threat of divine retribution triggered by broken promises, as well as shame if one proves false.

As well as that divine witness, oaths must be freely sworn before others of legitimate authority. Consequently, oaths evoke a hierarchical social order. They serve to bind but also to name that which is most morally valued in society. Part of the ritual of oath-taking means that they must be made in places that are special or set aside from normal, everyday events, follow set rules and texts, and involve obligatory gestures such as raising a hand or touching ritually significant objects such as a sacred book, weapon or regalia. Although demanded by law, they serve no legal purpose in this instance because Charles will already hold the office of king; rather, they are important speech acts that create and perform a new identity.

In Western societies, oath-taking extends back to classical times: Homer's *Iliad* revolves around broken oaths. Then as now, oaths could be used to assert honesty or promise something about the future. Today, oaths commonly mark forms of legal, bureaucratic or religious intentions, such as marriage, legal testimony and oaths of office. Throughout the Commonwealth, people take swearing-in oaths as they commence new and authoritative roles, such as parliamentarians, vice-regals, the military, police, lawyers, judiciary and jurors. As in citizenship ceremonies, oath-takers swear allegiance to the sovereign as well as invoking the divine.

The practice of oath-taking also conforms to Durkheim's (1915) maxim that ritual requires unity of action rather than belief. In Australia, despite widespread republican sentiment, public oaths explicitly make Queen Elizabeth their focus. Indeed, in the UK, Australia and New Zealand the parliamentary Oath of Allegiance is 'I, [name], do swear that I will be faithful and bear true allegiance to Her Majesty Elizabeth the Second, Her heirs and successors according to law. So help me God!' Swearing allegiance to a monarch remains discordant for some. Canada has seen an ongoing civil liberties campaign to remove the obligation for new citizens to swear allegiance to the Queen (*McAteer* v. *Canada (Attorney General) ONCA 578* [2014] emphasised the right of new Canadians to disavow their loyalty oath to the monarch). In 2011 in New Zealand, parliamentarian Hone Harawira was ejected from Parliament for attempting to swear to the Treaty of Waitangi rather than Queen Elizabeth (Watkins 2011; see also Chapter 5) and in Australia Malcolm Turnbull swore allegiance to Queen Elizabeth in 2015 in order to take up the Australian prime ministership despite his republican reputation (Wright 2015).

As ritual acts, oaths work by publicly moving people between social states using a sense of the sacred in a highly choreographed yet ambiguous way. They have efficacy because they evoke a wide array of values and significance and people infer from them the diverse interpretations which community solidarity seems to require. In any case, communication via symbols often evades the consciousness of those most entangled in them. And the most richly symbolic ritual, the coronation, will occur up to a year after these oaths are sworn, marking the culmination of the high ceremony and pageantry of sempiternity that began with the previous monarch's funeral rites.

The Crown's Material Role

On the wall of the Jewel House at the Tower of London where Queen Elizabeth's televised coronation is played on an endless loop, a sign explains that a monarch is crowned because 'authority passes from one monarch to the next through the symbolic use of the Crown Jewels during the coronation ceremony'. In fact, the coronation makes no difference to the monarch's formal status, because their reign will have already begun (for instance, Edward VIII abdicated before being crowned). Rather, the coronation makes the symbolic transition of heir's accession into a social reality.

The coronation ceremony is also when the overtly religious acts occur, hidden from public view. During the religious high point of the ritual, the monarch and the Archbishop of Canterbury (head of the Church of England and the worldwide Anglican Communion) withdraw to a private space. The archbishop anoints the monarch with holy oil. Queen Elizabeth herself stated that this is the coronation's climatic action: 'It is only when the holy oil touches me ... [that] I am transformed and brought into direct contact with the divine' (Atlantic Productions 2018). Then the heir and the archbishop return to the ceremony and, in the most dramatic moment, the archbishop places St Edward's Crown on the monarch's head. (By law, only three people are permitted to hold St Edward's Crown: the monarch and the archbishop may touch it; the third, the royal jeweller, must wear gloves.) By crowning the monarch, the Church of England asserts its key constitutional function: anointing the monarch as God's servant, legitimising the monarch by consecration and uniting sovereign and people before God.[2]

In anthropological terms, the death of a ruler leads the people into a liminal period, when symbols take on greater resonance, when greater effort is expended on their interpretation, when the established order is undermined or threatened and could potentially be upended. The risk of pollution posed by a ruler's death to the symbolic order is a classical anthropological concern (Lienhardt 1961; Douglas 1966; Turner 1969; Bloch and Parry 1982; Hertz [1960] 2004). The ruler's death is initially marked by rites of rupture, cessation and cutting (van Gennep [1909] 1960). After a suitable time, the disorder of communal grief will then ordinarily be resolved by rites of reaggregation which reaffirm the social structure. Of course, reaggregation may mean reformation, which is what republicans are betting on. Like republicans, monarchists, politicians and public servants also recognised the symbolic value of royal funerals and coronations as opportunities to shore up the social order – or to open the

[2] The Crown Jewels were first filmed by the makers of the documentary *The Coronation*. The filmmakers were prohibited from filming the two crowns used in the ceremony from above because that vantage point is reserved for God (Atlantic Productions 2018).

doors to reform. But will this efflorescence of ritual really create the optimal moment to pursue constitutional reform?

Ritual and Reform

The written constitutions of Canada and Australia represent formidable barriers to constitutional reform because of the very high levels of public support required to enact change. Constitutional monarchy is integral to Canada's national identity, far more than is the case in either New Zealand or Australia. Canadians have little popular appetite for reform and organised republicanism is generally weak, as it is in the UK. The country with the greatest popular appetite for reform is Australia, where the Crown is least visible in everyday life and which faces demanding constitutional hurdles to reform. New Zealanders seem ambivalent about monarchy, but there are few significant technical barriers to reform: the country's lack of written constitution and unicameral parliament means change can be as simple as a parliamentary vote, there is no legal need for a referendum, and while bipartisan support and consensus are preferred, they are not required. While the technical barriers to reform remain formidable in Canada and Australia, there are also complex social barriers in each country we researched.

Besides issues of national identity and indigenous importance, the death of the Queen and the coronation of King Charles will foreground issues that may be awkward to resolve. The new king will no longer be young. His adult sons are more popular than he is. There may well be little public affection for his wife as Queen Camilla. Further, Queen Elizabeth's role of 'Head of the Commonwealth', largely of her own invention, is not hereditary, though the Palace successfully lobbied Commonwealth members to have Prince Charles succeed his mother in this position. But there was clearly deep debate within the Commonwealth Secretariat, and the Queen herself had to publicly commend Charles' suitability for the job.

The overtly Church-of-England nature of the coronation may sit uneasily with contemporary expectations of religious diversity. In 1953, despite vigorous international decolonisation movements and the pluralism that is often a hallmark of postcolonial societies, the explicitly ecclesiastical coronation reflected the religious hegemony common in settler societies over which Queen Elizabeth reigned. Freedom of religion and its implications for public rituals are regularly considered in Commonwealth courts and parliaments, and human rights law considers non-discrimination as foundational. If the next coronation retains an overt religiosity, or fails to signal enthusiasm for multiculturalism, it risks having the monarch being perceived as out of touch with contemporary society.

The question of what happens to the monarchy when a monarch dies highlights what is required to create one. It illuminates the distance between legal form and social reality that ritual must fill. Whether this time of transition could also be the right time for reform remains largely redundant. There is no pause button on a monarchy. Should Queen Elizabeth die during the Australian night, Charles will already be King of Australia by the time Australian republicans wake up, with his kingship shored up by the momentum of public grief, statecraft rituals and religious pageantry. While succession may be automatic and constitutionally protected, it comes with considerable challenges. Issues of reform will have to be considered separately from the life cycle of the monarch, but the widespread perception that the time will come at the end of Elizabeth's reign implies that the appetite for reform may overcome the inertia which has characterised republican efforts at the end of Elizabeth's long life. However, the legal barriers to reform found in Canada and Australia may remain intractable.

One major argument Australian monarchists use to defend the status quo is that nothing would really change under a republic. Indeed, how republican reforms would affect the prerogative powers remains open. Despite criticism of the royal prerogative, most governments find these uncodified powers extremely useful, while critics remain suspicious of prime ministerial powers expanding into any space vacated by constitutional monarchy, as we highlight in the next and final chapter. We also set out the case for why transitioning from constitutional monarchy to a republic is far more complex than simply substituting state for Crown or codifying the powers of the sovereign.

References

Atlantic Productions. 2018. *The Coronation*. Television documentary. 60 minutes. London: Atlantic Productions.

Australians for Constitutional Monarchy. 2016. *The Crowned Republic*. Website. Accessed 10 January 2016 at www.crownedrepublic.com.au/index.php.

Bagehot, Walter. (1867) 2001. *The English Constitution*. Edited by Paul Smith. Cambridge: Cambridge University Press.

BBC. 2015. 'Australian Labor Party to Reignite Republican Debate.' *BBC News*, 22 July. Accessed 10 January 2016 at www.bbc.com/news/world-australia-33618520.

Bloch, Maurice and Jonathan Parry (eds.). 1982. *Death & the Regeneration of Life*. Cambridge; New York: Cambridge University Press.

Bonney, Norman. 2013. *Monarchy, Religion and the State: Civil Religion in the United Kingdom, Canada, Australia and the Commonwealth*. Manchester: Manchester University Press.

Brett, Judith. 1996. 'From Monarchy to Republic: Into the Symbolic Void?' *Journal of Australian Studies* 20(47): 17–32.

Butler, Judith. 1997. *Excitable Speech: A Politics of the Performative*. New York; London: Routledge.

Cochrane, Peter. 1996. 'Britishness in Australia.' *Voices: The Quarterly Journal of the National Library of Australia* 6(3): 63–74.

Connors, Jane. 1993. 'The 1954 Royal Tour of Australia.' *Australian Historical Studies* 25(100): 371–82.

Douglas, Mary. 1966. *Purity and Danger: An Analysis of Concepts of Pollution and Taboo*. London: Routledge & Kegan Paul.

Durkheim, Émile. 1915. *The Elementary Forms of the Religious Life*. Translated by J. Swain. London: Allen & Unwin.

Flint, David. 1999. *The Cane Toad Republic: Why to Vote No*. Kent Town, South Australia: Wakefield Press.

Godfery, Morgan. 'The Crown: Is It Still 'White' and 'English-Speaking'?' *The Round Table: The Commonwealth Journal of International Affairs*. 107(4): 493–506.

Hertz, Robert. (1960) 2004. *Death and the Right Hand*. Abingdon, Oxon: Routledge.

Herzfeld, Michael. 1990. 'Pride and Perjury: Time and the Oath in the Mountain Villages of Crete.' *Man* 25(2): 305–22.

Hirst, John. 1994. *A Republican Manifesto*. Melbourne: Oxford University Press.

Keating, Paul J. 1995. *Australian Republic: Information about the Government's Proposal*. Canberra: Australian Government Publishing Service.

Kerrigan, John. 2011. 'Shakespeare, Oaths and Vows.' *Proceedings of the British Academy* 167: 61–89.

Kirby, Michael D. 1992. 'Constitutional Rethink: A Crowned Republic?' *Australian Law Journal* 66: 777–78.

Knight, Sam. 2017. '"London Bridge Is down": The Secret Plan for the Days after the Queen's Death.' *The Guardian*, 17 March. Accessed 30 January 2018 at www.theguardian.com/uk-news/2017/mar/16/what-happens-when-queen-elizabeth-dies-london-bridge.

Lagassé, Phillipe. 'Royal Succession and the Constitutional Politics of the Canadian Crown, 1936–2013.' *The Round Table: The Commonwealth Journal of International Affairs* 107(4): 451–462.

Lienhardt, Godfrey. 1961. *Divinity and Experience: The Religion of the Dinka*. Oxford: Clarendon Press.

Matike Mai Aotearoa. 2016. *He whakaaro here whakaumu mō Aotearoa [Towards a Republican Constitution]: The Report of Matike Mai Aotearoa – The Independent Working Group on Constitutional Transformation*. Accessed 8 March 2018 at www.converge.org.nz/pma/MatikeMaiAotearoaReport.pdf.

McKenna, Mark. 1996. *The Captive Republic: A History of Republicanism in Australia 1788–1996*. Cambridge: Cambridge University Press.

2004. *This Country: A Reconciled Republic?* Sydney: University of New South Wales Press.

2016. 'Waiting to Die? The British Monarchy in Australia, New Zealand and Canada, 1991–2016.' In *Crowns and Colonies: European Monarchies and Overseas Empires*, edited by Robert Aldrich and Cindy McCreery, 309–24. Manchester: Manchester University Press.

Nairn, Tom. 1988. *The Enchanted Glass: Britain and Its Monarchy*. London: Radius (Century Hutchinson).

Quick, John and Robert Garran. 1901. *The Annotated Constitution of the Australian Commonwealth*. Sydney: Angus & Robertson.

Republic Advisory Committee. 1993. *An Australian Republic: The Options*. Canberra: Australian Government Publishing Service.

Roy, Eleanor Ainge. 2018. 'New Zealand Likely to Become a Republic in My Lifetime, Jacinda Ardern Says.' *The Guardian*, 30 March. Accessed 15 May 2018 at www.theguardian.com/world/2018/mar/30/new-zealand-likely-to-become-a-republic-in-my-lifetime-says-jacinda-ardern.

Sawer, Geoffrey. 1967. *Australian Federalism in the Courts*. Melbourne: Melbourne University Press.

Smith, David. 2005. *Head of State: The Governor-General, the Monarchy, the Republic and the Dismissal*. Paddington, New South Wales: Macleay Press.

Stephens, Māmari. 2017. 'The Crown isn't just Pākehā. It is also Māori.' *e-Tangata*, 8 October. Accessed 30 January 2018 at e-tangata.co.nz/news/the-crown-isnt-just-pakeha-it-is-also-maori.

Tennyson, Alfred. (1873) 1897. *Idylls of the King: In Twelve Books*. London: Houghton, Mifflin and Company.

The Economist. 2012. 'The Still Centre: How a Failing Institution Was Successfully Revived.' 9 June. Accessed 20 May 2018 at www.economist.com/node/21556592.

The Prince of Wales. 1994. 'A Speech by HRH the Prince of Wales at the Australia Day Reception, Darling Harbour, Sydney, Australia.' Transcript of speech given 26 January. *The Prince of Wales and the Duchess of Cornwall*. Website. Accessed 10 January 2016 at www.princeofwales.gov.uk/media/speeches/speech-hrh-the-prince-of-wales-the-australia-day-reception-darling-harbour-sydney.

Turnbull, Malcolm. 2016. 'Speech to Australian Republican Movement's 25th Anniversary Dinner [*sic*].' Transcript. *Malcolm Turnbull*. Website. Accessed

30 January 2018 at www.malcolmturnbull.com.au/media/speech-to-australian-republican-movements-25th-anniversary-dinner.

Turner, Bryan S. 2012. 'In Defence of Monarchy.' *Culture and Society* 49(1): 84–89.

Turner, Victor. 1969. *The Ritual Process: Structure and Anti-structure*. Chicago: Aldine.

Twomey, Anne. 2017. 'Royal Succession, Abdication, and Regency in the Realms.' *Review of Constitutional Studies* 22(1): 33–53.

van Gennep, Arnold. (1909) 1960. *The Rites of Passage*. London: Routledge & Kegan Paul.

Verdery, Katherine. 1999. *The Political Lives of Dead Bodies: Reburial and Post-socialist Change*. New York: Columbia University Press.

Walsh, John. 1965. *Sydney Morning Herald*, 4 June, p. 4.

Warhurst, John. 1993. 'Nationalism and Republicanism in Australia: The Evolution of Institutions, Citizenship and Symbols.' *Australian Journal of Political Science* 28(4): 100–20.

Watkins, Tracy. 2011. 'Speaker Refuses to Swear Harawira In.' *Stuff*. Website. 14 July. Accessed 30 January 2018 at www.stuff.co.nz/national/politics/5284635/Speaker-refuses-to-swear-Harawira-in.

Wells, H. G. (1922) 1958. *A Short History of the World*. Harmondsworth: Penguin Books.

Wright, Tony. 2015. 'Malcolm Turnbull, Republican Prime Minister, Is Sworn in by an Absent Abbott's Knight.' *Sydney Morning Herald*, 15 September. Accessed 30 January 2018 at www.smh.com.au/politics/federal/malcolm-turnbull-republican-prime-minister-is-sworn-in-by-an-absent-abbotts-knight-20150915-gjn46o.html.

Waitangi Tribunal. 2011. *Ko Aotearoa Tenei: A Report into Claims Concerning New Zealand Law and Policy Affecting Māori Culture and Identity*. WAI 262. Wellington: Waitangi Tribunal.

12

Conclusion

The Future of the Crown in an Age of Uncertainty: Sempiternal or Crumbling Foundation?

CRIS SHORE, DAVID V. WILLIAMS AND SALLY RAUDON

In the northeast corner of Parliament Square, opposite the Palace of Westminster, stands a large 3.7-metre bronze statue of Winston Churchill, dressed in military greatcoat and resting on his walking stick. During the 1950s, when plans for the redevelopment of the square were being drawn up, Churchill, ever conscious of his place in history and of the symbolic importance of the Westminster Parliament, had apparently pointed to the spot on the map and declared, 'This is where my statue will go.' His views on parliamentary democracy are encapsulated in his well-known aphorism: 'Democracy is the worst of all forms of government, except for all those other forms of government that have been tried from time to time' (Churchill 1974: 7566). Monarchists and legal theorists sometimes make similar comments about the Westminster model of constitutional monarchy. As one former UK cabinet secretary put it, 'What we have done is develop a way of organising society, for defence and law and order and all the other activities that you associate with the state, in a way which is adaptable and flexible and meets the needs of society as it advances and changes' (Wilson, Interviews, 2016). According to David Flint of Australians for Constitutional Monarchy (Interviews, 2015), constitutional monarchy is a 'tried, true and tested' system that has been refined over 'a thousand years of history'. Similar arguments about the virtues of stability, flexibility and political neutrality are often expressed by supporters of the Crown and constitutional monarchy in Australia, Canada and New Zealand. For example, as one former legal adviser at the New Zealand Department of the Prime Minister and Cabinet put it:

> I come to this debate not with any abiding affection for the form of constitutional monarchy as it exists in our country, Aotearoa New Zealand, but rather a practical acknowledgement, grudging respect even, for the robustness of our constitutional form.
>
> We have taken the majesty of monarchy, placed it on the bi-cultural compact that forms the foundation of the country, and then shaped a constitutional monarchy to the needs of a closely-knit independent nation. We may not have chosen the form of our constitution, and would not likely choose the current form if asked to design it today, but we took a non-bespoke constitution and fashioned it to our needs. What could be more New Zealand than that?
>
> (Sutton 2016)

In Australia, advocates of constitutional monarchy give a different and perhaps more conservative twist to such arguments about the localisation or patriation of the Westminster system of government – sometimes sweeping over millennia of Aboriginal occupation to do so. As the national convenor of Australians for Constitutional Monarchy, David Flint, argued:

> Whether we like it or not, the Crown remains the nation's oldest institution, above politics, central to its constitutional system . . . It was under the Crown that the nation was founded, it was under the Crown that responsible government was granted, it was under the Crown that the nation federated and it was under the Crown that Australia attained its full and complete independence.
>
> (2007: 33)

According to this line of reasoning, the essential task of government is not so much about distinguishing right from wrong, delivering social justice or enacting the will of the people; rather, it is about the maintenance of sovereignty and the preservation of order. Indeed 'peace, order and good government' (or POGG) are the words historically used to express the legitimate objects of legislative power conferred on colonial parliaments, including Ireland in 1920. This phrase, also deployed in the imperial statutes setting up colonial administrations, echoes Thomas Hobbes's ([1651] 2005) belief that government exists to deliver us from our natural barbarism. In this respect, as Doyle (1993: 123) observed of Australia, monarchy acts as a mythology for political conservatism by representing itself as a 'transcendental moral order'. Supporters of the Westminster model often compare constitutional monarchy favourably to the US system of government, which they say – as one former senior

British civil servant put it – 'is not fit for purpose' (Wilson, Interviews, 2016). By that he meant the system of primary elections, the role of the presidency and the frequent standoffs between the different (and competing) branches of government. The Crown, it would seem, has been particularly effective as a bastion of constitutional stability and continuity and a bulwark against undesirable revolutionary change. Or is this really the case? Robert Morris from the UK Constitutional Unit (Interviews, 2016) called this 'post-hoc poppycock' and argued that the monarchy's survival is primarily because of the relative stability of those countries where it still exists. From a comparative perspective, constitutional monarchy may have delivered continuity and stability to the postcolonial settler governments of Canada, Australia and New Zealand, but it was notably ineffective in providing stability or protecting democracy in Fiji, Grenada or many of the British colonies. As noted in Chapter 10, the British government used Crown prerogative and the cloak of the Privy Council to strip the local population of the Chagos Islands of their human rights in what was a clear abuse of executive power (Bradley, Interviews, 2016).

Such contested claims about the benefits of constitutional monarchy bring us back to the questions raised at the outset of this book. Four of these questions merit particular consideration:

1. What is the nature of the Crown, and exactly how 'divisible' is it? If it is a 'convenient fiction', for whom is it most useful, and how? What are the merits of constitutional monarchy as a system of government?
2. If the Crown is the embodiment of state authority, how is it embodied and personified, and how do people make sense of it?
3. How has the Crown evolved in the different realms and what role has it come to play in the constitutional ordering of society and the structure of governance?
4. Which of the four realms discussed in this book is most likely to be the first to adopt a republican constitution?

This final chapter tries to address these questions from both a theoretical and ethnographic perspective. Drawing on our fieldwork interviews and comparative observations from New Zealand, Australia, Canada and the UK, we illustrate the complexities, legacies and lingering confusions that continue to shape the way the Crown is conceptualised, enacted and strategically deployed in the discourses of political actors, government officials and legal experts.

Anachronistic or Indispensable? The Merits of Constitutional Monarchy

Most monarchists and supporters of constitutional monarchy see it as a stabilising force in the world, providing a trusted and flexible set of constitutional arrangements. More importantly, it 'works'. Some maintain that constitutional monarchy comes embedded in the system of Westminster-style responsible government, including the rule of law, cabinet responsibility, impartial public service, an independent judiciary and democratic elections – all of which would be jeopardised by the move to a republic. As Winston Peters, New Zealand's deputy prime minister and leader of the New Zealand First party, put it, 'We are only one of nine countries that's had an unbroken line of holding elections in the last 150 years. Only nine countries can make that claim – we're one of them' (Peters, Interviews, 2014). The tenth, he added, used to be Chile.

The merit of constitutional monarchy, advocates insist, is that its head of state rises above politics, providing a benign, impartial but patriotic leadership which effectively checks abuses of power by elected officials. The monarch's independent wealth protects against corruption. That they were raised with the singular purpose of dedicating their lives to public service negates the craven ambition and venality that characterises the role of head of state in many republics. Supporters also argue that constitutional monarchy is highly efficient and provides good value for money. As Winston Peters observes, presidents 'cost a fortune' whereas constitutional monarchy is cheap:

> What is it costing us to have the Queen? Nothing. What does it cost us to be in an arrangement with one quarter of the world's legitimate governments? Nothing. I kind of think we're doing pretty well out of it because of that, because the alternative is very expensive.
>
> (Peters, Interviews, 2014)

Some advocates go further and insist that monarchy delivers major economic advantages. A 2017 Wharton School study even claims to have found 'robust and quantitatively meaningful evidence' that monarchies economically outperform other forms of government (Guillén 2018). In the UK, such arguments are bolstered by the Royal Family's marketing and tourism earnings, its contributions to trade and its role in diplomacy. For Britain, the monarchy is a powerful symbol of nationhood and a focus of popular allegiance, yet even beyond the UK the British monarchy is held up as the preeminent example of its kind. From prominent monarchists internationally, including Count Tolstoy-Miloslavsky, head of the International Monarchist League, and the Reverend Canon Kenneth Gunn-Walberg, leader of the Monarchist League's chapter for the eastern US states, the appeal of monarchies is simple: 'There is style, a mystery and ethos with a monarch. Presidents come and go. There's a continuity, a sense of history with the monarchy' (Wayne 2018). Bagehot's analysis, written over a century ago, still holds true: the monarchy endows dry, dull cabinet government with majesty, dignity and spectacle, making it the hidden wiring that enables parliamentary government to work (Bagehot [1867] 2001).

For some Canadian, Australian and New Zealand descendants of colonial settlers, the monarchy still symbolises connection between their countries and the wider family of Anglophonic settler societies that share a common history, language and culture. For indigenous peoples in Canada and New Zealand, their relationship with the Crown is part of a historic bond that transcends national governments. The Crown is seen as partner to important treaties, such as New Zealand's Treaty of Waitangi (1840) and Canada's Royal Proclamation (1763), which are the basis of a raft of rights and reparations (see Chapter 4). In New Zealand, the Crown concept has been elevated – and massively inflated – by the Treaty of Waitangi settlement processes; as New Zealand's former attorney general noted, 'We talk about the Crown because Māori talk about the Crown' (Finlayson, Interviews, 2013). Indeed, for many New Zealanders, especially Māori, Crown and Treaty have become 'a contemporary basis for negotiation and participation in national life' (McAllister 2012: 190). While constitutional lawyers may insist that the substance and *mana* (efficacy, authority) of the Crown's Treaty obligations would simply be transferred to a republican state, many treat such reassurances with scepticism. Māori worldview is predicated on relational engagement (Marsden 2003) in which *wairua* (spirit) is a constant unseen presence (Tate 1990). For Māori, Treaty matters are based on personal relationships between people in one another's presence, enriched by ancestral ties, and these personal commitments cannot be meaningfully replicated by an anonymous state or government or a revolving cast of its representatives. Consequently, many see republicanism as a threat to this foundational bond and the state honouring its commitments to Māori (cf. Godfery, 2018).

Some Canadian monarchists rationalise that the Crown is necessary *because* of its unique social and legal relationship with indigenous peoples. In the early 1980s, believing that Pierre Trudeau's proposed patriation of the Canadian Constitution would limit their rights, First

Nations peoples protested by travelling to Ottawa via hired trains in what became called the 'Constitution Express'. They took a case to the Court of Appeal in England arguing that the imperial Crown of the Royal Proclamation 1763 remained indivisible in 1982. They lost that case, but a belated insertion of Section 35 into the Constitution Act stated that 'the existing aboriginal and treaty rights of the aboriginal peoples of Canada are hereby recognized and affirmed'. This has proved to be potent in litigation since 1982, developing the notion of the 'honour of the Crown' in dealings with First Nations. Monarchists in the UK and Australia tend to the conservative end of the political spectrum, and indigenous rights feature little or not at all in Australian arguments in support of the monarchy. However, some prominent advocates of constitutional monarchy that we interviewed in Canada, such as Nathan Tidridge and Peter Russell, placed much emphasis on the importance of the relationship between the Crown and indigenous peoples in affirming and legitimating the position of the Queen in right of Canada.

In Australia, monarchists argue that constitutional reform is futile because Australia is already functionally a republic with a figurehead monarchy. In rebutting the monarchist case, republican and historian John Hirst (1994) notes that Australians for Constitutional Monarchy, 'unique among lobby groups, argues not how great, but how small is the influence of the institution it protects' (44). Monarchists and republicans are surprised to agree that Australia is already 'only a hair's breadth from a republic', and, remarkably, each employs this point as evidence of the logic of their own position.

Monarchist arguments typically end with the adage, 'If it ain't broke, why fix it?' Despite its idiosyncrasies and imperfections, constitutional monarchy works and has been tested and refined over centuries. Its supporters claim that it is stable, responsive, flexible and surprisingly efficient to run. Why, therefore, would any right-thinking person put this at risk? One response to that question is to pose another: given that few people understand what the Crown and constitutional monarchy are, what exactly does it mean to say this system of government 'works', or might need fixing?

Corporation Sole or Aggregate? The Many Faces of the Crown

This question is further complicated by the Crown's polysemic and shifting nature. As we have illustrated throughout this book, the Crown can be both a singular entity and a multifaceted, divisible phenomenon.

That divisibility increased profoundly after the 1931 Statute of Westminster, which led to the development of separate, national Crowns and the legislative independence of the self-governing Dominions of the former British Empire. Yet much of the legal debate has historically hinged upon the question of whether the Crown is best understood as a 'corporation sole' – a unified and indivisible form of authority – or a 'corporation aggregate' (composed of multiple members). The reality is that it can operate as either of these, or as both. There is little agreement even among lawyers about which definition is most accurate, and the case law on this issue remains ambiguous. The Crown is thus variously constructed as (1) a part of the executive, (2) a body that stands between government institutions and citizens and (3) a detached, independent higher-order entity that represents both government institutions and the people. One British official likened it to a hydra-headed monster. Yet some of our expert informants rejected the notion of the Crown as a corporation at all, arguing that technically 'it cannot be a corporation' because 'the monarchy is overarching' and 'bigger than the concept of a corporation' (Wilson, Interviews, 2016). Corporations, as Wilson explained, are creations *of* the monarchy, not external to it.[1] This argument echoes claims by ardent royalists who insist that the Queen has not ceded her powers to ministers of Parliament but merely 'delegated' her authority to these usurpers. After all, as we were often told, the government is always Her Majesty's Government and the UK Parliament meets in what is still a royal palace. Such arguments rest on the assumption that the sovereign's power is inalienable and remains the ultimate source of all state power: hence, the origin of the term 'sovereignty'.

Maitland saw the idea of the Crown as a corporation sole as the greatest of all legal fictions (see Chapter 3), and in this he was probably right given the way it is endowed with seemingly metaphysical properties. Yet his ironic statement that 'the crown does nothing but lie in the Tower of London to be gazed at by sight-seers' (Maitland [1908] 2001: 418) is misleading. While the Crown today is a highly circumscribed legal fiction whose powers can only be exercised through the institutionalised channels of ministerial seals, it nevertheless remains the source of all state

[1] The original chartered corporations such as the British East India Company (1600) and the Virginia Company (1606) were created by the monarch through letters patent, and members of the Royal Family were among their shareholders. Today's corporations, by contrast, are created by legislation, external to monarchy and to the idea of privilege conferred by the state (see McLean 2004).

authority and has considerable political and symbolic agency. The Crown (or those who speak for it) has the power to declare war (as Prime Minister Blair did against Iraq), create treaties (such as the Treaty of Lisbon or the Comprehensive and Progressive Agreement for Trans-Pacific Partnership), prosecute criminals and issue passports. As one British constitutional expert put it, 'the Crown can create universities, the Crown can free people from prison, the Crown can disband the armed forces and can make a peace treaty. I think it was Bagehot who observed it can even cede Cornwall without Parliament's approval if it wishes' (Wilson, Interviews, 2016). In fact, Bagehot's depiction of the Crown's powers was even more expansive:

> [W]ithout consulting Parliament ... by an act of prerogative ... [the Queen] could disband the army; she could dismiss all the officers ... she could sell off all our ships of war and all our naval stores; she could make a peace by the sacrifice of Cornwall, and begin a war for the conquest of Brittany. She could make every citizen in the United Kingdom, male or female, a peer; she could make every parish in the United Kingdom a 'university'; she could dismiss most of the civil servants; she could pardon all offenders.
>
> (Bagehot [1867] 2001: 32)

This statement evokes the idea of a singular and all-powerful sovereign, vested with unchallengeable executive, judicial, military and political powers. However, the Crown is not one thing but several, and it assumes multiple forms. In this respect it epitomises what Sherry Ortner (1973) called a 'key symbol': one that is simultaneously ambiguous, fluid and 'polyvalent' with a wide spectrum of different yet highly condensed meanings that shift according to context. This helps us to solve one of the riddles raised earlier: how is it possible for the Crown in New Zealand to simultaneously be treated as a constitutional partner and signatory to the Treaty of Waitangi, a manifestation of the general will of the people of New Zealand, and a 'convenient legal fiction?' The answer lies in its dexterity and efficacy as a political symbol. Legal fictions have very 'real' effects. Indeed, as noted in Chapters 3 and 9, they are often more powerful for being fictitious and therefore beyond the realm of rational deliberation and judgement.

This makes the Crown exceptionally useful and potent as a political instrument, and yet its cultural influence and political power are often masked by the way it has become normalised. The Crown appears as sempiternal: it was thus and ever shall be, an institution that can never die. To echo Bourdieu (1977), the naturalisation of its own arbitrariness has rendered the Crown 'doxic'. The term *doxa* refers to 'a kind of belief that is not even perceived as belief' (Bourdieu 2014: 184), that is, 'rules' that are arbitrary yet are experienced as self-evident, unquestionable and outside the field of opinion: *doxa* 'goes without saying because it comes without saying' (Bourdieu 1977: 167). It thus appears to many as timeless, unquestioned, axiomatic and an essential part of our constitutional order, yet it barely even registers in popular consciousness as something that could be questioned. This certainly helps to explain the Crown's utility as an instrument of government and why ministers – even those who wish to reform or abolish it – find it either too convenient or too difficult to relinquish. The Crown is useful to those inside as well as outside the government apparatus for at least three reasons: it offers an authority that can be appealed to as a source of legitimacy; it allows government ministers and officials to act under the umbrella of a united and sanctified sovereign body; and it endows political decisions of government with gravitas and permanence, as decisions made by the Crown are assumed to carry much greater weight and authority than decisions made by a minister associated with a political party. Ministers typically use the Crown to elevate decision-making to a plane that transcends parochial and partisan interests. One could argue that the Crown is extremely useful for democracy because it frames and legitimates the rules of the political game: the Crown itself assuming the symbolic role of umpire – setting limits and certifying outcomes – under which parties compete for office (to become Her Majesty's Government), pass legislation and implement policies within a constitutionally bounded space. It does not 'play the game' because it is above the game, and yet the game cannot be played without it. It also acts to unify the separated powers within a common normative order. This perception of an apolitical and transcendent Crown is shared by both state and non-state actors including tribes, community groups, sports clubs, charities and ordinary citizens – all of whom can petition the Crown.

The Crown is also a particularly useful fiction for indigenous peoples. As Chapter 1 and Chapter 4 showed, in New Zealand and Canada it has provided a potent instrument for holding past governments to account and for redressing historical grievances. It elevates the state above partisan politics and gives Crown–indigenous relationships a special, perhaps even transcendent, status. At the same time, it also provides a platform for governments to display generosity regarding past grievances and goodwill for building future relationships. In New Zealand and Canada, Supreme Courts have held there is a 'fiduciary' relationship between the

Crown and indigenous peoples, and the 'honour of the Crown' has become a key principle in redefining that relationship.

The answer to the question 'for whom is the Crown a convenient fiction?' seems to be that it is useful for political, legal and administrative elites, for indigenous groups and for groups and institutions that receive royal patronage. If the notion of a personal relationship between the monarch and indigenous peoples was an effective instrument of imperial statecraft, it also makes the Crown a key site for resolving Māori grievances over broken promises made on behalf of Queen Victoria. As Janet McLean (2015: 187) argues, the Crown concept has been particularly important in redressing the historical wrongs of colonisation in New Zealand. As McLean explains, the monarch is imagined as 'an individual person, an abstract body vested with a moral personality, and is institutionally distinct from the ordinary Crown in Parliament. She represents statehood and continuity in ways that government, as we typically understand it, does not do' (196). The monarch is also the person who bears responsibility for the honour of the Crown, who can be held culpable for its omissions and commissions, and who has 'duties of sincerity [and] fair dealing' in her relationships with Māori (211). Endowing the Crown with moral personality and continuity can help counter objections to accepting contemporary responsibility for historic wrongdoing, neutralising common arguments such as 'why should I be held responsible for the actions of people who were not my ancestors?'

McLean concedes that having the Crown perform this work avoids or 'fudges' some issues. However, it is important to consider some of the problems that this creates. Three merit particular consideration. The first is that this narrative paints a simplistic and misleading picture of the Crown as continuous and unchanging. The Crown of 1840 (British, imperial, pre-democratic) is depicted as the same historical actor as the Crown of 1904, 1944, 1984 and 2018. This is a convenient fiction that both sides of the Treaty of Waitangi settlement process exploit. However, as historians complain, this conflation flattens the past and 'obscures the complexity of our history. . . . It means we avoid looking at policies of particular regimes, particular governments, and don't need to understand the nuances of our colonial politics' (Hill, Interviews, 2013; see also Shore and Kawharu 2014). Second, while making the Crown the villain of history and scapegoat for colonial wrongdoing is expedient for postcolonial reconciliation, it also renders the Crown as quintessentially 'other'. The Office of Treaty Settlements argues that in today's democratic New

Zealand the Crown stands for 'all New Zealanders', yet the message often conveyed by Treaty of Waitangi settlements is that the Crown remains a colonial institution that represents the interests of Pākehā (New Zealanders descended from European settlers). Far from 'unravelling the effects of colonisation', it could be argued that this perpetuates and cements them. Third, and to echo Maitland, we need to ask what 'difficult questions' this fiction prevents us from asking. As McLean (2015: 191) notes, for the most part the Waitangi Tribunal is only empowered to make recommendations to government and does not have jurisdiction even to *recommend* the acquisition of private land or property by the Crown and its return to Māori. In other words, only public land can be used to compensate claimants. Historically, much of the dispossession and appropriation of Māori lands resulted from the actions of rapacious settlers and private individuals, but the possibility of returning wrongly taken and now privately owned land is one that this form of postcolonial statecraft has completely ruled out.

The Crown as Metonym for the State?

Both the Crown and the state are symbols of overarching political and legal authority; both are historical actors that claim sovereignty and permanence; both are personified through the office of a head of state yet include a complex apparatus of auxiliary institutions and officials; both demand the loyalty of their subjects and citizens; and both are extremely hard to pin down or define with accuracy. It is tempting to conclude, therefore, that the Crown is just a metonym for the state. Metonymy refers to the substitution of a word for something that it is closely linked to. However, while one could argue that the Crown incorporates the state, these terms are not coterminous, nor do they cover the same conceptual ground. This has important political and constitutional implications. Anne Twomey notes that in New South Wales (NSW) law, if someone did a global search on the law statutes and substituted 'Federal or State government' for 'Crown' the result would be legally viable in only about 80 per cent of the instances. Some NSW legislation is significantly older than that of other states, and in the intransigent laws where substitution fails, where it is unclear what the original drafters meant by references to the Crown, 'you would have actually had to have gone back . . . even to medieval times to draw out exactly what was meant' (Twomey, Interviews, 2015). That body of mismatches would include the reserve powers of the sovereign, the royal prerogative powers exercised by ministers and government departments, and other powers incidental to government. This may or may not include all the rights, privileges and powers of a natural person, or what Bruce Harris has termed the government's 'third source' of authority, in addition to powers derived from statute and prerogative (2007).

If the state is a complex and opaque assemblage of individuals, institutions and ideological effects – a vast abstraction and apparatus of power that sometimes appears to have metaphysical qualities – these characteristics are even more pronounced in the Crown. Unlike the state, which the British Westminster model does not recognise as a legal person, the Crown has legal personhood and is a recognised *persona ficta*, or a non-human juridical person. Insofar as the Crown is always embodied in the figure of Her Majesty the Queen (or King), it is also a natural person. Yet when we try to 'pierce the corporate veil' and analyse how those natural persons acting on behalf of the state operate, the task is further complicated by the Crown's metaphysical qualities and the fact that its power can only be attested through the ancient seals of the Queen's office, which is summed up by the phrase 'what the Queen in Parliament decides' (Figure 12.1).

Harold Laski, writing almost 100 years ago, captured this idea of the Crown as a cloak 'that covers a multitude of sins' when he wrote:

> The Crown is a noble hieroglyphic; and it is not in the Law Courts that effort will be made to penetrate the meaning of its patent symbolism. Crown in fact means government, and government means those innumerable officials who collect our taxes and grant us patents and inspect our drains. They are human beings with the money-bags of the state behind them. They are fallible beings because they are human.
>
> (Laski 1919: 472)

The literature on the Crown repeatedly returns to the foundational theory of the king's two bodies (Kantorowicz [1957] 1997) to explain the medieval origins of the Westminster system of constitutional monarchy, but this concept is notably absent in theories of the modern state. One reason for this is that the state is typically imagined as an apparatus or contraption rather than as a dualistic person, even though some heads of state may act in ways that appear monarchical or portray themselves as embodiments of the nation. Yet what makes the Crown more than some mechanistic contraption – or noble but untranslatable hieroglyphic – is precisely the fact that it helps to personify the state.

Figure 12.1 Queen Elizabeth II wearing the Imperial State Crown to read the 'Speech from the throne' during the State Opening of Parliament in the House of Lords at the Palace of Westminster in London, UK; 18 May 2016
(Alastair Grant – WPA Pool/Getty Images)

Personified, Popular and Particular: Crown Effects and Crown Affects

The personification of the Crown is a fundamental aspect of its significance. Many people in Australia, New Zealand and Canada, including republicans who would like to abolish the monarchy, feel affection for Queen Elizabeth as a person. Australia's prime minister, Malcolm Turnbull, famously described himself as both a republican and an Elizabethan (and in Australian interviews, both monarchists and republicans claimed personal bonds with the Queen). That admiration sometimes extends into perceived bonds of kinship and genealogy. Queen Victoria was often described as a 'mother figure' by imperial subjects across the Commonwealth, and the idea of 'our royals' and 'beloved grandmother' found in monarchist discourse still sums up the way some indigenous communities perceive their genealogical ties to the monarchy (see Figure 12.2). For Māori, the ability to *whakapapa* (draw ancestral links)

Figure 12.2 Stanley Park, Vancouver: Monument erected to 'Victoria the Good' (Cris Shore)

between the descendants of the *rangatira* (chiefs) who signed the Treaty of Waitangi and the present monarch and her heirs is extremely important. Despite the fact that most Commonwealth countries are republics, many informants descended from imperial settlers talked about the

Queen as the head of a 'family of nations'. In Britain, as well as among monarchists in New Zealand and Australia, the 2017 Brexit vote has given new impetus to those who would like to revive that relationship.

The human persona of the monarch and her dualistic nature is one of the key elements that serves to differentiate the Crown from the state. As Chapter 3 illustrated, the Queen, as a warm-bodied and sentient being, stands in sharp contrast to the distant and impersonal state, Hobbes's ([1651] 2005) cold-hearted Leviathan. It is precisely these human qualities that enable the Crown to forge enduring personal relationships with its subjects. As many of our indigenous research participants noted, you cannot *whakapapa* or have a personal relationship with an office that shifts from person to person. By contrast, the Crown is enduring, recognisable and approachable: it has a 'face' that people know and can see daily on their coins; it is someone who can be petitioned, spoken to and held to account; it can express feelings of regret, remorse, humility and responsibility. People can engage personally with the Crown, and its personification can engage with the people

Another advantage in personifying and personalising the Crown is that royal bodies can be circulated and displayed throughout the realms and often engage in activities and events in performances of local identity (see Chapters 5 and 7): sailing in New Zealand, conducting 'working' tours of Canada, going walkabout in the Australian Outback, or simply waving to the crowds from the balcony of Buckingham Palace (see Figure 12.3). Life events of the Royal Family often act as touchstones for the media and the public, but most importantly the Queen and the Royal Family demonstrate the ceremonies and spectacles of stately authority through crowns, costumes, rituals and palaces. Representations of the Crown appear wherever political authority is claimed, no matter how trivial: coats of arms, military insignia, courts, hospitals, educational institutions, coins and currency, sport clubs and throughout government offices and buildings. While these vernacular signs of the Crown often go unnoticed, they nevertheless serve as an important backdrop to hone a sense of national identity.

The Crown is also manifest in the institutions of the state through the oaths of allegiance that every judge, minister, military officer, soldier, senior public servant, police officer, Scout and new citizen proclaims, not simply to the state but specifically to Her Majesty the Queen. Elsewhere, the Crown is manifest as the state's authority figure: the bearer of radical title, the prosecutor of crimes, the grantor of citizenship, the owner of public lands and the ultimate inheritor of

Figure 12.3 Queen Elizabeth II (wearing the Imperial State Crown) and the Duke of Edinburgh waving from the Buckingham Palace balcony, after the Coronation; 2 June 1953
(Keystone/Getty Images)

vacant goods. These are just some of the many faces of the Crown and its 'state effects' (Mitchell 1999).

Mapping Meanings: How the Crown Developed in the Different Realms

The notion of the Crown as an indivisible entity of imperial unity was the starting point for the imposition of British rule on its colonies. In Canada, Australia and New Zealand, the Crown was central to the establishment of colonial government and, more importantly, in the claims to legitimacy made by subsequent settler governments. As Paul McHugh and Lisa Ford note (2012: 28), New Zealand's settler governments used the *mana* of the Crown instrumentally, transforming it into something far more absolutist and extending and deepening its authority in order to hasten the process of land dispossession and acquisition. They 'also harnessed the regalia and authority of the Imperial Crown in its diplomatic form [so that] [t]he aura of the Imperial prerogative . . . was redeployed and magnified' (28). The Crown and its rhetoric of 'protection' thus furnished both the rationale and legitimation for the consolidation of settler sovereignty, framed through the usual imperatives of providing peace, order and good government.

A key finding of this study is that the Crown manifests differently in each of the different realms. This is partly due to the different historical trajectories and pathways by which the Crown arrived and the evolutionary processes that followed the divisibility of the Crown, especially in the period following the Statute of Westminster in 1931. The British government is still officially called 'Her Majesty's Government', and the party with the second largest number of MPs is usually termed 'Her Majesty's Opposition'. But loyalty to 'Her Majesty' remains integral to the oaths and obligations of Crown servants – civil as well as military – in each of the realms. In New Zealand, since 1955, groups of new citizens have publicly sworn allegiance to the Queen and loyalty to New Zealand by oath or affirmation, before singing 'God Defend New Zealand' (Green 2005):

> *I, [name], swear that I will be faithful and bear true allegiance to Her Majesty Queen Elizabeth the Second, Queen of New Zealand, Her heirs and successors according to the law, and that I will faithfully observe the laws of New Zealand and fulfil my duties as a New Zealand citizen.*

Significantly, the oath here is to Elizabeth the Second, Queen of New Zealand. Canada's citizenship ceremony also demands a 'declaration of fealty' to the *Canadian monarch* and a promise to abide by Canada's laws and uphold the duties of a Canadian citizen. By contrast, the Australian citizenship pledge is 'to Australia and its people, whose democratic beliefs I share, whose rights and liberties I respect, and whose laws I will uphold and obey' (Australian Government 2018). The wording of these oaths highlights important differences in the way the Crown is configured in these three realms. In New Zealand, unlike Australia, national identity did not demand abandoning the Crown, but it did demand that it transform into a national Crown (Cox 2002). Paradoxically, New Zealand is unique among countries for having two national anthems: 'God Defend New Zealand' *and* 'God Save the Queen'. In Canada, by contrast:

> There was a deliberate rejection of the historic Crown with its anthem, emblems, and symbolism, which made accessible a past the government

> of the day rejected. The new Crown was to be 'rooted in the future, not in the past' . . . This did not mean rejection of the Crown, but moulding it to a new form, one symbolic of multiculturalism and modernity.
>
> (Cox 2002: 146–47)

Yet in all of these countries, there is a dissonance between constitutional arrangements and public perception. As Claudio Kullmann observed:

> In popular perception Elizabeth II is still regarded as the 'Queen of England' rather than the (independent) Queen of Australia or New Zealand. In this sense, the monarchy continues to symbolise a link with the former mother country, which many consider inappropriate for sovereign nations.
>
> (Kullmann 2008: 446)

The fact that there is no such office as 'Queen of England' highlights the extent of that dissonance. Of all the four case studies that we have investigated, New Zealand stands out as the country where the conceptual inflation of the Crown is most evident. The Crown 'acts' in all kinds of ways, from the mundane practices of government and administration to the daily work of the courts, Parliament legislature, the cabinet and the executive. It has become an everyday term of use, and indeed many issues and institutions cannot be referred to without the Crown, such as Treasury, criminal prosecution, the Treaty and even quasi-non-governmental organisations like power companies, national museums and airlines (known as Crown entities). This adds a further layer of complexity and ambiguity to the protean Crown in New Zealand. In Canada, the Crown also occupies a prominent place in political discourse and the public imaginary and is today a significant focus for postcolonial national identity. This was particularly evident in the process surrounding the patriation of the constitution in 1982. Part of its elevated status lies in the fact that the Crown is the institution that most visibly distinguishes Canada from the Unites States. In Australia, by contrast, the Crown is not an everyday term of use, though the constitutional structures are remarkably similar to those of Canada. As Cox (2003: 13) says, 'unlike in Canada, in Australia the Crown was not generally seen as a source of state authority because the Constitution itself assumed much of this function'.

Fifty years ago, Australia, Canada and New Zealand shared a much closer view of the Crown and of themselves as loyal Dominions. One explanation for the curious expansion of the Crown's meanings in New Zealand and Canada – and apparent dissipation in Australia – is the prominence of issues concerning the place of indigenous peoples in each nation's history and ongoing constitutional arrangements. In Australia, the doctrine of *terra nullius* and the country's early history of military governments were major factors in the absence of any treaties with indigenous peoples. One of the very few places where the Crown appears in Australian law is, since 1991, in relation to native title over Crown lands. Curiously, public discourse around the Crown is not especially prominent in the UK, with the exception perhaps of Northern Ireland where it has long been the talisman for loyalist Protestant identity (and Catholic republican animosity). The Crown is not used as a moniker for government, the state or legal authority. However, the Queen and the Royal Family, and the legacies of royal patronage, still feature prominently in national life and popular culture.

Regina Mortua Est – In Rem Publicam Vivat

> We suffer in this country from a lack of emotional focus . . . New Zealand will become a republic just as Britain will be blurred into Europe. David Lange, former New Zealand prime minister
>
> (1993)

In 2014 when we started this project, it seemed almost inevitable that Australia would be the first of the four realms to become a republic. It has a strong history of republican sentiment, a recent and serious republican referendum and an everyday public discourse from which the Crown in singularly absent. Politicians in Australia and New Zealand had long assumed the inevitability of the move to a republic, although the exact timing remained suitably vague. That timing continues to be unclear. As the quote at the start of this section suggests, politicians gazing into their crystal balls sometimes get things wrong. Lange miscalculated on Britain and Europe; was he equally wrong about the move to a republic?

In 2018, there seemed undeniable momentum for another republican push in Australia: the front bench of both major parties in the Australian Federal Parliament are almost all republicans; all Australian premiers and first ministers but one issued a statement calling for a republic on 26 January 2016 (Australia Day); Australian Republic Movement (ARM) claims its membership has quadrupled over the 2016 period; the Labor government appointed MP Matt Thistlethwaite as shadow assistant minister for an Australian head of state in October 2017.

However, political will only carries so far. Reform would require politicians to spend political capital on this issue rather than on others which may be more important to voters, and Australia's current government holds only a slim majority. Constitutional change requires almost overwhelming public support – and only eight of the forty-four referenda taken to the vote have ever passed. While opinion polls show public appetite for a republic is strong, this may not reach the overwhelming support required for constitutional change. Without a political crisis to galvanise action, without properly funded technical work to embed the necessary statutory changes and without the community work needed to establish popular republican symbols, the ARM's minimalist aspirations show little sign of success.

Canada will not be in the running for the republic stakes for two reasons. First, because Section 41 of the Constitution Act of 1982, which asserts the status of the Queen as Queen of Canada, is one of four elements of the constitution that cannot be changed without the unanimous consent of the legislatures of all ten provinces and resolutions of the upper and lower house of the federal Parliament. Such a degree of unanimity on constitutional issues has never been achieved in Canada since its origins in 1867. Second, there is little popular appetite for republican reform. As previously mentioned, constitutional monarchy is widely understood as a helpful differentiator from the United States, whose political difficulties are often offered as an example of the deficiencies of republican government.

Consequently, one of our conclusions is that New Zealand could well be the first realm to replace constitutional monarchy with a republic. There are several reasons for this. One is the constitutional simplicity of doing so. New Zealand lacks the impediments to constitutional reform found in Australia and Canada; it has one house, no federal structure, no entrenchment and simple legislative processes for reform based on simple majority. Another is because debate within Māoridom has moved towards refiguring the constitutional status of the Treaty as a critical focus (Matike Mai Aotearoa 2016).

The Sacred and the Profane: The Crown and Constitutional Legitimacy

What, then, can be said about the future of the Crown and the monarchy given its supposed sempiternal nature and its extraordinarily ability to survive and adapt to the changing circumstances of the present? What explains its continuing resilience and relevance? Once again, it is worth returning to Kantorowicz, Maitland and Bagehot, whose analyses continue to provide critical insights into the Crown's complex nature.

One reason for the Crown's popularity and success, according to Kantorowicz, is its theological and mythic qualities. We have become 'seduced by our own fantasies and creations', he argued:

> That kind of man-made irreality – indeed, that strange construction of a human mind which finally becomes slave to its own fictions – we are normally more ready to find in the religious sphere than in the allegedly sober and realistic realms of law, politics, and constitution.
>
> (Kantorowicz [1957] 1997: 5)

Maitland, like many contemporary constitutional reformers and republicans, also sought to demystify the Crown and democratise the state, showing how the Crown's mystical trappings served to camouflage the operations of government and provide a cloak for the accumulation of executive power. Yet as Loughlin noted, 'when Maitland spoke of the Crown as a convenient cover for ignorance, it is not a naïve ignorance, it's an ignorance that is an expression at the same time of statecraft' (Loughlin, Interviews, 2016).

This definition of the Crown as cover for ignorance, convenient fiction and expression of statecraft echoes materialist conceptions of the state as not simply a theological or metaphysical category but part of an ideological apparatus that works to buttress exploitative class relations and mask a feudalist set of institutions. This is also the classic Marxist interpretation of how the state operates and how 'tradition' serves the interests of the rich and powerful. While these arguments doubtless have merits, they nonetheless beg questions about what role myth or religion might play in the construction of a constitutional legitimacy that is not simply one of instrumental mystique, deception and disguise. Moving beyond critiques of political mystification, are there some merits to the notion that successful constitutions necessarily require a measure of sacredness? By this we mean 'sacred' in the Durkheimian sense of being 'set apart from' the mundane world of political and economic interests. As Peter Boyce argues, 'the image of the Crown ... transcending the elected government has helped idealise the state and divorce the routine performance of governmental functions from the more sordid partisan struggles for political power' (Boyce 2008: 5). Perhaps elevation beyond 'sordid partisan struggles' is no bad thing. As Sir Paul Reeves, the first Māori to be appointed governor-general, put it in a radio discussion, 'The Crown for me represents the whole centre of the fabric of our government. There are things which are above the ins and outs of political life, things which are embedded, and I think the Crown represents that, and I think the Crown represents continuity' (Reeves 2008).

Several interviewees made similar arguments, noting that most constitutions have elements of transcendence and mystique in some form or another. As one veteran British civil servant put it, 'we need to recognise a power that is not "man-made", that stands above us'. Taking the doctrine of parliamentary sovereignty as a case in point, he added:

> No one really understands the origins of parliamentary sovereignty, and nowadays you've got judges saying it's a product of the common law. Now there's debate about this, but most people would say the judges did not create sovereignty. And if they did it's a pretty frightening thing, because that which we've created we can destroy. We can unravel parliamentary sovereignty. Of course sovereignty ultimately goes back to the Crown because it's the Queen in Parliament. The Queen as head of this is largely symbolic. But the sovereignty of Parliament is a useful fiction because ultimately in a society like ours, we have a number of different players (including) Parliament, the executive, the people, the press, the media, the civil service and the army. Of all these players, you've got to have one that trumps, because otherwise you're just going to have civil war. So it's a useful fiction. It's a necessary fiction – otherwise where is the trump card?
>
> (Wilson, Interviews, 2016)

Martin Loughlin makes a similar argument:

> I think that humans don't revere the things that they've made. They become artefacts, instruments. You can make it, you can destroy it. So having elevation of a monarch that is sort of divine or something above something we've just made gives us a symbol of continuity, of identity, of stability – however fake that might be in the world in which we live.
>
> (Loughlin, Interviews, 2016)

This goes beyond claims about the need for political neutrality in the appointment of a head of state: transcendence, it seems, is a key ingredient in the construction of political and constitutional legitimacy. Republicans and constitutional reformers often adopt a rationalist approach to the law and the constitution, believing that democracy and good governance are best guaranteed by political and legal systems based on rational, codified and transparent rules, and that unwritten and uncodified forms of government are invariably archaic, backward, irrational and inferior. However, they typically overlook the importance of symbols, myth and transcendence in the constitution of society.

Peter Boyce, writing about Australia, Canada and New Zealand, argues that enshrining state authority in the Crown 'has provided an effective mask for the steady expansion of power within the political executives' (Boyce 2008: 244). 'Monarchy', he adds, has 'ensured a much more pervasive and celebrated role for state institutions, with the Crown conveying a more benevolent and protective role for government' (Boyce 2008: 246).

> The challenge ... to retain monarchy is how to sustain respect for the Crown as political apparatus while preventing or discouraging undue identification with a monarch who is unavoidably British.
>
> (Boyce 2008: 250)

Therein lies the difficulty faced by all those who seek constitutional reform. If republicans seek only to replace a British monarch with a local citizen as head of state, the 'steady expansion of power' in the hands of the executive will continue without any effective bridling of executive power. As Chapter 2 noted, simply moving to a republican constitution entirely misses 'that part of our constitutional structure most in need of change: the limited role of representative institutions in checking the exercise of executive power' (Sharman 1994: 113). The common law tradition has sought to constrain the overweening power of the executive – whether Stuart royal despots, their Whig gentry successors or modern cabinet ministers and prime ministers using Crown powers to minimise accountability to Parliament or the electorate. Yet granting more power to unelected judges to control the exercise of prerogative powers, or to strike down legislation that is inconsistent with fundamental principles of legality, raises another area of debate about constitutional reform. Outside Australia, a strong appetite for significant constitutional reform was not evident in the interviews we conducted for this project in the present Queen's realms. There are many, perhaps, who are happy with *de facto* republican rule, though governments purport to act in the name of an ambiguous, shapeshifting Crown. Maybe the political landscape will indeed change when the Elizabethan age comes to an end. If that is to come to pass, however, then those seeking change still have their work cut out to prepare the way efficiently for new constitutional structures, for different symbols of the state and for clarity as to the future of prerogative powers. Above all, they need to devise new and more appealing accounts of how power should be exercised in the name of the people.

References

Australian Government. 2018. 'Australian Citizenship Pledge.' *Department of Home Affairs*. Accessed 23 February 2018 at www.homeaffairs.gov.au/trav/citi/pathways-processes/citi/australian-citizenship-pledge.

Bagehot, Walter. (1867) 2001. *The English Constitution*. Edited by Paul Smith. Cambridge: Cambridge University Press.

Bourdieu, Pierre. 1977. *Outline of a Theory of Practice*. Cambridge: Cambridge University Press.

2014. *On the State: Lectures at the Collège de France, 1989–1992*. Translated by David Fernbach. Bristol: Polity.

Boyce, Peter. 2008. *The Queen's Other Realms: The Crown and Its Legacy in Australia, Canada and New Zealand*. Annandale, NSW: The Federation Press.

Churchill, Winston. 1974. *Winston S. Churchill: His Complete Speeches, 1897–1963, Vol. 7*. Edited by Robert Rhodes James. New York: Chelsea House.

Cox, Noel. 2002. 'Republican Sentiment in the Realms of the Queen: The New Zealand Perspective.' *Manitoba Law Journal* 29(1): 121–47.

2003. 'The Development of a Separate Crown in New Zealand.' *SSRN Electronic Journal*. Published online 18 August 2003. DOI: 10.2139/ssrn.420026.

Doyle, Timothy. 1993. 'The Conservative Mythology of Monarchy: Impacts upon Australian Republicanism.' *Australian Journal of Political Science* 28(4): 121–35.

Flint, David. 2007. 'The Indispensable Crown.' *The Quadrant* 51(3): 30–38.

Godfery, Morgan. 'The Crown: Is It Still "White" and "English-Speaking"?' *The Round Table: The Commonwealth Journal of International Affairs* 107(4): 493–506.

Green, David. 2005. 'Citizenship – Becoming a Citizen.' *Te Ara: The Encyclopedia of New Zealand*. Online resource. Accessed 24 February 2018 at www.TeAra.govt.nz/en/citizenship/page-5.

Guillén, Mauro. 2018. 'Symbolic Unity, Dynastic Continuity, and Countervailing Power: Monarchies, Republics, and the Economy.' *Social Forces*. Published ahead of print, 4 May 2018. DOI: 10.1093/sf/soy037/4992685.

Harris, Bruce. 2007. 'The "Third Source" of Authority for Government Action Revisited.' *Law Quarterly Review* 123: 225–50.

Hirst, John. 1994. *A Republican Manifesto*. Melbourne: Oxford University Press.

Hobbes, Thomas. (1651) 2005. *Leviathan*. New York: Continuum.

Kantorowicz, Ernst H. (1957) 1997. *The King's Two Bodies: A Study in Mediaeval Political Theology*. Princeton, NJ: Princeton University Press.

Kullmann, Claudio. 2008. 'Attitudes towards the Monarchy in Australia and New Zealand Compared.' *Commonwealth & Comparative Politics* 46(4): 442–63.

Laski, Harold. 1919. 'The Responsibility of the State in England: To Roscoe Pound.' *Harvard Law Review* 32(5): 447–72.

Maitland, Frederic W. (1908) 2001. *The Constitutional History of England: A Course of Lectures Delivered*. The Lawbook Exchange.

Marsden, Māori. 2003. *The Woven Universe: Selected Writings of Rev. Māori Marsden*. Otaki, New Zealand: Estate of Reverend Māori Marsden.

Matike Mai Aotearoa. 2016. *He whakaaro here whakaumu mō Aotearoa [Towards a Republican Constitution]: The Report of Matike Mai Aotearoa – The Independent Working Group on Constitutional Transformation*. Accessed 8 March 2018 at www.converge.org.nz/pma/MatikeMaiAotearoaReport.pdf.

McAllister, Patrick. 2012. *National Days and the Politics of Indigenous and Local Identities in Australia and New Zealand*. Durham, NC: Carolina Academic Press.

McHugh, Paul and Lisa Ford. 2012. 'Settler Sovereignty and the Shapeshifting Crown.' In *Between Indigenous and Settler Governance*, edited by Lisa Ford and Tim Rowse, 22–34. New York: Routledge.

McLean, Janet. 2004. 'The Transnational Corporation in History: Lessons for Today?' *Indiana Law Journal* 79(2): 363–77.

2015. 'Crown, Empire and Redressing the Historical Wrongs of Colonisation in New Zealand.' *New Zealand Law Review* 2015(2): 187–212.

Mitchell, Timothy. 1999. 'Society, Economy, and the State Effect.' In *State/Culture: State-Formation after the Cultural Turn*, edited by George Steinmetz, 76–97. Ithaca, NY: Cornell University Press.

Ortner, Sherry. 1973. 'On Key Symbols.' *American Anthropologist* 75(5): 1338–46.

Reeves, Paul. 2008. 'The Sunday Group.' Radio interview, 1 June. *Sunday Morning* programme, Radio New Zealand. Accessed 17 May 2018 at www.radionz.co.nz/national/programmes/sunday/20080601.

Sharman, Campbell. 1994. 'Reforming Executive Power'. In *We, the People: Australian Republican Government*, edited by George Winterton, 113–24. St. Leonards, NSW: Allen and Unwin.

Shore, Cris and Margaret Kawharu. 2014. 'The Crown in New Zealand: Anthropological Perspectives on an Imagined Sovereign.' *Sites* 11(1): 17–38.

Sutton, Steven. 2016. 'Constitutional monarchy allows for democratic innovation.' *A Constitution for Aotearoa New Zealand*. Website. Accessed 17 May 2018 at constitutionaotearoa.org.nz/the-conversation/monarchy-innovation/.

Tate, Henare. 1990. 'The Unseen World.' *New Zealand Geographic* 5(Jan–Mar): 87–91.

Wayne, Leslie. 2018. 'What's the Cure for Ailing Nations? More Kings and Queens, Monarchists Say.' *New York Times*, 6 January. Accessed 6 January 2018 at www.nytimes.com/2018/01/06/world/europe/monarchy-us-advantage.html.

INDEX